Merry Christmas 1969
Mrs. Steffan

the sound of soul

the sound of soul

phyl garland

HENRY REGNERY COMPANY
CHICAGO

To my parents

Hazel and Percy A. Garland

who first turned me on to the magic of music

Parts of "Recording in Memphis," "Aretha Franklin: Sister Soul" and "Requiem for Trane: Another Kind of Soul" appeared first in Ebony *magazine. The author wishes to express her thanks to* Ebony *for permission to reprint these sections.*

Manufactured in the United States of America
Library of Congress Catalog Card Number: 73-88845

CONTENTS

INTRODUCTION

Today soul music, a vastly embracing but only vaguely defined phenomenon, has become a prime cultural force in both America and the world. Sales charts that announce the success of popular recordings are dominated by this music and its leading interpreters, while it is also known in its related forms of gospel music, the blues, rhythm and blues and the sort of infectious jazz that makes it difficult for one to sit still while listening. The mystique of "soul" even has been carried over into other areas of life, for there is something about the very sound of the word that connotes the warm and compellingly real. So "soul" and soul music are definitely "in."

However, the deeper meanings of this music and its origins are too often overlooked, as has commonly been the case with black music once it becomes popular and lucrative. Since those other than its originators like it, sing it, play it and make money from it, sufficient credit seldom is given to those who created it. It should always be remembered that soul music in all of its forms is the aesthetic property of a race of people who were brought to this country against their will and were forced to make drastic social adjustments in order to survive in a hostile environment. This black experience provided the foundation for the popular art of today.

How deeply has soul music penetrated the cultural core of modern America and how did it all come about?

This book has been undertaken as an attempt to answer that question. In the process it examines some of the ethnic forces that have gone into the making of this music, by recreating some of the color and feeling of that special society-within-a-society that gave birth to it and by presenting the attitudes of the musicians toward their music and the world in which they have had to live. This has been done by tracing the development of black music in America from its roots in Africa, by relating this cultural evolution to historical events and by surveying the current scene to determine its pervasiveness, the methods by which it is produced and the way in which it is regarded by performers and their audiences. The purpose of the book, in short, is to reflect some of the attitudes of blacks and the contemporary black mood. Thus, much of this musical portrait has been filled in by comments of the musicians themselves. They have revealed their deepest personal feelings about their art and the conditions that have helped to shape it. Quite a bit of the story is really theirs.

The total body of soul music is treated in a broad sense, going beyond the music that has gained popularity with the general public. Appealing as commercial soul might be, it is but one offshoot from a musical tree with many branches, and all of those branches are interrelated. If popular soul music is, as it often has been defined, a fusion of blues, jazz and gospel, the other forms of music must also be examined for their bearing on the subject, though it is not within the scope of this book to provide detailed explanations of every branch of black music; they can be found elsewhere, for much has been written on jazz and the blues, though gospel music has been woefully neglected. I have steered clear of technical musical analyses and have used a minimum of formal musical terms because they are usually confusing to the general reader. Then, too, in my opinion, no plethora of words can effectively recreate an actual musical sound. And since the music is its own best witness, a brief discography is presented at the end of the book.

Though a great deal of research and interviewing has gone into this book, it is not to be considered a scholarly treatise in sociology or musicology. Instead, it should be looked at as an informal account designed for the reader who likes the sound of soul and possesses an interest in the meaning of this music, in the world from which it has sprung and in the gifted people who create and perform it. And, it is to be hoped, thereby the book will be entertaining as well as informative.

Thus we come to what might be considered a peculiarity of this book. At this, the very beginning, I must state that I, as a black woman writing from out of my own experience and that of so many others, have not attempted to adopt a pose of Olympian objectivity. My perspective is a black one, and I have concentrated on the work of black musicians simply because I believe them to be the most vital factor in the development of modern music.

From the standpoint of other books in this field, I am deeply indebted to the poet, playwright and social commentator LeRoi Jones, whose pioneering book, *Blues People,* contains a wealth of fresh insights and should be considered a prerequisite for a deep understanding of what this whole thing is about. A vote of thanks also must be accorded Charles Keil for his stimulating work, *Urban Blues,* and the late Marshall Stearns. If there are others who have inspired me by the sheer force of their being, they are the historian Lerone Bennett Jr., a compassionate scholar who has *felt* everything he has written, and the poet Gwendolyn Brooks, who has shown me, by her accomplishments, that a black woman living in the strife-torn world of today can still become a full and creative human being.

Introduction

For an understanding of what is happening on the current scene, I am indebted to the musicians who gave freely of their time, even when their schedules were pressing. For some understanding of what has happened in the past, I bow in gratitude to the men and women of the black press, particularly William G. Nunn Sr. of the old *Pittsburgh Courier,* who gave me my first job in journalism, and the editors of *Negro Digest, Ebony* and *Jet* magazines. Long before blackness became a focal point of national interest, they chronicled the achievements and struggles of a people ignored by other journalistic organs.

Yet there are more definite acknowledgments to be made. Without these people, this work, such as it is, would not have been possible. First among these is John H. Johnson, editor and publisher of *Ebony* magazine, who enabled me to acquire national exposure as a writer and so kindly granted me an extended leave-of-absence that I might devote time to this project; Herbert Nipson, executive editor of *Ebony,* and Era Bell Thompson, international editor of *Ebony,* both of whom showed all consideration and offered much needed encouragement; Lucille Phinnie of the Johnson Publishing Company library, who gave me access to valuable materials others not available; Brenda Biram of the JPC book division, who dipped into her expertise in the book publishing field to prepare me for the unknown. Above all, a special thank you goes to my friend and colleague Basil Phillips, without whose aid and thoughtfulness this project never would have materialized.

Phyl Garland

CHICAGO, 1969

1

SOUL MUSIC: AN OLD SOUND OF NEW SIGNIFICANCE

Sometimes it is the gusty cry of a blues singer standing in a smoke-dimmed room where sweaty scents are compressed before a faceless but responsive audience of the "never-hads and never-wases," shedding his own private tears of conjugal misalliance through a song-story half-talked and half-sung in down-home phrases punctuated by slurred notes sustained on an amplified guitar. And as the shouts of "Do your *thing*, baby!" come back from all corners of the room, a musical performance is transformed into a ritual of release.

At other times, it is the sudden scream, the grunt, the wail of James Brown gyrating about a stage, dancing like a demon dispossessed, falling to his knees, projecting with his movements and his rough-edged voice a mood of irrepressible joy. Certainly it accounts for that twist of gospel stomp in just about everything Aretha Franklin does.

But it can also be the deliberate "thoooomm . . . thoooomm . . . thoooomm" of a steadily "walking" bass; the sensuous growl of a tenor sax ripping melodies to pieces while reconstructing them in some new and more fascinating form; a rhythmically repetitive phrase rising with a strange insistence, like an ancient incantation alien to these shores.

Its presence is felt when Mahalia Jackson vocally embraces the phrase "Lord o–of lo–o–ove" in Duke Ellington's moving invocation *Come Sunday,* bending the notes with her incredibly rich, black velvet contralto and exhorting a silent God to "Pu-*leeeeeez* look down . . . and seeeee . . . my people through." And it is the solid thud of the good two-hundred-pound Baptist sisters marching proudly down the aisle of many a black belt church on just that kind of Sunday morning as their strong but wavering voices proclaim, "Jeeeee*eeee-sus!* I-a *love* you!"

Always, it is to be found in the streets of urban ghettos, where snatches of radio broadcasts issue indiscriminately from littered doorways, and on the main drags, where tinny speakers, set above the smeared windows and faded displays of ramshackle record shops, blast out with the latest "rhythm and blues"-cum-"soul" hit, chanted lyrics mingling with the din and dirt of too many people with too little to live on in too "raggedy" a place.

Sometimes it seems to be a profane liturgy of the doomed and the despairing, but more frequently it is a hymn of hope or an unbridled affirmation of dark defiance.

This, then, is the sound of soul as it is manifest in the overlapping forms of blues, jazz, gospel and popular music. Its essence is indisputably black; for in the long and dismal decades that must have seemed like eons to those forced to endure them, chants and hollers not markedly unlike those to be heard in the popular music of today were sent up from rural Dixie's cotton fields by sackcloth-clad black men and women who labored under a relentless sun from predawn to postdusk knowing that no matter *how* hard they worked or how many bales they picked, tomorrow would be no better than today and might well be far worse. In the low, vibrato-laden drones emanating from the black slave's religious meetings (forbidden at first, the meetings were later encouraged as a possible preventative of insurrection), the spirituals were born and seeds were sown for their procreation through a stepchild called the blues and its close relative, jazz. Throughout two hundred and fifty years of slavery and yet another century of pseudo-freedom, the permutations of this compellingly human sound have developed. And suddenly, in the crushing tumult of mid-century America, the sound has become a very big thing.

By the end of 1968, "soul music," as it has evolved from rugged roots into a modified but highly popular form, accounted for a healthy chunk of the unprecedented $1.1 billion gross income for that year in the recording industry. This was indicated by the fact that in *Billboard* magazine's year-end assessment of individual popular record sales—based on a system that takes into consideration the number of top-selling records an artist has had during the year along with the number of weeks each hit appeared on the charts and its standings—black soul artists or those commonly identified with this phenomenon held sway. They accounted for seven of the top twelve chart positions, and Aretha Franklin, that blues-based, gospel-steeped singer-pianist from Detroit ranked as the year's number one artist. Not too far behind her were James Brown, the "dancingest," "shoutingest" singer of them all, known as "Soul Brother No. 1"; the late Otis Redding, the leading exponent of the Memphis soul sound, who only after his death in a private airplane crash near the end of 1967, achieved a popularity in the musical mainstream that had eluded him in life; Dionne Warwick, a dusky, honey-voiced chanteuse of pop-oriented soulful ballads; several stalwarts from Detroit's fabled Motown stable of "pop-soul" talent, most notably the musical torrid duo of Marvin Gaye and Tammi Terrell; and Motown vice-president Smokey Robinson with his singing Miracles. Along with these outstanding successes were representatives from New York's Atlantic Recording Corporation, which has capitalized on soul sounds for more than a decade: Archie Bell and the Drells and a white soul quartet called the Rascals, who admit that they got their start by listening to Ray Charles, that blind "genius of soul" who laid the groundwork for so much of the contemporary scene.

Of course, the Beatles, the remarkable British quadrumvirate, were there and have long paid tribute to their sources of soulful inspiration. In the area of album sales, which are a little less capricious than the thrust toward "hot" singles, Motown stalwarts such as Diana Ross and the Supremes, the "sultry sirens of soul," were represented by more than one top-selling LP, along with their male counterparts, the Temptations, a group of Southern-born harmonizers from whose ranks a notable single artist has emerged: David Ruffin, their former lead singer.

Even in the realm of jazz, originally an improvised sort of stompingly jubilant music that lent itself readily to dancing but has, in recent years, become increasingly introspective and convoluted, the soul sound seemed to dominate from the standpoint of record sales. Wes Montgomery, a virtuoso guitarist who had spent nearly twenty years plucking octave statements from his "box" with a thickly calloused, brine-soaked thumb (used in lieu of a pick), was the top-rated "boss" of them all. Ghosts seem to haunt these charts, and, sadly, Wes Montgomery, who, like Otis Redding, struggled so long for recognition, was dead in 1968 before his star had ascended. But his spirit lingered in recordings of his pungently alive interpolations of popular material like *Goin' Out of My Head* and *California Dreaming*, which first captured public interest as hit tunes. Nestled just beneath Montgomery on the ladder of popular jazz were artists such as Jimmy Smith, a "funky" organist who has managed to make his "mojo work" on behalf of mainstream success; Eddie Harris, a tenor saxophonist whose best-selling renditions of movie themes from *Exodus* and other films preceded his experimentation with the electronic effects of "electrifying jazz," though his sound remains in the same easy-listening groove; Ramsey Lewis, the pride of Chicago pianodom and one of the first jazz artists to make a big splash in the popular vein with his 1965 recording of the Dobie Gray rock 'n' roll hit *The "In" Crowd.* Interestingly enough, the other two-thirds of Lewis's original trio, bassist Eldee Young and drummer Isaac (Red) Holt, who had split off from the pianist in the midst of the group's rise to national prominence, rode high on the charts of 1968 with a hit called *Soulful Strut,* recorded under the name of their own new group, Young-Holt Unlimited.

Even apart from trends documented on the *Billboard* charts (the recording industry's equivalent of television's Nielsen ratings), other notable events are taking place. It was that good year 1968 when Aretha Franklin was invited to sing the national anthem at the Democratic National Convention and forgot the words. When José Feliciano, a blind Puerto Rican singer-guitarist who had wailed his way into the hearts of youthful hordes by begging them to "light" his "fire," performed the same honors at baseball's World Series, he was publicly criticized for injecting a few soulful "yeah, yeah, yeah's" into lyrics of the *Star-Spangled Banner.* Meanwhile, perennial blues artists whose following had been restricted to the black underground were discovered by enthusiastic audiences of young whites. B. B. King, the "Beale Street Blues Boy," was acclaimed as a "new blues find" after struggling along in the field for twenty-one years, and Albert King, a towering left-handed guitarist from Mississippi, was playing the same type of twanging, country music he calls "blues power" at "electric circuses," "kinetic playgrounds" and San Francisco's Fillmore Auditorium, the Lincoln Center of hippiedom. And 1968 was also the year that marked the emergence of Janis Joplin, an uninhibited, gravel-voiced college dropout from Texas, as "the greatest white blues singer of all time," something virtually unheard of since the reign of singer Mildred Bailey, the "white soul sister" of the late thirties and early forties.

So it seems that soul was "all over top of the scene." No doubt these developments prompted *Billboard* to select as its "artist of the year," Jimi Hendrix, a soul-rock-pop guitarist ironically called "the black Elvis," after the favorite hip-wiggling son of Memphis, Tennessee. As leader of a group called "The Jimi Hendrix Experience," he was cited by *Billboard* for making "the most significant contribution to popular music during the year" through "his fusing of the highly-amplified music of today with the purer sound of the blues." Perhaps more than any other artist, Hendrix, who dropped out of high school in Seattle, Washington, in 1962 and found fame in England five years later, has captured the fancy of young whites, not only through his psychedelic sound and fantastic guitar technique, but also through almost unimaginable actions during his deafening performances. He sometimes plays the guitar with his teeth, tearing out the strings at high decibel levels, and, as a climax, batters an instrument to pieces or burns it up onstage. In *Eye* magazine, a lively periodical geared to the tastes of "the rock generation," Michael Thomas has dubbed Hendrix's style "crotch-rock," due to his manner of playing the guitar from between his legs, and has called him "the ranking psychedelic super-spade heavyweight of pop."

Perhaps all of this is merely a fad, but that is doubtful. None of this has happened overnight, and the sound of soul has crossed oceans to titillate foreign musical appetites. As long as five years ago, when I visited Europe and walked with a friend into a quiet Brussels bistro, the first silence-shattering sound I heard was that of a blasting jukebox as some Belgian buff put in his franc for a hearing of *Delivre-Moi.* It seemed strangely familiar and did, indeed, turn out to be a French group's translated version of the Ray Charles hit *Unchain My Heart,* delivered with Gallic exuberance and the same rhythm and chord changes utilized in the original. This was true of the popular music to be heard in other European cities, from Paris to Istanbul, and, except for the gratuitous absence of Muzak, it was difficult at times, musically speaking, to discern that one had left the United States at all. Just before his death in 1967, for example, Otis Redding was voted England's most popular male vocalist in Great Britain's *Melody Maker* magazine poll, toppling Elvis Presley from the number one position he had held since 1956. America's most popular soul artists frequently are invited to appear abroad. Dionne Warwick enjoys, proportionately, as large a following in France as in this country. Motown Records, founded twelve years ago by a Negro former assembly-line worker named Berry Gordy and now a prime multimillion-dollar force in the pop record field, maintains a special international division to handle foreign record sales and to book artists in other countries where its products sell. And in early 1969, Nina Simone, that cello-throated, classically trained pianist known as the "high priestess of soul," has had hits top the record charts in both England and Holland.

Developments of this sort have led a leading musicologist, Henry Pleasants, to observe that the world might well be moving into an epoch of Afro-American dominance in music. In his book *Serious Music—and All That Jazz,* Pleasants draws parallels between musical events of this era and those that took place in Europe during previous centuries, when attractive new music rooted in the cultural traditions of various countries brought about a shifting in academic or formal musical styles from that of the Renaissance to those of the Baroque, the Classical and the Romantic. Applying this principle to the present, he states:

> If we look for a corresponding national domination and a continuity of the pattern of successive national or cultural dominations, we can find persuasive evidence that we are now in the midst of what future musical historians may well designate the Afro-American Epoch.

Citing the tendency of scholars to overlook popular music as "presumably inferior," he continues:

> Popularity is blithely dismissed by a musical Establishment whose own new music long ago ceased to be popular, and so the new idiom is scorned precisely because of the popular acceptance that is the most irrefutable evidence of its validity.

Tracing the roots of this popular music to its sources within the new civilizations of Africa and America, Pleasants points out:

> One thinks of America, too, of course, as a new continent, but as far as music is concerned, America became new only as the African contribution became conspicuous. What distinguishes America's indigenous music today, in the purely technical area, is the *explicit* beat and the musician's swinging relationship to that beat. And this new element is African—and rhythmic.[1]

Thus soul music and its fraternal, beat-driven twin, rock, might be here to stay for far longer than most have dared to consider. And there are even extra-musical factors that should not be ignored. Ever since the terms "soul brother" and "soul sister" were impressed upon the national consciousness through reportage on the 1965 racial uprisings in the Watts district of Los Angeles, the word "soul" has taken on a connotation of social identity linking those rebels who find some revitalizing sustenance within its aura with those of a similar bent—regardless of color—and thereby separating them from others who would willingly perpetuate the society-at-large as it is. Thus the identification linked with racial rebellion has been broadened to embrace iconoclasts identified with social rebellion, and at its purest level the terms of soul and soulful have been willingly proffered by some blacks to whites who openly reject prevailing social values. On yet another level, followers of fads who possibly might be seeking some accessible mode of personal release have adopted the more superficial aspects of a life style assumed to be the special province of black folks who have soul.

Even "soul food" has shared the vogue for things soul, though black people have been eating greens, cornbread, red beans and the cheaper, less meaty portions of the hog for almost as long as they've been in this country—and not always by choice. Now white aficionados of soul venture into offbeat markets to procure chitterlings and collards for their "novelty" buffets, thereby competing with disgruntled black consumers who resent the rise in prices that has accompanied the increased salability of these items. Black restaurants have not benefited greatly from this trend because the highly publicized spiraling racial tensions within the hostile, crumbling enclaves that are the black urban ghettos have given rise to a situation in which it is no longer advisable for outsiders to go to the Harlems of this country, as they did in previous decades, for "exotic colored entertainment."

Regardless of these racial antagonisms, an enthusiasm for soul seems to be everywhere. Aretha Franklin has been featured on the cover of *Time* magazine, though the inside article was more than a little condescending. *Esquire,* the "magazine for men" that is read equally by women, has presented a four-color special section on soul as "the new thing," complete with a cover picture of the dethroned heavyweight boxing champion Muhammad Ali (nee Cassius Clay). In the summer of 1968, *Book World,* a weekly literary review, featured an article on soul itemizing "32 meanings not in your dictionary." Possibly the most readily applicable described soul as "Black motherwit as opposed to white theory." Even in so unlikely a place as *The New Yorker* magazine, famous for its glorification of urbane indifference, a cartoon appeared in which a becrowned dowager asked her mirror on the wall who was the fairest of them all. In its reply, the mirror paraphrased a classic joke of the black in-group, as well as the fairy tale, by saying: "Snow White, but you got *soul,* Baby!" (If you want to know what that other joke is, ask some "black brother," but be ready to run when you do so.) Certainly, one of the strangest sights to be seen on television in recent years was James Brown's early 1969 guest appearance on a late-night show that simulated the sort of party to which a onetime Alabama shoeshine boy never would have been invited, had he not been *the* James Brown. Singing to an integrated audience of mod-types arranged in calculated casualness about a plush setting, Brown went into his "thing," thrusting his fist into the air and shouting his familiar "Say it *loud!*" as all (whites included) answered back gustily, "I'm black and I'm *proud!*"

At this point, one begins to wonder exactly what it is that has provoked this strange inner odyssey on the part of the American mainstream in its quest for soul. Perhaps it is the implication of an inviting warmth and genuine feeling embedded in the mystique of soul that leads so many to seek within it an antithesis to the cold, computerized society of today where the need to dominate and to acquire things for oneself has squeezed out a deeper consideration of human values. In view of the racial polarities frequently, but not always, involved, the search for soul might spring from a stumbling but gnawing need on the part of the dominant nine-tenths of the nation's population to reclaim a rejected portion of the self by looking repeatedly to that oppressed black tenth for some absolution of a festering guilt through the reassuring sound of dark laughter and song, but without regard to dark tears. Here, in the black man's tenacious ability to survive and even to forgive, there might be some indication that there do still exist the greater human possibilities so many so long ago abandoned.

There is a certain magic in the very sound of soul. Here there might be a chance to free oneself for a greater indulgence in life, as exemplified in some nameless street-corner scribe's description of the ghetto: "Jews own it, whites run it and black folks enjoy it." Here one might find release from the rigid rules restricting self-expression that are so refreshingly contradicted in a remark attributed to the lengendary blues singer-composer "Big" Bill Broonzy. When questioned about the use of folk idioms in his music, the artist replied: "All music's folk music. I ain't never heard no horse sing a song." And there might also be a chance to fulfill the elementary need for sex without shame, as set forth by Jackie "Moms" Mabley, that matriarch of black comediennes, when she jokingly announces her intentions of moving into the White House as "the first common-law First Lady."

There must, in fact, be a great deal more to it all than just the music. As the historian and social commentator Lerone Bennett Jr. has pointed out in his essay "Passion: A Certain Dark Joy," "Men cannot live without machines in the modern world but they assuredly cannot live by machines alone. In the long sight of history, it may be more important to influence the non-machine aspects of a people's life than their technology." Focusing on the meaningfulness of the black man's special "zest for life, a creative capacity for meeting adversity and transcending it," Bennett goes on to state:

> Americans who have—generally speaking—externalized almost everything, who live by machines and die by them, who mortgage their souls for pieces of tin and split-level caves in middle-class hells; Americans who have lost the capacity for enjoying themselves and others, who are lonely and frightened and afraid—Americans could use some of that life-giving force.[2]

The tragedy is that America has tended to reach out to the black man with hands that too frequently want to take without giving, with tongues that seek to savor the sweet without tasting of the bitter. This has been most apparent in the quest for cultural vigor, particularly in the field of music. Unfortunately, it has been a part of the American pattern for the originators of black music to be shunted into the background once their creations have been adopted by whites and made lucrative as well as popular. This is what happened during the thirties and forties when jazz, which had picked up a great deal of biracial sophistication on its long journey from New Orleans, by way of Chicago and Kansas City, to the "Big Apple" of New York City, set the tone for the swing era and the hegemony of the big bands. Big-band music resulted from an unusual cultural meeting of Africans and Europeans, both transplanted to the fresh soil of America—the black group by a special "invitation" imposed against its will and the white group almost always as a matter of choice. But it, too, sprang from black roots. Musicologists have pointed out that early black Americans supplied the rhythmic fire and other elements harking back to their African past but transformed by an encounter with the scales, melodic emphasis and musical forms carried over to the new continent from Europe. Whites who adopted the new music supplied a certain style and polish of their own. Had not American music been subjected to this unique meshing of cultural forces, jazz, as well as the popular music of today, might never have evolved, for these types of music are indigenous to neither Africa nor Europe; they must be regarded as part of an American music. However, social circumstances traditionally have made it easier for whites to exploit this music than the blacks who must be considered its fundamental contributors. (That is why, during the swing era, white bands, frequently using black arrangers to create the music they played—but working behind the scenes—were projected into the spotlight.) This matter will be further explored in the following chapter, but even here it must be noted that the workings of this system have left a certain bitterness in the hearts of black musicians and have not escaped the attention of some who have looked to their music for aesthetic gratification. Referring to that memorable Jazz Age and its subsequent "swing era," the late Marshall Stearns, a redoubtable lecturer and writer in this field, noted in *The Story of Jazz:*

> If Benny Goodman (a white virtuoso jazz clarinetist who pioneered in the use of black musicians in his band) became the "King of Swing" in 1935, reaping all the publicity and profits, the man behind the throne was Count Basie (a perennially popular black bandleader whose music, once called "jump," must be considered part of the backbone of

> all jazz conceived for dancing). For it was the Basie band that gave depth and momentum to the whole swing era while planting the seeds that later gave birth to bop and the "cool" school of jazz.[3]

Stearns traces the way in which white bands came to dominate this era, in terms of public popularity, to the point where they were acclaimed for playing literal copies of black music while black musicians were not even accepted in these white aggregations, and then he goes on to detail the way in which mixed bands gradually began to be accepted during the late thirties and the reason that their emergence had been so difficult: "The reason was simple: on the one hand, Negro musicians were outstanding additions to white bands; on the other hand, Negro bands—no matter how good—were paid about half as much as white bands."

The tendency of white America to accept black or hybrid music only when performed by whites has been equally apparent, though less blatantly, during the fifties and early sixties, which have been marked by the emergence of rock, a modified form of rock 'n' roll, as the dominant popular music of young whites. In *The World of Rock,* John Gabree credits rhythm and blues, the black popular music of two decades, as being one of the two major building blocks of modern rock, the other being country and western music, which, as critic Martin Williams has written, also contains elements of the black blues. Gabree notes the way in which old R&B (as rhythm and blues was called) songs known to the black underground were picked up and popularized by white artists operating within the musical mainstream. The examples are too numerous to be recounted, though the most memorable are Little Willie John's *Fever,* which became a big hit when done by Peggy Lee; LaVerne Baker's renditions of *Tweedle Dee* and *Jim Dandy,* which were redone by Georgia Gibbs; the old bluesman Joe Turner's *Shake, Rattle and Roll,* which became the first rock 'n' roll hit for an early white rock group known as Bill Haley and the Comets. Gabree explains that covering records, as these copies are known, are common to the industry, but he adds: "The only catch is that it usually works when whites do it to records by blacks and not the other way around."[4] A most interesting demonstration of this phenomenon may be found in the chain of events that have led to the development of the current rock movement.

As just about everybody with ears knows, white youngsters of today have adopted rock, with its amplified guitar whangs and pulsating electric bass tones, as their music. Something cradled within the urgency and insistence of this pulsating hybrid of black and white folksy music seems to move them, and they have made culture heroes out of its leading artists. Foremost among these are the Beatles, the long-haired English imports who have, since their introduction to the American public in 1964, triggered a movement among the young that has resulted in the popularization of a music geared to their peculiar tastes, performed and frequently produced by those of their own generation. This has been one of the most significant developments in mid-twentieth-century pop culture, and it has been a prime contributing factor to the rapid growth of the recording industry, for it is now known that most popular records are deemed so by the tastes of purchasers under the age of twenty-five.

In recent years, the Beatles have moved toward musical experimentation and pensive lyricism contiguous with the development of their own "thing." However, it cannot be forgotten that the Beatles forged the basic elements of their style by listening to recorded imitations of black American artists as performed by white artists and heard in England during the mid-fifties.

In *The Beatles,* published as "the authentic unexpurgated biography" of this remarkable quartet, Hunter Davies describes the way in which John Lennon, who collaborated with Paul McCartney to become the driving creative force within the group, was affected by the music of Bill Haley and the Comets when he heard them perform the theme song for an American movie called *Blackboard Jungle* in the early fifties. (Haley, not entirely incidentally, had listened long and hard to the music of a black group called Hank Ballard and the Midnighters.) Lennon also liked the sound of British "skiffle" groups, composed of youths playing simple tunes on homemade instruments. However, what impressed him most deeply was a 1956 initial hearing of Elvis Presley doing his big international hit *Heartbreak Hotel.* In the book, Lennon is quoted as saying, "Nothing really affected me until Elvis." This was borne out in his efforts to reproduce Presley's kind of sound in his early outings with a group that came to be known as the Beatles, Liverpudlian accents and all. But where had Elvis come from?

He was a native Texan bred in Memphis, Tennessee, heart of the black blues country. Though Presley first appeared professionally as a country and western singer billed as "The Hillbilly Cat," he was exposed to the music of black lay and professional blues singers throughout most of his life. There is, after all, something in the very atmosphere of Memphis, with its lazy, hazy, Southern slow-pace that seems to perpetuate the spirit of the blues. By its mere vantage point at the head of the Mississippi Delta basin, Memphis inherited the spontaneous musical expressiveness of newly freed slaves who made their way north from plantations further down the river, after the Civil War. The essence of their songs became a part of the local fabric but were transformed in texture by a new black urbanity. Even in those post-bellum days,

Beale Street, now a shabby ribbon of concrete dotted by pawn shops and joints, was a main drag for black folks, though it was W. C. Handy, an early innovative professional, who first popularized the town, with his *Memphis Blues,* published in 1912, and his *Beale Street Blues,* which followed four years later.

This was the musical milieu in which young Elvis reached his adolescence, absorbing a certain throbbing pulse from the air around him, even as early as 1953, when he was earning $35 a week as a truck driver. Among the more immediate black musical influences to which Presley was exposed was that of Chuck Berry, a fun-loving singer-guitarist whose fanciful composition *Mabel-lene,* published in 1955, later came to be regarded as the first rock hit, possibly because its splashy rock style was more whimsical than bluesy. Berry also helped to popularize the term "rock 'n' roll music" with his 1957 song written under that title. He is now considered the most influential single black contributor to the evolution of white rock, and it is said that his stage style inspired Elvis's suggestive pelvic movements during performance.

Presley found a clever manager in Colonel Tom Parker. By melding his country and western roots with the infectious beat of R&B à la rock via Berry, Presley came up with an appealing beat-heavy basically black sound that captivated white youngsters from Los Angeles to Liverpool, where John Lennon was steadily listening. Some of his material was new, but other songs were not, though they were unfamiliar to the youngsters who first heard him do them. Many of them had existed all along in the black underground of "race" records and R&B radio broadcasts. Outstanding among these was Presley's best-selling rendition of *You Ain't Nothin' but a Hound Dog,* which had been popular among blacks in a version done by "Big Mama" Willie Mae Thornton as early as

1953. The difference between the two was in the fact that Elvis had gained the adulation of a large white public while "Big Mama" would hardly have been accepted in those days before the big pop-folk-rock-soul explosion of the sixties.

Nearly a decade later, the Beatles reintroduced to this country a modified version of Presley's sound, noticeably altered by the use of group singing, which had become popular among blacks (through the Clovers, Spaniels, Coasters, Drifters and others) during the intervening years. Their success was such that they gave rise to a virtual flood of long-haired, guitar-plunking young white rock groups named after insects, beasts, reptiles and even psychical phenomena. Some of these groups soon drifted back into a well-deserved obscurity. Others, who possessed actual talent and were merely seeking a more palatable and challenging outlet, stayed on to develop styles of their own and to gain the respect of musicians on both sides of the racial fence. They have formed the foundation for the emergence of modern or progressive rock, in which various types of musical influences are apparent, among them classical, jazz, the folk ballad and even the exciting raga of India. However, progressive rock is directly related to soul music and other offshoots of the black musical tree, for its main distinguishing characteristic remains the explicit beat, and that beat is, again, as Pleasants observed: "African—and rhythmic." Many of its followers have appropriated from the black sub-society both musical elements and a certain cool and easy style of movement—loose-jointed and bobbling—along with the black's special jargon: "Like, Man," the whole "scene" has gone into a different kind of "groove," with "all kinds of cats" beginning to "put down" whatever they consider to be "jive" and a "drag," learning instead how to get "out there" by "blowing their minds," getting into their "bags," really "sockin' it to 'em" by "doing their own thing" with "sounds" that are sometimes "outa sight."

Thus in the mutual use of rhythm and ingredients of the blues, plus syncopated techniques developed within jazz, the relationships between rock and soul music are quite clear. However, one of the major factors distinguishing these two types of related music is this: rock has evolved more directly from black music as played by whites, with a sizable injection of white folk idioms; soul music leans more heavily toward its gospel, blues and jazz roots and always has been, regardless of the name by which it was called in past decades, the dominant music of both sacred and secular popularity among blacks. And proof of this latter statement lies in the fact that there is no conspicuous generation gap among blacks, so far as music is concerned.

Though black adults do not spend as much time listening to records as the younger generation (since they are called upon to make a living) and less frequently run down to the corner to pick up on the latest hit by Aretha Franklin, Marvin Gaye or Sam and Dave, they will certainly listen to it and tap a foot to it when their children bring it home. And in many a black physician's or dentist's office, if you listen carefully, you'll find that he has his personal desk radio tuned in (but very softly, so as not to clash with his recently acquired middle-class bearings) to the soul stations of WVON in Chicago or WLIB in New York's Harlem. On the other hand, white adults, who grew up to the sound of Frank Sinatra and the Andrews Sisters at best, or *Mairzy-Doats* at the very worst, commonly prefer the subdued sounds of Lawrence Welk or Herb Alpert's peppy but polite Tijuana Brass, seldom regarding the blues-rock idols of their children as anything more than mere makers of noise and caring very little about the whole matter. With the black adult, this is hardly the case.

So far as I am concerned, an interesting example might be found close to home. In fact, it *is* home. My mother, a singer-turned journalist who once dreamed of trailing Lena Horne into the Cotton Club chorus line, can remember hearing as a child all the old blues hits of the mid- and late-twenties when they were released as "race" records. With a bit of encouragement, she can come up with a solid rendition of *Down Home Blues* as it was sung by Ethel Waters, one of the early black queens of stage and screen, or some of the more rugged blues like *Aggravatin' Papa, Backwater Blues* or *Trombone Cholly*, which was a big hit for the empress of all blues singers, Bessie Smith, who died tragically in 1937, as the legend goes, when she bled to death after an automobile accident because she allegedly was refused emergency treatment at a "white" hospital in Clarksdale, Mississippi. (This not completely substantiated legend inspired Edward Albee's play *The Death of Bessie Smith.*) Bessie was but one of several blues-singing women of that period named Smith, all of whom were said to be unrelated (among the others were Mamie, Clara and Trixie). Some of these singers' stylistic differences remain fresh in my mother's mind. And she can recall the way that her father, who loved this music called the blues more than anything other than his own family, would come home from work in the evening and sit in his favorite chair with a little secretly procured "taste," listening to those blues records, with eyes closed, until the music moved him so much that he would shout out, "*Sing* it!"

My father, a trombonist turned businessman who once played professionally in all sorts of bands staffed by musicians I'm certain nobody ever heard of, can still beat out on the piano some of the ragtime favorites of *his* father. Proudly he mentions the time he heard, as a small boy, the fabled 125-piece band of Lieutenant James Reese Europe, General Pershing's black bandmaster of World War I, rocking out in concert with what is regarded as the first symphonic jazz. And he will discuss at length, with anyone who happens to ask him, the way he happened to be sitting in Harlem's Apollo Theatre that night in 1935 when a plump, teen-aged orphan named Ella Fitzgerald won the amateur contest, "sounding just as good as she does today and wearing the first natural [hairstyle] I ever saw, though that might not be what she had intended it to be."

As the child of parents anxious to give me the advantages they had not enjoyed, I was exposed to classical music—which I prefer to call formal music as a generic term—and soon developed an abiding love for it. But as I labored over all those tedious piano exercises inflicted on generations of youngsters by Czerny and his ilk, wondering why pieces that sounded transcendingly beautiful when played over the radio were slaughtered beyond recognition at my fingertips, there remained one instrument of release: the jukebox that my parents, in all their youthful enthusiasm for music, kept in the corner of our living room—a rather soulful thing in itself. The jukebox had been rigged so that no one in the constant troop of neighorhood visitors had to feed it a nickel or dime to make it work. One had merely to push a button to be serenaded by the great big-bandmasters of the thirties and forties, Duke Ellington, Jimmie Lunceford and Count Basie, as well as a bit of Tommy Dorsey and Benny Goodman. One holdover from 1940, a mainstay, was that gloriously gritty and grinding "Negro national anthem" called *After Hours,* as done by Avery Parish at the piano with the Erskine Hawkins Orchestra. It was the kind of music that made some folks in those still-lean, postwar years sit down with cup after cup of black coffee, puffing on homemade cigarettes rolled from pipe tobacco in newspaper, just listening and trying to get it all "together" in their minds.

On that same jukebox, one could also hear the blues by Basie's shouter from the southwest, "Little" Jimmy Rushing, called "Mr. Five-by-five"; T-Bone Walker and Louis Jordan with his Tympani Five, who also came out of that blues-rich part of the country in the late forties; colorful musicians with colorful names—Bullmoose Jackson and Ivory Joe Hunter—who helped shape the urban blues style of the fifties; and, of course, "The Queen," Miss Dinah Washington, regarded by the British-born musician-critic Leonard Feather as probably the most important R&B find of the late forties and early fifties. "The Queen" *really* did her "thing" back then, blowing her top in tempo and shouting out to all the world about walking down the street wearing nothing but a smile.

Throughout the fifties, the jukebox offered the "new sounds" of Charlie Parker and Dizzy Gillespie as they were giving birth to bebop and the silken song phrasings of Sarah Vaughan and Nat "King" Cole. The latter two, of course, had to fight it out, as the sixties dawned, with the gutsier sounds of bluesmen Bo Diddley and Muddy Waters. Then, too, there was a series of popular singing groups; the Mills Brothers, who were held over from 1931, when they had become the first black regulars on national radio; the Charioteers, who were radio features on Bing Crosby's Kraft Music Hall from 1942 to 1947; the Ink Spots of that same era, led by Bill Kenney's quivering high tenor; the Ravens, who followed the Ink Spots closely, with their swooping, deep bass lead into *Old Man River;* the Clovers with their R&B classic *One Mint Julep* in the early fifties; and the others who, throughout the following decade, helped usher in the era of soul.

Many of the sounds with which I was virtually saturated are not readily identifiable as those akin to soul music. But the rhythm and the feeling were always there, in the lilt of a popular ballad, in the unbridled stretching out of a big brass ensemble and in the buoyancy of a blues shout. Somewhere along the way, our jukebox was replaced by a high-fidelity system—and may the proverbial God rest our jukebox's soul wherever it now happens to be. But I might add that it was not located in New York, Chicago, Kansas City or some other hotbed of musical activity. When we owned it, it was tucked away in a small western Pennsylvania town where the majority of the residents were European immigrants. And that all just goes to show you that black people, no matter where they go, will take their music with them or seek it out when they get there.

A corroborating factor demonstrating the continuity of soul music in essence as well as chronology lies in its close relationship to the tambourine-shaking, hell-defying sound of gospel music. Partially this relationship is owing to the fact that so many of today's leading soul artists began their careers, often at an early age, as gospel singers, pianists or organists, performing every Sunday and usually throughout the week at the "Triumphant, Monumental, Leading Light" Baptist and Sanctified God-In-Christ Methodist churches of metropolitan ghettos, while also going on the road to "stir the flocks" at revivals and concerts in backwoods towns. Among those who shared these experiences are Ray Charles, Lou Rawls, Nina Simone, Wilson Pickett, Johnnie Taylor and too many others to be catalogued. And it is important to note that this strain precedes the rise of W. C. Handy, whose father and grandfather were ministers in Alabama before the turn of the century. And it reaches all the way into today, embracing popular and jazz musicians such as Sarah Vaughan and the late Nat Cole, who got their start in church, as well as blues-oriented artists such as the late Dinah Washington and Sam Cooke, an R&B star of the early sixties who was a gospel singer when he first met and influenced a very young gospel star named Aretha Franklin, little more than a decade ago. As a child, Aretha toured on the gospel circuit with her father, the Rev. C. L. Franklin, of Detroit. Rev. Franklin's incantatory use of rhythm in his sermons, captured in more than a score of long-playing records under his name, has been ineradicably impressed on his daughter's musical style. As one of her popular female competitors says of her: "Aretha's still singing the same thing she used to sing in church, except now instead of saying 'My Lord,' she says 'My man.' "

There is some truth in this, for in her singing and her playing I have heard many of the techniques familiar to my own Baptist upbringing. Similarly, when Ray Charles comes to the end of a chorus and lets loose with a half-chanted and half-sung cluster of improvised lyrics building up to a screamed *"Yeeeeee–aah!"* that seems to batter at the very gates of heaven, whipping the audience into a state of deliciously unbearable tension that inflames it to the point of shouting back its own unison *"Yeah!"* I am more than a little reminded of the prancing, perspiring, hymn-humming preachers of my youth who could take a list of biblical names, linking them only with the rhythmically injected word "begat," and produce such an intoxicating effect that the "sisters" of the church would "get happy" and "shout," springing up from the pews, evidently borne heavenward by shrieks of a frightening unexpectedness, and breaking into the frenzied, foot-stomping, fist-flailing, dancelike movements that anthropologists have traced to African origins. Not infrequently, the sisters would climax their fits of "possession" by "the spirit" by bursting into seemingly uncontrollable tears, or by collapsing in the aisles as forlorn Sunday-best-dressed-up heaps destined to go out and do "day's work" in somebody's kitchen the following Monday and, possibly, for every Monday after that. There was something deeply moving in their pain-provoked and penetrating cries, something that lingers in my mind and in the music called soul.

It would be strange if it were any other way with this music, for the church, with its unfulfilled promise of salvation, has been one of the few constants in the black man's long and tortuous travail in America. It was his "balm in Gilead" throughout the interminable dark night of slavery, and he carried its sweet sustenance along with him into another period of less formalized suffering, reaching out through it to a "precious Lord" who could take his hand and lead him to "the upper room" because this passionately revered Savior most certainly knew how much he could bear. In his church, whether a remodeled, secondhand edifice deserted in its socially transitional locale as a result of affluent America's retreat to the suburbs, or a storefront "tabernacle" on a garbage-strewn side street, the black man and his woman could unleash the rejected love within their hearts while reclaiming a sense of personal worth without fear of reprisals, exploitation or humiliation. Beyond the gospel shouts and jubilant cries heralding an imminent salvation, it was the only place where a weekday maid called "Mary," or some other disrespectful first name, might wear some weekend dignity by ushering others, just as proud and poverty-stricken as she, to their seats. It was the sole arena where a chauffeur or a handyman, reduced to facelessness and namelessness by his employers and often mute within his own home, might speak with some seldom exercized authority as a deacon of the congregation. And as the preacher would wail out his message, calling down death and destruction upon the oppressors as well as wrongdoers in the mass of the oppressed, all might resolve their feelings of frustration: "Pa–*raaaaaais*–se the *Lord!*"

No writer has captured so completely and compassionately the essence of the black man's religious experience in America as the essayist and novelist James Baldwin, in *The Fire Next Time.* A product of Harlem's asphalt jungle, Baldwin fought against a nullification of the self that was a built-in risk of black existence. Regarding the insidious destruction of those who had grown up with him, by their desperate retreat into the nightmarish obscurity of drugs, alcoholism, pandering and prostitution, he frantically drowned himself in religion, seeking within the folds of a fervent but not always honest evangelism an opiate that might fortify him against a relentless pain. As a man whose rendezvous with truth was inescapable, Baldwin soon shed his pentecostal robes, though his experiences as a boy minister are frozen in words that burst from the printed page in a virulent and gorgeous plea for man to be more than he is, to live up to his capabilities. Baldwin, too, recalls the special sound of those religious meetings, noting:

> There is no music like that music, no drama like the drama of the saints rejoicing, the sinners moaning, the tambourines racing, and all those voices coming together and crying holy unto the Lord.

He goes on to state:

> I have never seen anything to equal the fire and excitement that sometimes, without warning, fill a church, causing the church, as Leadbelly [the deceased folk-blues figure, Huddie Ledbetter] and so many others have testified, to "rock."[5]

Baldwin is clear about it. He thinks that the underlying meanings of this mode of expression, which contains certain elements found in jazz and the blues as well as in some gospel songs—"something tart and ironic, authoritative and double-edged"—is to be attributed to sensuality, explaining: "To be sensual, I think, is to respect and rejoice in the force of life, of life itself, and to be *present* in all that one does, from the effort of loving to the breaking of bread."[6] This is, perhaps, the most eloquent and concise definition of soul and all it entails ever to be set down on paper.

Considering all of these things, is it any wonder that blacks are so reluctant to share something so close to the secret core of their ability to survive and even to transcend pain. This is, indeed, an inner property that is jealously guarded. And yet, without any acknowledged premeditation, this black possession, this valued form of defense, has been lifted from its underground sanctuary and prostrated before the blistering neon rays of contemporary commercialism. Soul has always existed in black music, but now it has become popular, and, inevitably, its sound and its style have been adopted by others who react to it from their own nuclei of fundamental feeling. And that, of course, returns us to the matter of "blue-eyed soul" and whether or not this overtly black music when played by white artists is "for real."

Like so much of art, in any time and any culture, soul music has reached out from the environment of its incubation to become a popular form that can be learned and copied by others who do not share the heritage that went into the making of it. Thus, several white artists have been able to approximate the black soul sound so closely that they have been able to "fool" black music fans. To a great extent, this was true of the Righteous Brothers when they first gained acclaim in the early sixties. Many black listeners believed that this this soulful sounding duo who did neat arrangements of old Ray Charles tunes must, indeed, be black, too—until they saw on television a pair of country-looking, blondish-haired gents who obviously were not. The same can be said for Bobbie Gentry whose *Ode to Billie Jo* had more than a few black fans believing that this shapely, white California coed had spent half of her life clinging to the rail of the Tallahatchie Bridge spanning a Mississippi river.

In the area of instrumental music, race has been even more difficult to determine when the music has combined deep feeling and an ability to play with and against the beat, regardless of its complexity. In the realm of jazz, who would have thought, from simply hearing the music, that Joe Zawinul, who supplies that funky electric piano background for the popular soul tunes of alto saxophonist Cannonball Adderley, was pale-pated and Austrian-born. Of course, his name sounded a little bit strange, but one can't always go by that in a country where miscegenation has been practiced secretly for more than a century. And how many ardent devotees of Nina Simone, a one-of-a-kind artist who has managed to parlay songs of protest into a popular commodity, realize that she has employed white musicians, including a tambourine-wielding organist, in her instrumental ensemble? As one dips deeper and deeper into the subject of who does or doesn't have soul, so far as sheer sound is concerned, it all begins to bubble up into a moot point.

Musicians, who have long been known for their sense of fair play, are reluctant to discredit anybody, generally considering other artists on the basis of their ability and little else. Some who are relishing their first taste of success within a multiracial mainstream are grateful for the role white soul-blues-rock practitioners have played in popularizing this type of music, thereby opening new opportunities for them. As one yet-struggling black folk-ballad singer has unashamedly admitted: "The Beatles really made it for everybody. Chuck Berry ought to be more grateful to them than anybody else because they brought him back in the sixties." And it cannot be ignored that the recent domination of black artists on the record sales charts has been due to the black musicians' ability to break out of the black underground into the general market, where consumers of many ethnic backgrounds purchase their wares purely on the basis of appeal. When it comes to the power of the dollar, it is difficult for all the black consumers, functioning as a separate entity, to compete with the gyrating hordes of youngsters who comprise the mainstream. And, increasingly, black performers, even of the most soulful sort, are focusing their attention on this lucrative mainstream. This is what Dionne Warwick always has done, and no small part of her success has been due to the skillful arrangements of Burt Bacharach. This is what Otis Redding was beginning to do just before his death, and this is what James Brown and Aretha Franklin have recently been able to do, though their popularity among blacks has been long-standing. A very few black artists have made the most of this trend. Foremost among these is blues-rock guru Jimi Hendrix. His appeal is almost exclusively to whites. As Michael Thomas has noted in *Eye:* "Hendrix does for white audiences what James Brown does for black audiences. He makes their juices run. But he hasn't been to Harlem. At his concerts there are few Negroes."

On the other hand, the picture is quite different from the standpoint of black music fans whose loyalties are intense and are not easily recaptured once they have been offended. Free of the prospect of any personal financial gains, blacks are more concerned with the matter of preserving special rights to those areas they consider to be their own "thing." This is particularly true of those of a militant political bent, but it is also often true of those claiming no such abstract alliances. Immediately, there comes to my mind one mid-twentyish friend. His attitude toward political and social problems is one of a towering indifference—so long as he's doing all right for himself. But let one white performer appear on television doing a song originally recorded by a black, and he will fly into a rage, shouting out the name of the black performer or group with an earlier claim to the tune, as well as the year in which they did it and the label on which it was recorded. He is but one of a great block of grumbling black music-lovers who "put down" Motown's Supremes after they played the Copa in New York and began building a substantial following among white adults. Then the Supremes' style, previously considered so teasingly appealing, was dismissed by many as mere "slick soul done for white folks." Such reactions are as common to the well-heeled black matron who complained about not being able to enjoy the Temptations when they appeared at an Eastern supper club because "the place was filled up with all these hippie-type white kids" as they are to the bean-eating project-dweller who would not have been able to afford the cover charge.

Seldom are blacks avid fans of white soul performers, with the exception of José Feliciano—and he is Puerto Rican, which is excused as being not exactly the same thing as being white—and even he has not held their favor. One black buff who possesses a collection of several hundred records replied when I asked his opinion of Janis Joplin, "Who's she? I never even heard of her." On being given an explanation, he commented curtly, "Why should I buy her imitation of something Erma Franklin or Big Mama did when I can have the original?" Yet he loves Dionne Warwick, apparently being willing to overlook Bacharach in the background.

The disinterest of blacks in popular music by whites might be partially explained by the fact that they have, indeed, heard so much of it before in "the original." But even when the white material *is* original, they are not likely to hear it, for there is a definite difference between the type of music programmed for R&B or soul radio stations, aimed at black audiences and featuring black deejays, and that played on the "Top 40" and "underground" rock stations directed toward whites. Only the biggest hits with the most universal appeal are to be heard on both. Of course, purists might point to an actual difference in the resonance of black and white voices, since so many white musicians have demonstrated that they, too, "have rhythm" or have been capable of developing it. Yet none of these arguments completely explains unfavorable black reactions to white-made music, for the judgments previously described are not always musical ones. However, these seemingly unjustifiable adverse reactions cannot be easily disregarded. In fact, they are rather revealing.

The relationship of the black listener to the music that he regards as "his" always has been a very deep and personal one, quite often reflecting a great deal about his subordinate position in the society. In contrast to all the things the black man has not had in this country, he has always had "his" music. This has been his special province, and any infringement upon it, either by whites seeking out black music as presented by black performers or by white artists offering convincing duplications of black music, is likely to be resented.

Thus, when the black man reacts with coolness toward Tom Jones, the British soul singer, it is not necessarily because he dislikes the way Jones sounds but more because he resents the fact that Jones has a regular television show on his own while black singers, whose ancestors have been Americans for generations, do not and commonly appear on the electronic tube only as "guests." Blacks find it difficult to forget that only a few years ago, when popular white singers such as Perry Como and Andy Williams were able to retain long-running television shows, Nat "King" Cole, both a singer and a pianist, was quickly squeezed out of his pioneering fifteen-minute show because he was unable to get a sponsor —in spite of the fact that he had been more successful in developing a mainstream appeal than any black artist of his day and, perhaps, of all time. They recall the countless musicians and entertainers who never got an even break or made big money, whose works earned millions when copied by others. They do not begrudge Elvis Presley royalties from the two hundred million records he sold nor the one hundred thousand dollars he can command for a single week-long personal appearance but are angry and disheartened because their artists have never had an opportunity even to approximate that kind of success, no matter how formidable their talents. Only recently has a breakthrough been made with the burgeoning popularity of soul music, and only of late has due credit been accorded black sources of musical inspiration. Thus the Righteous Brothers have begun to shout out, when appearing on television, "Now here's to the Number *One* soul team of Sam and Dave!" before performing the black duo's hit *Hold On, I'm Comin'*.

But there remains another fundamental reason for the black attitude of rejection.

Black artists, and particularly those in the soul vein, have not always chosen music as their life's work because they were driven by aesthetic proclivities or saw art as a means of protesting social injustice. Quite often it was simply because they wanted to eat and to eat well, to have a mink coat or a Cadillac and a home in the better part of the ghetto. Throughout the years, even prior to the late thirties and forties when star athletes such as Joe Louis and Jackie Robinson opened the door to success in professional sports, the field of musical entertainment, both in a sacred and a secular sense, was one of the very few ways of "making it," of acquiring money and recognition, accessible to blacks in a world where opportunities were woefully restricted.

One of the most telling examples at hand is that of Mahalia Jackson, a former washwoman from New Orleans who rose to become the internationally acclaimed "queen of gospel." In her autobiography *Movin' On Up,* she recounts the way she was born in 1911, in that early melting pot of jazz, to a poor but clean-living family that resided in "a little old 'shotgun' shack" where "it rained about as much inside our house as it did outside." Her father moved cotton on the docks of the Mississippi River by day, worked as a barber by night and as a preacher on Sundays. Her grandparents on her father's side had been born slaves, and her mother's relatives were plantation sharecroppers who earned 75 cents for a twelve- to fourteen-hour workday, purchasing the necessities of life on credit at a company store where the black people never caught up with their supposed debts. Some of her father's people were in show business and toured with Gertrude "Ma" Rainey, called the "Mama of the Blues." They encouraged young Mahalia, who had an exceptionally strong voice even as a small child, to join them, but religious influences within her home dissuaded her from doing so. Living in an area called the Front of Town, located between the railroad and the waterfront, she dwelled in an atmosphere filled with music, within hearing distance of the now-defunct Storyville section, with its cabarets and "sportin' houses," where early jazz musicians such as Ferdinand "Jelly Roll" Morton got their start. But she never did succumb to these temporal influences.

Her mother died when Mahalia was five, and she was passed on to a series of strict, God-fearing relatives who helped consolidate her ties with the local Baptist church.

However, she also recalls the more powerful and consuming sound that filtered into her life from the Southern sanctified and holiness churches near the house where she lived.[7]

By the time Mahalia was seven, she was working as a nursemaid for white families, and though she aspired, from those days, to become a real nurse, the kind that could wear a crisp white uniform, circumstances prevented her from doing so or from going beyond the eighth grade in school. When she was sixteen, Mahalia moved north to Chicago, as did so many other hopeful blacks of that era, searching in vain for "a city called heaven" on earth. Finding no such "promised land" at hand, she "paid her dues," as blacks would call it, by commuting to the suburbs and doing housework for whites and by working as a beautician, "straightening heads" for South Side Negroes. Her residual energies, meanwhile, continually were channeled into the church, and it was there that she was able to make a little decent money by singing at conventions and, consequently, being invited to appear at churches throughout the country. In this way Mahalia acquired a substantial black following long before she stunned the musicologists and critics at a special folk music session conducted in conjunction with the Newport Jazz Festival in 1950. The invitation had been issued by Marshall Stearns, an astute, veteran scholar of black music, and as a result of her appearance, Mahalia Jackson, who had had only one formal vocal lesson in her life—and it had been notably unsuccessful—went on to become the leading recording star of gospel music and an international concert artist. But even at the height of her success, Mahalia was unable to forget the black experience that had spawned her. She understood the reasons that she could not get a national sponsor when she had her own radio show on CBS in Chicago, in 1954, but found it difficult to believe that whites who flocked to her concerts, both in the United States and abroad, could claim as brothers-of-the-skin those who shot bullets through her windows when she bought a home in a previously white Chicago neighborhood in 1955.

It might be argued that Mahalia Jackson was born more than a half-century ago and that the social circumstances that limited her prospects do not apply to younger artists. Unfortunately, this is not true, for the highly touted "progress of the Negro," in areas unrelated to self-realization through identity, has been more theoretical than tangible. More than 40 per cent of the nation's black people continue to subsist at a level of poverty considered by the U.S. government to be barely sufficient to sustain life, and an average black college graduate still earns a mere six thousand dollars a year, compared to almost ten thousand granted a white with a similar background. Indeed, the "black bourgeoisie" itself, the black middle class, has only become a recognizable factor since World War II, and its members remain a very small minority of all black people in this country. Moreover, the development of a black middle class, and the economic and sociological shift that development represents, has come about too late to effect sweeping changes in the life patterns of black artists and potential musicians who have reached maturity in this decade, as a look at those who have more recently come upon the scene and at the role music played in their very special set of circumstances makes clear.

In 1967, when he died at the age of twenty-eight, Otis Redding had earned more than six hundred thousand dollars from personal appearances alone that year and owned a three-hundred-acre ranch near Macon in his native Georgia. A high school dropout, he had become a wealthy and publicly acclaimed man. But he had worked as a chauffeur and valet until his first records were cut and his ballad *These Arms of Mine* had established him as an artist. One cannot help but doubt that a man of his humble beginning, and particularly one who lived in the South, might ever have reached such a high level of professional and economic success if it had not been for the outlet provided by his music.

In mid-February, 1969, James Brown, who spent three years of his teens in a Georgia reform school, was featured on the cover of *Look* magazine beside a picture of former Democratic Vice-Presidential candidate Senator Edmund Muskie. *Look* posed the question: Was Brown, whose recordings and investments grossed $4.5 million in 1968, the most important black man in America? The question was answered wordlessly in the picture that showed him signing an autograph for a black youngster and casting down upon the lad a stern but affectionate look that seemed to tell the boy that he must become his *own* symbol of black manhood.

Since his early teens, twenty-six-year-old Curtis Mayfield has been a successful singer, guitarist and songwriter, though he cannot read music. As leader of the popular vocal group called the Impressions, who have been described by critics as "the modern Ink Spots," he has become an important figure in the pop music field and has helped to mold the careers of other talented people, including a family singing group known as the Five Stairsteps and Cubie. Mayfield grew up in Chicago with several musically inclined youngsters, among them Jerry Butler, who went on to become a star with his recording of *For Your Precious Love*. Mayfield did not finish high school, though he strongly advises others not to follow his example and recalls of his childhood: "I suppose we were poor, but everybody else we knew was poor so I guess we didn't notice it."

The three original members of the Supremes, the jewels in Motown's crown, were not always known for their glamour, polish and expensive wardrobes. Lead singer Diana Ross, Mary Wilson and former Supreme Florence Ballard became buddies as little girls growing up in a Detroit lower-income housing project where a college education and a comfortable future were *not* among the things they could take for granted.

Martha Reeves of Motown's Martha and the Vandellas came from the same sort of semideprived but respectable background and readily acknowledges the role it played in her development. After graduating from high school, she took a job as a secretary at Motown in 1962, hoping to worm her way into a singing career by way of the back door. "I had to get in some way," she says of the then-young Motown firm. "Everyone was so young there and there was such a feeling about it." She sang every chance she got, hoping to be overheard and discovered. Eventually, Martha and two other girls were called in to back up Motown star Marvin Gaye on a recording session. That was the beginning of the group that later recorded such hit tunes as *Come and Get These Memories, Heat Wave* and *Dancing in the Street.* In 1968, when Martha, a willowy, cocoa-colored young woman, replaced the two other girls in her group with new Vandellas, one of the additions was her younger sister, Lois, whom she had groomed for that purpose. Then it was that Martha told this writer that her search for success was motivated not only by a desire for personal stardom but also by a need "to get some butter for the others," namely, her brothers and sisters. "I wanted to see that they had the new dress for the prom, the graduation clothes and other things I couldn't have," she explained. "I wanted them to know there was a better chance ahead."

Of course, all black artists have not come from such backgrounds. Some, such as Booker T. Jones, leader of the integrated instrumental group called the M.G.'s (for Memphis Group), have college degrees, and a few have come from upper-middle-class origins, among them the soulful composer-balladeer Oscar Brown Jr., whose family has considerable real-estate holdings in Chicago. But this type of black musician has tended to be the exception, and the black public knows this. Thus the black has often come to resent any "borrowing" of his music. To him it has seemed that those who have every other conceivable way of "making it" have, perhaps inadvertantly, taken something away from those who have possessed so small a share of life's material rewards—and that once again brings us back to the question of "blue-eyed soul."

If middle-class Negroes such as Booker T. and Oscar Brown can play and sing the blues, shouldn't the same privileges be extended to white artists such as Janis Joplin, who is the daughter of a refinery company executive; John Hammond Jr., whose father, through his position at Columbia Records, has discovered and shaped the careers of black artists such as Billie Holiday, Count Basie and innumerable others; Paul Butterfield, a comfortably brought-up blues singer and harmonica player who listened carefully and even sat in with groups led by men such as Muddy Waters before organizing his own blues band? If rigid racial lines are to be drawn, then what is the black operatic prima donna Leontyne Price doing singing Puccini and Verdi at the Metropolitan? Shouldn't she be shouting out the blues or recording hit tunes for Motown?

An answer to this lies in the differentiation between music that can be learned and mastered as an art—a direction in which jazz has been moving—and music that is dependent on a certain ethnic authenticity, as the musical commentator Nat Hentoff has observed in his essay "The Future of the Folk Renascence."[8]

With regard to the young white performers, Hentoff advises, ". . . they will not only have to write much more of their *own* material, but they will also have to confront the present and future as *themselves*." (Hentoff's italics)

Yet it is becoming increasingly difficult to draw these ethnic lines. Of late, a black singer-guitarist named Charlie Pride has become a star in the country and western field—and that is supposed to be *white* folk music. Most notably, Ray Charles broke into the mainstream by doing bluesy versions of country tunes. It is unlikely that the day is just around the corner when we will be treated to the spectacle of an Oriental gospel singer, but blues guitarist B. B. King already has expressed an interest in Japanese koto music. And none of this should be surprising, for part of the magic of music, the purest and most pleasure-giving of all the arts, has always been its universality. It is indeed a shame when it has to be made into a battleground, as so often has been the case. But there are, as I have tried to indicate, valid reasons for the blacks' possessiveness. It should never be forgotten that the sound of soul has also been the sound of suffering. Behind the shout of the blues, there is the tear of the spiritual. I, for one, cannot listen to either one without recalling a summer night I spent in Mississippi, in 1966.

It was the year following the one in which idealistic students, black and white together, had come to the dusty backwoods town of Ruleville to participate in the voter registration and educational project sponsored by the Council of Federated Organizations. It had been a summer of brotherhood and learning on both sides. But this was a year later. Most of the young crusaders had returned to their homes in the North by then. James Meredith, the man who integrated "Ole Miss," to the accompaniment of a national rumbling, had just been shot while attempting to march alone from Memphis to Jackson. The late Dr. Martin Luther King Jr., the peace-preaching and footsore "messiah" of black people, had come south to complete Meredith's march and thousands had come with him, joining in one of the last of the dramatic civil rights demonstrations of the decade. But even they had marched far past Ruleville.

In that steaming, rural summer night, several of us sat in the small frame home of Mrs. Fannie Lou Hamer, the heroine of the Mississippi Freedom Democratic party who had been evicted from a plantation, harassed, jailed and beaten nearly to death because she tried to claim her right to vote in 1962. She, too, had gone to march with Dr. King, proudly limping along beside him on one leg that was shorter than the other because she'd been injured as a child but had not had access to medical treatment. She had come back, as she always did, to shed a little guiding light on her neighbors in Ruleville. Among these were the young people, some under ten, most in their teens and a few who had already crossed over into their twenties, in all hopelessness. Now they had gathered in her home, as they frequently did, coming together to ward off the shattering despair that had been their lot and that of so many before them. Mrs. Hamer, a dark, sad-eyed, full-bodied woman known throughout the Delta as a gospel singer, began to lead them in *We'll Never Turn Back,* which had been the theme song of the Mississippi Summer Project. Their voices rose through the ominous stillness of that night with a strength that was understated and a passion that was not self-pitying:

We've been 'buked and we've been scorned,
We've been turned back sure's you're born,

But we'll never turn back,
No, we'll never turn back
Till all people be free
And we have equality.

That, truly, was the most soulful sound I've *ever* heard.

1. Henry Pleasants, *Serious Music—and All That Jazz* (Simon and Schuster, 1969).

2. Lerone Bennett Jr., *The Negro Mood* (Johnson, 1964), p. 71.

3. Marshall W. Stearns, *The Story of Jazz* (Oxford University Press, 1962), p. 150.

4. John Gabree, *The World of Rock* (Fawcett, 1968).

5. James Baldwin, *The Fire Next Time* (The Dial Press, 1964), p. 47.

6. *Ibid.*, p. 57.

7. Mahalia Jackson and E. M. Wylie, *Movin' On Up: The Mahalia Jackson Story* (Hawthorn, 1966), p. 32.

8. Nat Hentoff, "The Future of the Folk Renascence," in *The American Folk Scene: Dimensions of the Folksong Revival*, eds., David A. DeTurk and A. Poulin Jr. (Dell 1967), p. 326.

2

A CONCISE NATURAL HISTORY OF SOUL

NOBODY KNOWS where the blues began, though the seeds for their development were planted in August, 1619, when an unknown "Dutch Man of War" deposited twenty Africans at the tiny settlement of Jamestown, Virginia. It was a year before the arrival of the famous "Mayflower" and it marked the beginning of the black man's history in America.

Those twenty human beings and the twenty million other blacks who were brought to the New World as chattels during the 244 years slavery was sanctioned by this country, along with their descendants, were to have a profound effect on the course of America's growth: economically, politically, sociologically and, in particular, culturally.

It was their unpaid-for labor that helped lay the foundation for the emergence of the richest nation the world has ever known. It was the problem of justifying their enslavement in a nation supposedly dedicated to the pursuit of democracy that was a contributing factor, though hardly the sole or precipitating factor, in a bitter civil war. It has been the question of defining their place, or, better yet, determining whether they are to have any place at *all* in the affluent society, that has provoked the shattering social convulsions that yet continue. And it has been the black man's peculiar ethnic background, his painful experience in a land where he has been denied access to the highly touted "melting pot," and his reactions to that experience that have found voice in a type of music not quite like any other.

This music has undergone countless changes and has reflected many influences during the black man's 350-year involuntary "visit" to the New World. It is unlikely that the slave chants of previous centuries would have made the hit parades of today, yet there are certain elements within today's black music that can be traced directly to ancient sources, and it can safely be stated that had it not been for the strange meeting of cultures concomitant with the black man's arrival in America, coupled with the circumstances surrounding his position, the moving music called soul, blues or any other name might never have come about.

In his penetrating study *Blues People,* LeRoi Jones has presented the idea that the blues, used as a common denominator of black music in the Western world, embodied the captive's adaptation of those aspects of his own cultural heritage he had retained to a situation in which much had to be reinterpreted. He proposes that the changes apparent in the course of this musical development reflect the transmutation of the African, who did not believe he would be here forever, into the black American, who knew his plight was irreversible and therefore had to find new methods of adjusting to a generally hostile and oppressive environment. According to Jones's thesis, the blacks were people reacting as people and not merely unfeeling social tools indifferent to the cold manipulations of cultural synthesis. It was the black man's reaction to the subhuman position imposed on him that led to the creation of a particular type of music, one that sprang from what he calls a blues attitude. Pointing up the importance of this reaction within a special set of circumstances, Jones states: "The African cultures, the retention of some parts of these cultures in America, and the *weight* of the stepculture produced the American Negro. A new race."[1] Using music as the prime referent to this change and citing the significance of the blues and its related forms as an index of it, Jones writes:

> It is a native American music, the product of the black man in this country: or to put it more exactly the way I have come to think about it, blues could not exist if the African captives had not become American captives.[2]

I am inclined to agree with Jones, and while some have quibbled over his emphasis on social context and human reaction as prime factors in musical development, there can be, at a more fundamental level, no doubt about the significance of the black man's peculiar role in the shaping of modern music. One of the supportive facts behind this whole approach has been succinctly stated by the composer-bandleader Noble Sissle, a major figure in the so-called Jazz Age of the twenties. In his introduction to black song-writer Perry Bradford's autobiography, *Born with the Blues,* Sissle singles out "the beat" as the distinguishing characteristic of all modern popular music, commenting: "Who created this 'beat'? The answer is—the American Negro, because none of the other immigrants brought it with them."[3]

In keeping with LeRoi Jones's line of thinking, I would suggest that anyone who wishes to understand the black man's music should first know his history. That history cannot be recounted here in detail. However, a few vital factors should not be overlooked, even in a survey of this sort.

As is the case with his music and its alien flavor, the black man's experience in America cannot be equated with that of other groups because he came from a totally different culture into a situation where the deck was stacked against him from the very beginning. Of all the diverse peoples comprising this mongrel society, the black man is the only one who was brought here against his will. For him, there was no quest for religious freedom or the possibility of becoming a landowner instead of a lackey. He came as a slave. There was no intention on the part of the embryonic establishment of ever letting the black man become anything other than a slave. Thus the whole frame of reference of blacks to American history is quite different from that of whites.

Among black schoolchildren, I have found no great affection for George Washington simply because he was supposed to be the father of "our" country. "Hip" kids are more inclined to think of him as a slave-owner and wonder why there are so many blacks who go by the name of Washington while rarely does one encounter a white with that surname. The same sort of icy response is likely to greet laudatory recitations of the exploits of the pilgrims and pioneers, who, though they certainly had it hard enough, gambled for a stake in the future and did not endure the black's constantly dehumanizing humiliation. Above and beyond the black man's celebrated loyalty and proven patriotism, he *is* quite a different kind of American because his initiation into this society was as a slave and not as a potential partner.

Certainly, slavery has been a common practice throughout the history of mankind, in Greece, in Rome, among competing tribes in Africa long before the mid-fifteenth century when some black rulers began trading off other blacks to the Portuguese and later to the Dutch and English who made regular trips to the continent to collect human cargo. However, the introduction of the African as a slave in the New World brought into play forces seldom apparent in the non-American examples.

First, the black was a lucrative commodity, and he was imported in great numbers. Yet he was a human being, and America was a place where the language, the customs, the whole pattern of living and problem-solving were completely different from that to which he had been accustomed. He was a non-Western man thrown into a Western culture and thus, above all other things, separated from the European whites who had come to colonial America as indentured servants. It was an uncomprehendingly bewildering experience for the African to find himself a slave in a place of strange customs. It was not enough that he was cut off from his past and systematically stripped (though not completely) of his heritage, but he was not accorded adequate indoctrination into the ways of the new world. From his vantage point in bondage, he had to develop his own patterns of adjustment as best he could. Throughout it all, he was regarded as a *thing*, for, as Jones has observed:

> It is certain that it was this foreignness and the reluctance of the white American to think of the African as another *man* that helped early to fix the African's and later the Afro-American's place in American society—just as the color of the African's skin set him apart from the rest of the society blatantly and permanently.[4]

This statement touches upon one of the reasons that the black and not the Indian or Caucasian was chosen to supply the inexpensive labor needed to develop the new land. Originally, it was not a matter of racial prejudice, for as Lerone Bennett has pointed out: "The rulers of the early American colonies were not overly scrupulous about the color or national origin of their work force." As for why this one group was singled out from others, Bennett explains:

> White men, for one thing, were under the protection of strong governments; they could appeal to a monarch. White men, moreover, were white; they could escape and blend into the crowd. Indians, too, could escape; they knew the country and their brothers were only a hill or a forest away.[5]

Thus the spotlight fell on the sturdy black, who was so inexpensive that he could be bought for life instead of for a few years, as was the case with indentured servants; who presented an unlimited supply of labor; who was unprotected by a strong government and was so visible by his blackness that he could run but not hide—or at least not for long.

The die was cast. The black man was brought to America to serve as a slave—for no other reason. The suffering began on the shores of Africa, it continued on the slave ships, and it grew in the New World—on the plantations of Caribbean islands and of South and North America, which half of the forty million blacks stolen from Africa lived to see.

When one searches for the roots of soul, one must therefore look to those plantations, especially to those in America's Dixie; for though the black man came to this country empty-handed, he carried within him many elements of his African heritage. Not the least of these were his music and its rhythm.

The distinguishing characteristic of African music is its polyrhythmic nature, the quality whereby different rhythms are piled one on top of the other and played simultaneously and somehow made to fall into place in constantly shifting patterns. As a simple experiment, one might try beating 4/4 time with one hand and 3/4 with the other. Now consider the effect when four or five such rhythms are played together while deliberately placed accents add yet another quality to this woven fabric of tempos, as is common in West Africa, from which the American black's ancestors came. A much simpler but similar use of rhythm is to be found in jazz and much of the popular music of today, where extra beats or accents are placed in all sections of the spaces between the regular beats. (For a taste of this phenomenon in one of its most popular forms, listen to Martha and the Vandellas do *Dancing in the Street.*) But this quality, as it is found in the music of today, becomes more apparent when one focuses on both the rhythm and the melody and harmony.

So long disregarded by the West as unbeautiful and barbaric, the music of Africa, with its rhythmic complexities and stylistic intricacies, has been thoughtfully reevaluated by anthropologists and serious students of music whose appreciation transcends the comfortably familiar. As Ivan Annan has written in his commentary on *Folk Music of Ghana*:

> The music of Africa, only a short time ago regarded as "exotic" and "primitive," is recognized today as a large family of musical idioms with common connections, as diverse as European music is diverse. It has come to be understood that our early conceptions of African musical "primitiveness" were completely erroneous. We are now fully aware of the sophistication inherent in much African music, not only in its rhythmic capabilities, but in its other aspects as well.[6]

Prominent among these other aspects is the use of antiphony, wherein there is an exchange between a leader and the chorus or audience. This pattern is quite noticeable on recordings of West African music and has its counterpart in black music of this continent. It can be found in the talked-shouted-sung sermons by preachers in Baptist and "sanctified" churches; that it is equally obvious in the AAB form of the classic blues, in which an observation is stated in music, repeated in slightly altered form and followed by a line of comment on the initial statement, frequently with enough space at the end of the sung phrases for an instrumentalist in the band to inject his "comments"; and it can be found in the repetitive ensemble brass riffs of big jazz bands as they answer the call of a saxophonist, trumpeter, pianist or vocalist. Today, this element can be heard in the soul music of Ray Charles in the raw or of Aretha Franklin with the Sweet Inspirations shouting out behind her.

In his authoritative anthropological study *The Myth of the Negro Past,* Melville J. Herskovits has dealt with this subject, tracing many of the black American's prevailing attitudes and cultural characteristics to their African antecedents. Detailing the retention of Africanisms in religious concepts (respect for supernatural forces in lieu of a strict reliance on human powers), speech, social attitudes and motor habits (walking, posture, movements while singing or dancing, etc.), he draws some comparisons between Negro music of the New World and that of West Africa, with its diverse lullabies, work songs, "signifying" songs of derision, social dance songs and sacred music. Qualifying his opinions and noting that any thorough study of the subject would be dependent on a more extensive examination of *all* such types of derivative music to be found in all the Americas, Herskovits suggests that the musical influence of blacks in this hemisphere has been notable not only in the music they have created themselves but in three other areas more closely related to the mainstream: the direct borrowing of Negro religious songs such as *Swing Low, Sweet Chariot,* which is now sung as frequently by whites as blacks; the use by white song writers of stylistic characteristics and progressions of this music in their popular songs; a similar use of these characteristics in works by "serious" composers such as Anton Dvorak, most notably George Gershwin and less conspicuously Aaron Copland.

Citing the ubiquity of the drum in African music and the corresponding emphasis on rhythm in black music of the Americas, Herskovits points to intangible similarities, such as "the close integration between song and dance found everywhere in Africa," the tendency of audiences or choruses to accompany musicians with hand-clapping and to "dance a song," in both sacred and secular music, and the widespread reliance on improvisation, which is "a deeply rooted device of African singing." He also notes the occurrence of antiphony and writes:

> The pattern whereby the statement of a theme by a leader is repeated by a chorus, or a short choral phrase is balanced as a refrain against a longer melodic line sung by the soloist, is fundamental and has been commented on by all who have heard Negroes sing in Africa or elsewhere. The relationship of the melody to an accompanying rhythm —carried on by drums, rattles, sticks beaten one against the other, hand-clapping, or short nonmusical cries—is also of the closest [derivation]. So prominent is the rhythmic element in Negro music that this music as ordinarily conceived relegates the element of melody to second place.[7]

Though much emphasis has been placed on the prominence of rhythm in this music, melody is no small ingredient, nor is harmony absent. Richard A. Waterman, an authority in this field, has drawn parallels between European and West African music, showing that both employ the diatonic, or seven-note, scale as well as harmony, which is not found elsewhere in folk music. The latter is noticeable in African group singing where long unison phrases often resolve into segments of "harmonizing" or singing in thirds. And Annan has written ". . . in the use of two-part singing, the African has no superior." Parenthetically, it should be noted that these similarities apply only to the folk music of these continents and not to classical or "formal" music, as Marshall Stearns has made clear, adding:

> The main difference is that European folk music is a little more complicated harmonically and African tribal music is a little more complicated rhythmically. They are about equal in regard to melody.[8]

Yet these African elements provided only a foundation for the new music that was to develop in the Americas. The full development of black music was closely linked to events in the New World. The pattern was different in areas outside the future United States. In the Latin-Catholic colonies of the Caribbean there was a more limited cultural exchange than in the British–Protestant colonies of North America. This difference was explained by Herskovits thus:

> The contact between Negroes and whites in the continental United States as compared to the West Indies and South America goes far to explain the relatively greater incidence of Africanisms in the Caribbean. In the earliest days, the number of slaves in proportion to their masters was extremely small, and though as time went on thousands and tens of thousands of slaves were brought to satisfy the demands of southern plantations, nonetheless the Negroes lived in constant association with whites to a degree not found anywhere else in the New World.[9]

This difference in the degree of association is generally acknowledged to be one of the main reasons that the drum-heavy ritualistic sounds of Haiti, where blacks waged a successful battle for independence against the minority of French planters, are quite close to the African originals. It explains why the highly rhythmic dances called the conga, rhumba, mambo and cha-cha, all basically African, did not originate in Virginia or New York but in Cuba, which was dominated by Spain, a nation whose own native music already reflected the black imprint of the Moorish invasion—in particular, in the flamenco, with its rhythmic clapping, stomping improvisations. In North America, the "Caribbean-style" pattern was to find its most dramatic expression in New Orleans, a French colony that was swallowed up by the British-derived United States. As we shall see later, the invasion of New Orleans by the "purer" African music of the Caribbean may have been the main reason that the music called jazz is commonly acknowledged to have been affected by developments in that city of so many cultural cross-currents.

Even from the beginning, the slave clung to some fragments of his indigenous music. Though it is difficult to set up a definite chronology of events, the birth cry of black music in this land may well have been heard in the work song with its set call and response form. Here there was a direct relationship with the African past, for on that other continent art is not separated from life, as is common in the Western world, but is interwoven with the activities of life as a functional entity. In Africa, music is one of the means by which cultural traditions are passed on from one generation to another. Through music, old men and women voice their philosophical attitudes and indoctrinate the young with the principles to which they should adhere. Through music, legends of history are transmitted, warriors are incited to fight. It is in Africa, for example, that the talking drum, which can be used to convey specific messages, is found. Then, too, music is used in connection with toil. As Stearns has stated: "In all parts of the New World, the work song is sung wherever Africans are found, for this type of music is an integral part of an African tradition of mutual help." And he also notes: "Within the United States, the work song was probably sung as soon as the first slaves were landed and put to work."[10] The work song is one of the forms that survived its plantation days and was carried out into the country's byways, where heaving manual laborers swung their pickaxes and hammers in perfect unison to a leader's chant. It was heard when the continent-straddling railroads were being built and on chain gangs composed of black prisoners who used it to boost their morale. And today it survives, virtually unchanged, in parts of the rural South. The public knows it in songs such as *Take This Hammer*, and in the traditional lament, *Another Man Done Gone*, in its clap-accompanied rendition by Odetta, the lady master of folk and blues.

Then, too, there was the field holler, derived from the West African whoop, shout or cry called the "falsetto break." Some have described it as a sort of eccentric yodel marked by a vocal "snap," a twisting of the voice with an abrupt breaking off at a higher pitch. In her writings on the slave songs of the Georgia Sea Islands,[11] Lydia Parrish tells how she heard Negroes calling to each other across the fields in a most unusual way: "The call was peculiar, and I always wondered how they came by such a strange form of vocal gymnastics, since I never heard a white person do anything like it."

What distinguished this call from other such expressions was not only the twisting and snapping of the voice but a certain melancholy, offbeat note found within it: the "blue note," which is found throughout black music of America and is produced by flattening the third and seventh notes of the scale in any key. This became the most important key to the blues and the blues effect as it was carried over into jazz where the "flatted fifth" was added as a third "blue note" with the arrival of the modernists at the halfway mark of the twentieth century. Some have theorized that this flattening of certain notes and distinctive slurrings resulted from the African's attempt to adapt his use of the pentatonic, or five-note, scale, which he had known in his homeland, to the Western diatonic scale. However, Waterman and others have, as we have seen, pointed out that the diatonic scale also is used in West Africa. Regardless of the reasons for the appearance of the "blue note," it was most definitely there in the field holler and is one of the roots of the more complex musical form called the blues that began to be acknowledged as a separate phenomenon around 1917.

While the blues were songs with a definite form and words that were sung by many, the hollers or cries were musical fragments sometimes used as "calling cards" by individuals as they made their way up country roads for a visit. The holler later found its way into the urban areas of the South and also of the North, where blacks sought a better life, as the street cry of vendors, and as such it remained recognizable until so recently that Oscar Brown Jr. has written a song called *Rags and Old Iron* that was inspired by the street cries he heard as a boy on the South Side of Chicago only thirty years ago. Brown's song comes complete with the vocal twist and snap. These shouts have been most widely popularized through George Gershwin's folk opera *Porgy and Bess* in the cries of the Crab Man and Strawberry Woman. (All jazz lovers treasure the Miles Davis rendition of these segments, particularly *Crab Man*, on which this trumpeter and flugelhornist imitates the undulations of the human voice as completely and as beautifully as has ever been accomplished on an instrument.)

From the church there came a shout . . .

Ebony

. . . reaching back to deep black roots . . .

Ebony

Columbia Records

. . . drawn from an essence that lingers today in the blues-tinged gospel songs of James Cleveland (above) and the moving spiritual entreaties of Mahalia Jackson (right) . . .

Stax

. . . while the Staple Singers have carried the sanctified feeling into the area of "soul-folk" music, singing powerful songs of protest and inspiration.

Ebony

From the touring road shows of the South, there came a young woman named Bessie Smith who sang of dark laughter and dark tears as she became the "Empress of the Blues," reigning over the underground era of the twenties . . .

Ebony

. . . while a cornetist named W. C. Handy set the black blues down on paper, informing a nation of their existence.

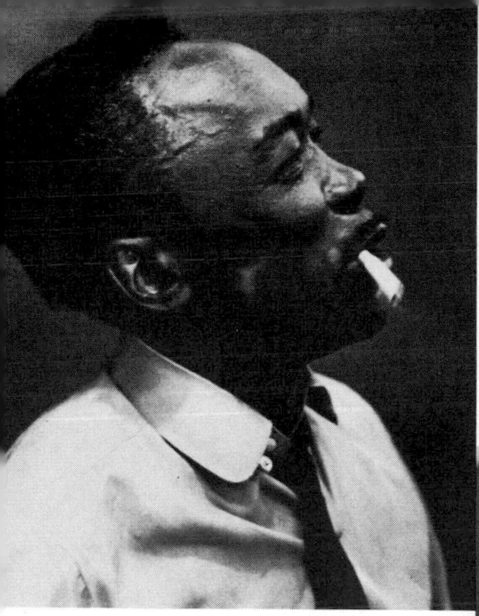

Stax

The blues have taken many forms throughout the years, and several of their greatest practitioners first learned what the blues were really about in their native Mississippi, among them John Lee Hooker (left), whose singing and guitar playing ring of the rural South . . .

CBS-TV

. . . Muddy Waters (right), whose "down home" style and "low-down" musings have been touched with an urban flavor identified with the city of Chicago . . .

Stax

. . . Albert King (left), who has bridged the racial gap to become a favorite among members of the hip generation.

B. B. King, once known as the "Beale Street Blues Boy," has crusaded for acceptance of his art form for 21 years, singing and playing music of an earthy profundity.

Those identified with jazz and popular music also spring from the soul tradition, among them (left to right) LaVerne Baker, whose rendition of *Tweedle Dee* was a big rhythm and blues hit of the 50's; Nat "King" Cole, a jazz pianist who became one of the leading pop singers of the late 50's and early 60's; Della Reese, whose range is from gospel to pop; Erskine Hawkins, of *After Hours* fame, whose big band of the 40's had a blues foundation.

Rhythm and blues singing groups of the 50's helped set the scene for the soul era, among them, the Coasters . . .

Atlanti

. . . the Drifters . . .

. . . the Platters.

An interesting story was told to me a few years ago by Helen Dowdy, who sang the part of the Strawberry Woman in the original 1935 production of Gershwin's American classic. At the time, she was a formally trained singer and a member of the Eva Jessye Choir that had been selected to do the difficult choral work in this unorthodox opera. Gershwin, who had soaked up black soul at its source by spending some time in South Carolina's Charleston area, where the work was set, had heard these penetrating and haunting cries there and had written them into his opus. However, on returning to New York, he found it next to impossible to locate a black singer who could duplicate them, because all the black singers he auditioned were professionals who had been trained in the European classical tradition of singing and had come to look down on black music and its very methods. The young Miss Dowdy was the next prospect for the part, and, thrilled at this opportunity to step out from the chorus and to perform as a soloist, she tackled her assignment with gusto. She practiced at home, singing all the written notes in the "proper" Western style, but her mother, who had grown up in the South and was familiar with the cries, overheard her and convinced her she was doing them "all wrong." She proceeded to teach her daughter the correct way of singing them, emphasizing the slurrings and snaps so vital to them. When Miss Dowdy showed up at rehearsal the next day and sang her little song the way her mother had taught her, Gershwin flipped, shouted "That's *it!*" and, in her words, "just about fell out of his chair." Thereafter performed always in this manner, the Strawberry Woman's cry, like that of the Crab Man, became one of the lasting highlights of the opera.

It has been said that all the blue notes are to be found in the cracks between the keys on the piano. One needn't bother looking for them there, but one can assume that black music employs quarter tones, as compared with the Western full and half tones between notes. (These "bastard" tones are to be found in some other non-Western music.) They can most easily be produced with the human voice, when notes are slurred into and out of. And since the attempt to imitate the human voice marked the black man's use of instruments, they are to be found in music he has played as well as sung. To those trained in the Western manner, the results give the impression of being "out of tune," though the effect is deliberate and the intention is *not* to hit the notes sharply on the nose, moving from one note directly to the next. Also, in this instrumental voice imitation, there is the use of vibrato, growling sounds and others that simulate vocal inflections. In short, the holler and its offspring have resulted in that which we now consider to be American music.

While the history of the field holler, the basic ingredient of much that was to follow, can be traced, the evolution of the spiritual is more nebulous. Here the European influence is more apparent, for much of the early black's religious music was based on white hymns, though they were greatly transformed when he applied his particular style to them. Thus it is difficult to distinguish the element in spirituals that is entirely the black man's creation from the element that is his variation on music that already existed.

The black man was exposed to white religious music during the period known as "The Great Awakening," which began in the early nineteenth century, when white ministers tramped throughout the country's frontier and rural areas conducting revivals and spreading "the word." Most often they were Baptists and Methodists whose approach to the gospel was fiery and emotional, in contrast to the austere restraint of the Calvinists. Their method, which prompted hardship-ridden frontier whites to "shout" and pass out, equally appealed to the blacks, whom they sought out to convert from "heathenism."

The white revivalists are considered to have been forerunners of the Abolitionists. Some of them came from New England, where the old British custom (now extinct) of "lining out," of having the minister recite a line of a song before the congregation sang it, for the benefit of those who could not read, bore some resemblance to African call and response patterns. The custom may have appealed to the slave, as may have the practice of immersion, which he might have fitted into the residual elements of African religious ceremonies, like that of the cult of the river spirits. Furthermore, he could identify with the dramatic stories of the oppressed "Hebrew children" and find refuge in the promise of a reward beyond this world for those who suffered. In this way, he came to worship a God who was *not* recreated in his image, and he was the only American to do so. Considering this background, it is easy to understand why most blacks, even today, belong to the Baptist or Methodist denomination, or to the sanctified church. Services conducted in the sanctified churches bear a much closer resemblance to African religious ceremonies than do those in any other church, and, as might be expected, they attract a greater percentage of poor blacks whose assimilation has been slighter than that of middle-class Negroes.

At first, slave owners tried to prevent their blacks from worshiping, for, as Jones has observed, if they were to be converted from "heathens" into Christians, they would have to be regarded as human beings and as such could not be dealt with under the complex system of rationalizations designed to justify their enslavement. Later, however, religious worship was encouraged, as a pacifier. The black, who came from an intensely religious culture, took to it readily, finding in it a new outlet when his own secret "voodoo" and cultist ceremonies were forbidden, to be practiced only in clandestine meetings and, in truer form, in the non-Protestant Caribbean.

As the slave came to conduct his own services, he brought to them particles of his indigenous black culture that, combined with the white biblical stories and songs he had heard, produced a hybrid sort of ceremony. Music was very much a part of it, as was the case in Africa, and so was a modified type of dance. A much-quoted description of an early black American church service deals with the basically African "ring shout."

> Very likely more than half the population of the plantation is gathered together; let it be in the evening, and a light-wood fire burns red before the door of the house and on the hearth. For some time one can hear, though at a good distance, the vociferous exhortation or prayer of the presiding elder or of the brother who has a gift that way and who is not "on the back seat"—a phrase the interpretation of which is "under the censure of the church authorities for bad behavior"—and at regular intervals one hears the elder deaconing [i.e., lining out] a hymn-book hymn, which is sung two lines at a time, and whose wailing cadences, borne on the night air, are indescribably melancholy. But the benches are pushed back to the wall when the formal meeting is over, and old and young, men and women, sprucely-dressed young men, grotesquely half-clad field-hands—the women generally with gay handkerchiefs twisted about their heads and with short skirts, boys with tattered shirts and men's trousers, young girls barefooted—all stand up in the middle of the floor, and when the "sperichil" is struck up, begin first walking and by-and-by shuffling round, one after the other, in a ring. The foot is hardly taken from the floor, and the progression is mainly due to a jerking, hitching motion which agitates the entire shouter, and soon brings out streams of perspira-

> tion. Sometimes he dances silently, sometimes as he shuffles he sings the chorus of the spiritual, and sometimes the song itself is sung by the dancers. But more frequently a band, composed of some of the best singers and of tired shouters, stand at the side of the room to "base" the others, singing the body of the song and clapping their hands together or on the knees. Song and dance are alike extremely energetic, and often, when the shout lasts into the middle of the night, the monotonous thud, thud of the feet prevents sleep within half a mile of the praise-house.[12]

The "spiritual" referred to in the above passage is not the professionally arranged version of *Go Down Moses* or *Nobody Knows de Trouble I've Seen,* as performed in song recitals today, but a music more likely composed of melodious fragments that erupted spontaneously from these gatherings. The black man's religious music includes not only the haunting songs easily identified as spirituals but also the ring shout, the still-flourishing shouted and sung sermons, the ecstatic jubilee heralding a release from the suffering of the flesh and this world with its popular equivalent, the gospel song of today. The spiritual as it is now known, in its polished concert versions, has been called, as it was by Alan Lomax, ". . . the most impressive body of music so far produced by America,"[13] perhaps because it is so close to European music in its melodies and form. With its frequent echoings of a reluctant resignation to things as they are in this world in the hope of catching up in the next world, with its voicings of penitence and quiet suffering, with its subdued rhythms and only oblique references to defiance cum Joshua, it is, and always has been, in all its gorgeousness, the black music most palatable to white tastes, though it remains, at its base, akin to the rowdy gospel shouts.

Perennially, the spiritual has been a symbol of the religiosity of subjection that blacks have presented to whites in an endless search for acceptance. The process dates back to 1871, shortly after the Civil War, when the Fisk Jubilee Singers, a group of students at one of the nation's oldest black colleges, left their adopted home of Nashville, Tennessee, and set out on a mission to raise twenty thousand dollars to construct a building to house newly freed blacks in search of learning. Under the directorship of their teacher, George A. White, they sang concerts of classical music (at first) and spirituals to audiences of sympathizers. At the beginning, their prospects of success were not bright, though the dark clouds of late Reconstruction reaction had not yet begun to roll over the land. In 1871, however, they toured the South and the West, garnering some financial reapings, but they were at a loss for friends when they finally reached that colossus of the East, New York City. They did, however, find two willing supporters in the Rev. Henry Ward Beecher, a Congregational minister who had been a leading exponent of the antislavery movement, and his sister, Harriet Beecher Stowe, whose novel, *Uncle Tom's Cabin,* had been a naively stated but effective plea for abolition. The two agreed that the Fisk Jubilee Singers should be presented at Plymouth Church in Brooklyn. Advance publicity of the concert was greeted with derision, but guffaws were quickly swallowed when papers reported after the concert that "Those black bards, with grotesque words and primitive melodies of the South, captured the hearts of the Brooklynites at the last night's concert." Other accounts noted the way a hush fell over the audience when one young woman in the group dramatized the way her mother had been sold on the auction block before the whole chorus rang out its own challenge in a resounding version of *No More Auction Block for Me.* In 1872, this group of "gospel singers," as they were billed, toured Europe to general acclaim, sang for Queen Victoria at Buckingham Palace and returned to America to perform before overflow audiences throughout the land. Instead of twenty thousand dollars, their concerts netted one hundred fifty thousand dollars from their seven-year journey and, for the first time, established black music as an art with powers to move anyone who heard it to extremes of emotion.

But this was only one side of the story. While the contribution of the Fisk Jubilee Singers should never be underestimated, there was another meaning of the spirituals not thoroughly projected in their presentations. This was the message they conveyed to so many enslaved blacks. In a social setting where open discussion among slaves was forbidden and where black insurrection was a constant fear of landed whites, spirituals were sometimes used to pass along information concerning operation of the Underground Railroad, the system whereby escaped slaves were aided by other escaped slaves and northern abolitionists who provided shelter along secret routes in order that the bondsmen might make it to the Canadian border and cross over into freedom. Perry Bradford, who was born before the turn of the century and through his immediate family had a direct contact with this period, wrote of the hidden meaning of the spirituals in his 1965 autobiography when he stated:

> Grandma Betsy Bradford (a former slave) once told me *Steal Away to Jesus* was another one of their spirituals with implications of hidden reprisals; which meant steal away from their bosses and beat it up north to the promised land.[14]

This defiance and rejection of things as they were are to be found in subtle thoughts underscoring the spirituals and other black music, especially the work song and some of the blues. But the quest for acceptance was to determine what portions of this music were to be offered for public consumption and even what black attitudes would be toward black music for many a year. There were interminable efforts to transform the original black music into something more "respectable." Even the spiritual, the most palatable of forms, was "adapted."

The highly Westernized arrangements of the spirituals as we know them today are the products of black composers who were among the tiny elite of the conservatory-trained around the turn of the century. Two names stand out. One is that of Harry T. Burleigh, a gifted singer born in 1866. As a child in Erie, Pennsylvania, Burleigh became fond of the classical music he heard in the white home where his mother worked as a maid. However, his development along the black side of the musical coin came during the years of his youth, when he sang with several Negro choirs and worked as a doorman before winning a scholarship to the National Conservatory of Music in New York in 1892. There he met the conservatory's director, the Hungarian composer Anton Dvorak, and a friendship developed. The young Burleigh sang Negro spirituals by the hour to the foreign visitor, who drew from their melodic essence in composing his *New World Symphony*. Burleigh later applied his classical training to his chosen task of setting down harmonically rich concert arrangements of the spirituals. His arrangements, which are the versions of these songs most frequently heard, are so numerous that they cannot all be set down here, though they include: *Ain't Goin' to Study War No Mo', By an' By, Deep River, Ev'ry Time I Feel the Spirit, Go Down Moses, Sometimes I Feel like a*

Motherless Child and *Wade in de Water.* During the mid-twenties when Burleigh's work was attracting attention, there arose a controversy over whether spirituals should be presented in such modern arrangements or only in their simpler state, which was the way many whites preferred them. Burleigh tried to justify his approach by saying, "The depth of harmonic effects which has been added is of universal quality which lifts them from the Negro as his peculiar property and gives them to the public at large." But fundamentalists asserted that when spirituals were accorded such treatment, "the soul is taken out of them."

The other name that stands out among arrangers of spirituals is that of R. Nathaniel Dett, who was born in Ontario, Canada, in 1882. A graduate of Oberlin with additional musical studies at Columbia University, the University of Pennsylvania and Harvard University, Dett was closely associated with Hampton Institute, a Negro college in Virginia where he served as a teacher and choral leader for many years. Though he was well known as an arranger, particularly of choral works, much of Dett's reputation was built on original compositions that dealt with both racial and nonracial themes. The racially flavored music, in which he utilized the feeling of the spirituals but in highly Westernized forms, is what has survived. His *Listen to the Lambs* is a standard for black choral groups, and his opera *The Ordering of Moses* was recorded by the Voice of America for broadcasting overseas and is frequently performed in middle-class black churches, though whites might be unfamiliar with it. Even before his death in 1943, six years after Burleigh's, Dett had been designated the man who brought dignity to the Negro spiritual. However, his identification with this "dignifying" process was carried so far that in 1929, when he was in his most creative period, the Negro press thus delineated his significance: "Before he began his revolutionary changes in the immature and unrefined chords of Negro melody, Negro music was immensely crude and unfit for formal church service." He was praised for his "ingenious treatment of Negro folk songs."

Those "immature and unrefined" sounds happened to be "the real thing," and they have survived in the gospel music of today that is gaining an ever broader audience for its leading interpreters, among them Mahalia Jackson, Bessie Griffin, Marion Williams, Clara Ward, Alex Bradford and James Cleveland.

Returning to a line of historical development, it has become apparent that while the various types of black American music developed from similar roots, they shot off in different directions, and that all of these forms later came to overlap, in the soul music of today. This separation of routes is most noticeable in the evolution of jazz and the blues that were incorporated into it, as both seemed to emerge at about the same time at the turn of the century.

Jones, for one, has questioned the general conception that jazz was born in New Orleans and made its way up the river to Chicago on the ground that primitive blues that were so much a part of this music developed simultaneously in several undefined rural settings. Furthermore, there was so much mass migration among Negroes after the Emancipation that cultural forces of this sort could not be easily contained. However, it can safely be assumed that New Orleans was a catalytic factor in the growth of jazz as a publicly recognizable type of music and its subsequent national popularization when it was carried to other cities, not only Chicago, but also Los Angeles and New York. And the special conditions that point to New Orleans as a prime place of musical incubation are considerable.

Until Napoleon sold the Louisiana Territory to the United States in 1803, New Orleans had demonstrated many of the characteristics common to Latin-Catholic colonial possessions, including the greater survival of Africanisms in music and religious practice. However, once the city began to feel the effects of the western migrations and began to take on a new role as a prosperous major port where mingled cultural forces represented by the infiltration of North Americans steeped in the British-Protestant tradition, the arrival of pure blacks from the West Indies and other countries, the existence of a considerable body of free blacks and mixed bloods who participated in the city's commerce and activities and the continuing French influence, the music that developed was bound to reflect various strains. Yet the way in which jazz is believed to have been developed presents an unusual story closely linked to the social situation.

From 1817 to 1885, African music could be heard in something that must have been quite close to its original state during the slave dances in an empty lot called Congo Square in New Orleans. Writers of that period were fascinated by these Sunday afternoon sessions that were sanctioned by the city authorities as a palliative. According to their reports, the drums and other exotic instruments played there, including a stringed ancestor of the banjo (called *banjor* by blacks), were essentially West African, as were the dances that were often part of the *vodun* or voodoo ceremonies. This was the only place in the young United States where these rituals were brought out into the open, since they were forbidden in the Protestant-dominated sections of the country. The rituals also tended to survive longer in the more permissive environment of New Orleans, though fragments of *vodun* beliefs and practices have been secretly carried over into what are outwardly considered the superstitions of some southern blacks.

However, already the Congo Square dancers were said to have sung in a French-Creole dialect, indicating a blending of African and European elements. And another major white influence came to the fore in the popularity of military bands, patterned after those fashionable in Napoleon's France. Any available excuse was used for a parade to be held, and bands played for all sorts of formal and informal affairs.

Even before the Emancipation, freedmen and privileged house slaves had had their own brass bands that performed along with whites at parades, but with the swelling of the black ranks after the Civil War, the number of these bands increased accordingly. Most commonly they were associated with the rash of secret fraternal organizations and "burial societies" that proliferated in the new black subsociety. Anthropologists have traced this tendency to form such secret societies back to Africa, and equivalent organizations are common throughout the Caribbean. For the newly freed slave who was trying to find his impecunious way through an unfamiliar course of life, the societies served many purposes, providing small benefits for the sick, a rudimentary form of insurance for families of the deceased and a sense of community or "togetherness" that offered a social outlet as great as that the church had offered in previous years when the blacks' activities had been more restricted.

The use of bands to accompany funeral processions had been common in New Orleans since the early part of the nineteenth cenutry, but they had generally played in the accepted European manner, since the house slaves and mixed bloods had followed the pattern set by their masters and former masters. But with the coming of these new post-bellum black bands, composed of those who had been less exposed to white life and who retained a greater portion of their elemental rhythmic affinities, something began to happen to the music. Processions to the cemetery remained solemn—hymns were still played—but after the graveside services, which often were marked by spectacular displays of emotion (it was not uncommon for members of the family to scream, faint or try to hurl themselves into the grave), a jubilant recessional followed. The bands would "rag" the music, breaking the stiff martial 4/4 time into a livelier 2/4 tempo. The songs they played were popular hymns or spirituals such as *When the Saints Go Marching In* and *Ain't Goin' to Study War No Mo'*, but all stops were let out in improvising on their themes and stirring up, with the accented beat, an intense heat that attracted crowds of bystanders who strutted alongside regular members of the procession. This joyful release following such an unlikely event as a funeral was said to be in keeping with the ancient idea that one should weep at birth and rejoice at death, when the spirit would be free to live on without the trials of earthly existence.

These funerals with their uninhibited post-service music were being conducted long before the turn of the century, and the secret societies with their frequent use of brass bands provided one of the earliest opportunities for the black musician to work as a professional, though only part-time. However, the date usually set for the emergence of what would today be identifiable as jazz is about 1900, and it is generally conceded to be the result of the outgrowth of another quirk of New Orleans culture.

One aspect of black life in America with which whites are not always familiar is that involving the distinctions made according to darkness or lightness of skin color and, secondarily, straightness or kinkiness of hair. This unfortunate line of thinking, which has played more than a small part in racial divisiveness until very recently, can be traced to the plantation. Since white slave owners had access to the black women at hand, even against the will of the woman or her mate, miscegenation was an everyday fact of life. Frequently, but far from always, the children of these illegitimate unions were given lighter tasks around the house instead of having to toil in the fields like their darker fellow men. The lighter-colored slaves did not constitute all the house servants—others were chosen because they possessed particular skills or "loyalty"—but they were more likely to be found there and more often were accorded special privileges. Through their closer association with the master and his family, the lighter-skinned blacks more quickly adopted white manners of behavior and were indoctrinated into white ways of thinking, chiefly coming to the conclusion that whiteness was better than blackness and that the less black one was the better. This type of thinking, which rubbed off on some darker Negroes in their lowly position on the social ladder, gave rise to feelings of shame on the part of many blacks and resentment on both sides. As a result of this pernicious theory, while some house servants, of all shades, preferred to remain in the general slave quarters, where they would not be so closely watched and often could sneak off to mingle with their brothers, others gloried in this separation since it set them apart from the mass. The slave owner, especially, benefited from this system, for by bringing some of the servants to identify with him, he could count on them to serve as informers on the others. It was an effective method of putting down slave rebellions before they had a chance to begin, and more than one carefully planned insurrection, particularly that of Denmark Vesey in 1822, was foiled by a squealing house servant.

Some of the mixed bloods who were taken into the house were among the first to be given a chance to learn how to read, a skill usually forbidden slaves on pain of severe punishment or mutilation. Numerous blacks achieved much in spite of their restricted circumstances, but as things went in general, mixed bloods or the lighter Negroes had a better chance of getting a break from whites. Thus, a disproportionate number of the earliest Negro college graduates, including quite a few of the Eton- and Harvard-educated representatives elected to office during Reconstruction, were medium brown or very light in color. Such selection had less to do with native ability than the fact that so many early black graduates happened to be the illegitimate children or close relatives of wealthy whites though they were often very black in their thinking. The same applies to many of the early Negro landowners, businessmen and educators. So deeply rooted is this pattern that in the so-called Negro Society of today one finds far fewer dark than light Negroes, with the dark ones having gotten "in" through distinguished lineage, exceptional accomplishments or money.

Within the past few years, the coming of the civil rights movement with its emphasis on unity and the rise of the militants with their turnabout slogan of "*black* is beautiful" have spelled out the death knell to this kind of prejudice among people already rejected by the society-at-large. But nowhere has this pattern been so dramatically demonstrated than in the New Orleans of the nineteenth century, where it had a decided influence on musical development. There it had been solidified into an actual caste system. The rich whites, of course, remained on top, but just beneath them was a separate class composed of mixed bloods called Creoles of Color. Products of unions between French or Spanish aristocrats and African or part-African slave mistresses, they or their recent forebears had been freed by their masters under the Black Code of 1724 that accorded slave children the status of their mothers. In other words, when the master freed his slave mistress, his children by her automatically were freed.

With their powerful connections, the children enjoyed far more privileges than poor whites. Though some simply became mechanics or small merchants, others acquired considerable wealth and became slave-owners themselves. Provided with the best of education—many were sent abroad for schooling—they were well steeped in European culture. Their children were taught classical methods of music by the finest instructors, while many regularly attended the opera, having their own special section. Though these Creoles would now, for the most part, be considered light-skinned Negroes, since the definition is social and not biological, they did not identify with or associate with the hordes of newly freed blacks who descended on the city following Emancipation. After all, they had long been free and they were not really black at all, if one considered the matter from the standpoint of biology, for a quadroon or an octoroon was only one-quarter or one-eighth black. Creoles continued to marry within their own group and to live as a special class-conscious elite while the "real" Negroes moved into the upper part of town. That was the section of the city where all the raucous funerals were held and where, a little later, strange slurring, rhythmic semi-march-like sounds were to be heard.

However, the tide began to turn against the Creoles in the 1870's and, more definitely, with the legislation of 1894, which segregated *all* persons of African ancestry. The Creoles had been *almost* white, but they had not been quite white enough. The arrival of a different type of segregation affected the total texture of their lives, and whereas Creole musicians previously had been welcome in downtown parades, they now found themselves unable to get the really good jobs. As a result, the Creoles began going uptown to play alongside their untutored darker brothers whose unorthodox approach to their instruments was based on a vocal tradition built around the principle that "If you can't sing it, don't play it." Students of jazz have suggested that it was the meeting between Creole musicians who knew how to read music and played in the "pretty" European style and the more free-wheeling, improvising, rhythm-conscious uptown black musicians that resulted in the creation of early jazz, which can be compared to what we now call Dixieland. This is probably an oversimplification, for the blues somehow found their way into the picture. However, Creole developments can hardly be ignored.

Histories of jazz are filled with stories of the colorful events and improbable persons who followed in this period of New Orleans domination and one should certainly look to the stories for details. There was the legendary Charles "Buddy" Bolden, who was said to be the hottest and loudest cornetist of all time, before he blew his top in 1907 and was committed to an asylum. There was Ferdinand "Jelly Roll" Morton, a Creole pianist of exceptional innovative abilities, who ran away from home and began his ascent to fame by tickling the ivories in a brothel, as was the custom in New Orleans's red-light Storyville district. There were the innumerable cabarets, joints and dives of that fabled Storyville where a small knot of white youngsters listened hard, copied well and moved north to win acclaim as the Original Dixieland Jazz Band (O.D.J.B.), making the first acknowledged jazz recordings in 1917. What the O.D.J.B. played was "original" only to those who had never heard it played by black musicians—which meant the rest of the world—but its playing set the pattern for just about everything that was to come afterward in terms of the recognition of black music when played by white musicians. It has been said that a Negro band called Freddie Keppard's Original Creoles had been invited to record before the O.D.J.B. but turned down the opportunity for some rumored reasons, mainly fear of imitation. The fact remains, however, that Freddie Keppard's band did *not* make those first recordings and there is speculation as to whether its efforts might have stimulated the same public enthusiasm as did those of the white O.D.J.B.

With the closing down of Storyville in 1917 and the subsequent dispersal of New Orleans musicians to other parts of the country, the O.D.J.B. was followed north by Joe "King" Oliver and his band, which the O.D.J.B. is said to have imitated. Oliver was joined in Chicago by a young trumpeter named Louis Armstrong, who also hailed from New Orleans, and the new music called jazz was never quite the same after Armstrong injected it with his fantastic skill for creating fresh and totally improvised statements based on simple tunes. Many others followed, too, but still the O.D.J.B. had been first and it inspired a whole school of white musicians, some of whom, among them the trumpeter Bix Beiderbecke, brought a polished talent of their own to the music. Gifted whites lent a certain ballast to the pattern; consequently Paul Whiteman made a fortune as the "King of Jazz," operating a nationwide network of bands that frequently played arrangements by black musicians such as Don Redman, whom he hired to rehearse whites who could play the arrangements only with great difficulty. Another one of the black arrangers employed by Whiteman in the twenties was a young man from Mississippi named William Grant Still, whose main area of interest was formal composition. Still later excelled in his preferred field and was acknowledged as the foremost black composer of "classical" music, though not one of his works is currently listed in the Schwann catalogue of available recordings.

It is also known that during that "flapper" Prohibition period of the Jazz Age, Whiteman, among many others, made frequent trips to Harlem, then an "exotic" urban playground for the rich folks from downtown who sought their after-hours kicks at nightclubs operated by gangsters and featuring black musical entertainment, though blacks were not admitted as patrons and the entertainers themselves were discouraged from using the rest rooms or mingling with the clients out front. One of the places Whiteman visited was the garish but singularly significant Cotton Club, where, late in 1927, a suave Washingtonian named Edward Kennedy "Duke" Ellington began a long-term engagement with his orchestra, instigating a one-man musical revolution by playing sensitive impressionistic original songs classified under the category of the "barbaric" and dissonances in advance of the time that set his "jungle music" apart from competing sounds of the era. Whiteman, like the others who heard Ellington, even in that early stage, listened and realized that his music could not be copied, though Ellington did not make very much money.

That was the way it continued during the Depression, which sent the nation to its economic knees, and during the resurgence of the late thirties, which ushered in the era of swing and the big bands. It was Benny Goodman who emerged as the "King of Swing," not Fletcher Henderson, who, after finding it impossible to keep his own pioneering big band together, was employed by Goodman as an arranger. Goodman, a virtuoso clarinetist who had tasted of subtle discrimination as a poor Jewish boy brought up on the South Side of Chicago, did help to break the ice by reputedly being the first to use black musicians in his band, among them the pianist Teddy Wilson and master vibesman Lionel Hampton, who went on to form his own popular band in the forties. But this concession was not enough to make up for the universal slight of those who made no similar move in this direction while the question was debated in show biz annals as to whether black musicians *really* should be allowed to play with white musicians.

As whites swept all the national music polls, which were not recognized by blacks, a few stepped forward to proclaim their convictions. Texas-born Harry James, for example, in 1939 refused to accept a national award as best trumpeter because he thought it should have gone to Louis Armstrong. He did not fear to say so to the press, though the majority of his colleagues remained mute. Admittedly, white musicians as a whole had not deliberately set out to squeeze out the black musicians whom they unabashedly copied or employed behind the scenes. They simply were in a better position to capitalize on the music and did not fail to do so. The system operated as it did in all areas of life when race was an issue. Thus when, with the coming of radio, a network program called the Fitch Band Wagon was inaugurated to feature a different big band each week, strangely enough none of them were black—that is, until October, 1939, when an aggregation led by Count Basie, the plucky kid from Red Bank, New Jersey, who had gone all the way to Kansas City to come rolling back into the bigtime with the Bennie Moten band, led the first black group to be broadcast coast-to-coast, from California.

An article written by Billy Rowe, the New York-based theatrical editor of the *Pittsburgh Courier,* which was the most widely read, nationally circulated black publication of the forties and early fifties, commented on Basie's performance during that memorable broadcast. Rowe wrote: "When asked about the great men of music in the world today, he spoke not of white men who claim greatness, but Negroes like Sonny Greer [a former Ellington drummer], Duke Ellington, Fats Waller, the late Bennie Moten, Meade Lux Lewis, Pete Johnson, Teddy Wilson and others who have achieved greatness in a world that they have created." Referring to the way in which Basie "shaved his whiskers, put Uncle Tom in a closet" to call the announcer by his first name (rare for blacks in those days), Rowe lauded the plump, plinking pianist, saying "he did the race well." Then Rowe addressed himself directly to the sponsors of the program: "We thank you for Basie, but we want others like Ella Fitzgerald, Duke Ellington, Louis Armstrong, Jimmie Lunceford, Erskine Hawkins, Cab Calloway, Andy Kirk and countless others whose names will undoubtedly liven the pages of musical history yet to be compiled."

Rowe's prediction was accurate, but immediate rewards for those involved were not forthcoming. Blacks continued to express their disgruntlement through their own publications by referring somewhat condescendingly to Artie Shaw as "the white king of swing" and to Glenn Miller as "the new ofay [pig-latin for 'foe'] swing sensation."

Meanwhile, throughout these formative years of jazz, other developments had taken place in black music at a level closer to the grass roots. These events centered around the emergence of the blues as a popular form—something that originally was and has remained, until very recently, basically and almost exclusively black.

Perhaps this process, too, began long ago, for in his introduction to Paul Oliver's documentary study *Blues Fell This Morning* (reprinted as *The Meaning of the Blues*) the late Richard Wright surmised that while the spirituals might have been sung by slaves closer to the "big house" of the plantation who got a secondhand whiff of Christianity, the devil songs and their derivative blues were more likely to have been shaped by the substance of field slaves and their descendants who were compelled to remain closer to what we might call the nitty-gritty. How else might one account for the fact that the blues do not cover up reality with starry-eyed illusions of a salvatory hereafter but, instead, come to grips with life as it is with its roughness, frustrations and bawdy personal encounters. For the ingredients of the blues exceed the previously analyzed blue note and other elements of the blue tonality. The blues are not purely a matter of form, though a definite blues form has been set forth. More than all these things, the blues must be regarded as intense, highly personal and telling depictions of the human condition expressed with a cutting candor. As such, they say much about the attitudes of those who created them. As Richard Wright has written of the blues: ". . . though replete with a sense of defeat and down-heartedness, they are not intrinsically pessimistic; their burden of woe and melancholy is dialectically redeemed through sheer force of sensuality, into an almost exultant affirmation of life, of love, of sex, of movement, of hope."[15]

In light of the significance of the blues as quite likely the most authentic musical documentation of black attitudes throughout the years, one might expect that careful records had been kept detailing their development from times unknown. Yet quite the opposite is true. And here one must confront head-on some of the reasons that black music, in general, has historically been dismissed as an important cultural force. How could the music created by a race deemed subhuman be considered on a level equivalent to the products of a "master" race? At best it could be thought captivatingly amusing, with its unrestrained "barbaric" qualities: "childlike" with its erroneous "imitations" of "finer" white sounds. Thus, even in its most Westernized forms, black music was seldom considered anything more "artistic" than a spontaneous eruption of an inner pain, as was the case with the early spirituals. Likewise, jazz, which was so easily identified with the brothels and dives where it was shaped and played by musicians who were more interested in earning a little cash than having a good time, was dismissed as "light" entertainment, just as its early exponents were called upon to "clown" as well as play. The blues, which blacks kept closest to themselves, were not noted at all until they were examined in the latter part of this century by white intellectuals whose interest in them is suspected to have stemmed from a "seek out the noble savage" attitude, from a desire to extoll the "simplistic" in lieu of a befuddling white "complexity."

For the same reasons that the black man's story has not found its way into the accepted textbooks on American history, his music has been excluded from supposedly comprehensive studies in this field. Always his music has been segregated from that deemed worthy of designation as "art." The fragmentary history of black music can be found only in separate volumes written on the blues and jazz and is ever isolated from the total picture. There comes to mind a famous multivolumed dictionary of music and musicians in which no black creation is noted, unless one includes Beethoven, who is rumored to have been half a "blood brother." Both European and American writers have ignored blacks while setting down voluminous treatments on "music of today," or of any other day, for that matter. As I write this, there is before me a four-hundred-page history of music in America in which careful attention is paid to everything from the arrival of the first organ in New England to the most obscure twelve-tone compositions. In it, some four pages are devoted to jazz and swing, with Paul Whiteman and Benny Goodman being pointed up as its most significant contributors; glancing historical mention is made of ragtime, a turn-of-the-century syncopated piano music closely patterned after European forms, though its "father," Scott Joplin, was a black man; a few black dances such as the Charleston and Black Bottom are briefly noted; the only other mention of anything black can be found in the brief summaries of the work of Ulysses Kay and Howard Swanson, contemporary black composers who write classical music. Black artists have even been denied credit for their creations. In 1893, for example, a German musicologist challenged the Negro's claim to the spirituals, and in at least one book on the history of jazz no black musician is mentioned and the O.D.J.B. is given full credit for origination of jazz.

Much of the blame for this gross insult can be placed on the doorstep of the white establishment, but a more tragic side of the story has to do with the way so many blacks long hated their own blackness and all things that might be considered a manifestation of this blackness. In his introduction to a volume on *The Negro in Music and Art,* compiled as part of the International Library of Negro Life and History, Lindsay Patterson has written:

> Unfortunately, the Negro as performer and composer, in light of the enormity of his gift to the world, has not derived the full benefit from his music. Most appalling of all, there are those who, even today, challenge his right to be called the creator of so much that is irrefutably his, Why? A partial explanation lies in the fact that the Negro has not documented his own contributions to most of the

musical forms he has spawned. This has resulted in a great deal of distortion historically, some of which has stemmed from persons who have had their own vested interests at heart. It is the intelligentsia who usually provide the most accurate records, but our Negro intelligentsia have concentrated their efforts and energies on the Negro in classical music—a form alien to America. It should be noted that no classical composer of color has employed the Negro idiom in the way that Bartok made use of Hungarian folk music.[16]

This black denial of black creativity has been consistently apparent and has been applied even to those efforts that were conceived as attempts to bring black music into the arena of Western forms through marked modifications. One notable instance involved the work of Lieutenant James Reese Europe, a classically trained black composer and conductor born in 1881 who wrote marches that were considered "worthy of the pen of John Philip Sousa," according to the *New York Tribune*. Europe did his stint as a musical director on Broadway in the second decade of this century, when black entertainment was all the rage, and became the manager of several New York dance bands that performed for the white aristocracy before becoming a commissioned officer of the 369th Regiment during World War I. During the war Europe organized a big band of symphonic proportions that played in a syncopated early-jazz style and later wowed Europe through his compositions and accompaniment for white ballroom dancers Vernon and Irene Castle. Even before the war, in 1914, Europe had been busy organizing the Clef Club in New York, a functional organization composed of highly trained black musicians who, in the words of the great stride pianist Willie "the Lion" Smith, "played for all the rich people, the classy people. . . . It cost one hundred dollars to join and your discipline had to be one hundred per cent."

Jim Europe's musical ambitions were as unlimited as was his imagination, and on March 11, 1914, he presented a concert by his Clef Club "Symphony" orchestra at Carnegie Hall. That one-of-a-kind orchestra, which used mandolins and banjos in lieu of second violins to give, in his words, a peculiar "steady strumming accompaniment to our music," was an unprecedented instrumental ensemble that included clarinets, baritone horns, trombones and cornets, against a background of ten pianos. It was composed of more than one hundred pieces and played the works of Negro composers. Explaining his methods in an interview with the *New York Evening Post,* Europe said: "You see, we colored people have our own music that is a part of us. It's the product of our souls; it's been created by the sufferings and miseries of our race."

Europe further attempted to utilize Russian and other European sounds in combination with black sounds—which was a notable move toward the Westernization of black music. Yet his concerts received mixed reviews. A white reviewer wrote in *Musical America:*

> If the Negro Symphony Orchestra will give its attention during the coming year to a movement or two of a Haydn symphony and play it at its next concert, and if the composers who this year took obvious pleasure in conducting their marches, tangos and waltzes, will write short movements for orchestra, basing them on classic models, next year's concert will inaugurate a new era for the Negro musician in New York and will aid him in being appraised at his full value and in being taken seriously.

This was, as might have been expected, the white attitude, but it was echoed in a letter of commentary written by Adolphus Lewis, a black music-lover from Philadelphia, who said of one of those concerts:

> Of course, the music was typical of the light, happy-go-lucky Negro, but there are those among us who are trying to master the classics in music as well as along other lines, and to say that the music satisfied this class, would be gainsaying the truth. . . . All races have their folk-song and dances, but all races try to develop their art from examples set by masters of other periods; and if we expect to do anything that is lasting from an artistic standpoint, we too, must study the classics as a foundation for our work.[17]

There are no recordings of Europe's work. Perhaps he was spared similar "put-downs" when he was stabbed by a drummer in his Boston dressing room on May 9, 1919.

If whites were so condescending toward music that was close in style to European music, was better treatment likely to be accorded the blues, which never were projected as anything other than sheer expressive blackness? In fact, part of the secret of the blues' survival might lie in the fact that they remained a part of the black subsociety and were not commonly presented to whites for acceptance, even after the advent of popular recordings around 1917. Blues records were sold as "race" records, released through outlets in black communities and available only on special order to others who might happen to know about them—which was, indeed, rare. And the survival of the blues, in spite of all efforts to discredit black music wholly, compares only with the survival of the black man himself.

Since no written records have been kept, it is impossible to note the year or even the period in which music even remotely resembling the classic blues began to be heard. Early jazzmen such as Jelly Roll Morton looked down on them and would hardly have gone out of their way to learn more about them, though they were closer to the source. Some major blues figures such as "Big" Bill Broonzy merely remembered that "The real blues is played and sung the way you feel," while others believe they were there all along, especially in the spirituals. In an interview with the Mississippi-born bluesman John Lee Hooker conducted by Pete Welding and published in *Downbeat* magazine, the artist said: "You take spirituals and the blues—maybe I'm wrong but I think I'm right—the blues come from spirituals. They are the background of all music. I don't want to argue the point. But they are: they use the same patterns."[18]

Yet the breeding ground for the blues seems to go back beyond all these casual reminiscences. Probably, they are rooted on the plantation, where blacks sometimes were called upon to present programs of improvised dance and song for their masters. They might even have preceded those ante-bellum presentations, for as the late Langston Hughes, a peerless chronicler of black expression, and Milton Meltzer wrote in *Black Magic:*

> The first stage for the captive Africans was the open deck of a slave ship. There on the way to the Americas, blacks in chains, when herded up on deck for exercise, were forced to sing and dance in the open air for the amusement of the crew. The log of the English ship *Hannibal* in the year 1664 recorded that the Africans linked together aboard that vessel were made to "jump and dance for an hour or two" every day when weather permitted them out of the hole.[19]

The use of the ability to entertain as one of the means of survival, in fact, was carried over to the plantation, where, as cartoonist E. Simms Campbell noted in 1939 in his essay on "The Blues":

> As court jester, the Negro had long since learned that his very existence depended upon his ability to please the white man. One was either a "good nigger," one who acquiesced to the wishes of the plantation owner or overseer and lived, or a "bad nigger," one who had decided ideas about what he would or wouldn't do, and who usually died.[20]

This tradition of providing instant entertainment for white masters is important, for though the blues might have been sung in secret, the way in which they became a publicly popular form was an outgrowth of touring road shows related to minstrelsy. These were the medicine shows, gillies and carnivals in which many black dancers, singers, comedians and all-around entertainers served their apprenticeship. It is scarcely necessary to state that all the entertainers came up the hardest of ways and within their ranks were a few who were to help immortalize the blues.

Minstrelsy is considered to be the father of vaudeville and the musical theater, even as it is known today, and it comprises one of the most schizophrenic of all chapters in American racial history. Though "blackface" shows were known in this country as early as 1810, their biggest boost is commonly linked to the career of Thomas D. Rice, a white actor who hit upon a golden idea when he visited Louisville, Kentucky, in 1828 or 1829 while touring the frontier territory with an itinerant show. As the oft-repeated story goes, there was a livery stable situated just behind the spot where the troupe had camped. There a decrepit and deformed Negro called Jim Crow went about his chores in such a painful but eccentric way that he attracted the attention of Rice, who overheard him singing a strange little ditty that went:

Wheel about, turn about,
Do jis so,
An' ebery time I wheel about
I jump Jim Crow!

Inspired by this seemingly weird character, Rice set about devising an exaggerated version of his song and movements and performed it on stage in blackface to great acclaim. He added other comic Negro caricatures to his repertoire, and another burned-cork entertainer, Dan Emmett, borrowed the "Jim Crow" song, carried it throughout the country and helped lay the cornerstone for minstrelsy, which was to become the most popular form of American entertainment for nearly a century. Yet there was a paradox in this series of events. These white minstrels who blacked their faces with cork to perform songs and dance-steps borrowed from blacks and strung together with jokes told in a ridiculously incorrect patter thought to be patterned after black dialect became darlings of the white public. The "cakewalk" of black house servants and the "stick dance" of field hands, as copied by white minstrels, created such an enthusiasm that poets such as Edgar Allen Poe wondered if their intricate rhythms might be worked into verse. But though the public loved the antics of these whites made up to look like blacks, Negroes were not admitted to the theaters and were barred from the stage as performers!

All of these ironies are brought to bear on the career of one man, a Negro composer named James Bland who was born free in 1854 in Long Island, New York. Bland was descended from a line of free Negroes, having a father who possessed a degree in law. Like the white youths of his day, Bland was intrigued by the minstrels but, at first, was unable to consider a stage career because blacks were not accepted. When Negro minstrel troupes began appearing after the Civil War, the door was opened for Bland, who had completed his courses at Howard University at the age of nineteen. He appeared throughout this country with groups such as Callenders' Original Georgia Minstrels and was acclaimed in England, where he gave a command performance for Queen Victoria and later drew $1,000 a week under his billing as the "Prince of Negro Performers." Bland remained abroad where he did not have to wear burned cork to cover up his rather light skin, as was the practice with many Negro entertainers, for some time. And though minstrelsy had passed from favor when he returned to this country in 1901 and his star descended during the remaining ten years of his life, James Bland is still known for the more than two hundred songs he wrote, all of them in the "sweet" white mode instead of in the black style. Among them are the old standards *In the Evening by the Moonlight, Pretty Little Caroline Rose* and *Oh Dem Golden Slippers.* The history of music in America on my desk makes no mention of him, but a somewhat detailed treatment is accorded Stephen Foster, the man with whom Bland was most frequently compared. Yet Bland has had a "last word" that is truly resounding, for his most famous composition, *Carry Me Back to Old Virginny,* was adopted as the official song of the state of Virginia—but only because it was not generally known that its composer was a black man.

When black minstrel shows became common during the latter part of the nineteenth century, they attracted many talented youngsters hungry for a touch of adventure in early "show biz." One of them was W. C. Handy, who joined Mahara's Minstrels in 1896 at the age of twenty-three. A minister's son who became a musician over the protests of his father, Handy taught himself how to play the cornet and studied music theory from books, becoming enough of a "trained" musician to qualify for the job of bandmaster. He had been inspired by the spirituals he heard in his native Alabama, later noting in a 1931 radio broadcast:

> Like tears, they were relief to aching hearts. Personally, I think these spirituals did more for our emancipation than all the guns of the Civil War. We thought that when freedom came, the day would be one of sunshine, but freedom was only nominal and the day a gloomy one and we needed another song to lighten our labors and make brighter the world in which we live. Here we record the birth of our secular songs which are known as banjo songs, plantation songs, "coon" songs, ragtime, jazz and the blues. The blues embody all the elements of the secular songs herein named and even take the pathetic melody of the spirituals.

Speaking of the blues compositions that made him famous and the sources from which he had drawn, Handy said:

> Behind the *Memphis Blues, St. Louis Blues, Beale Street Blues, Yellow Dog Blues, Aunt Haggar's Children's Blues, Joe Turner's Blues* and others that have been heard over the radio, were my personal experiences in rock quarries as a water boy at the much discussed Mussel Shoals, when I heard the labor songs of the steel drivers. . . . Personal experiences in the mines, steel mills around Birmingham where I worked as a common laborer; three years residence in Mississippi, where I saw the aesthetic value in the songs of the cotton pickers, and as a traveling minstrel from coast to coast with the opportunity to observe that some-

> thing within our group that takes us back to the shores of Africa from which we were transplanted, and that something was rhythm. . . . With the Caucasian, melody or harmony is paramount and regard for the written note imperative. With the American [Negro] rhythm is paramount, intensified or diminished by his varying moods, and to express "blues," one disregards convention and uses the written note as only a guide, whether in blues or spirituals.[21]

Though Handy often is referred to as the man who "invented" the blues, this is not the case, for they had existed as a folk form before 1909, when he composed a political campaign song that he called *Mr. Crump* that was published in 1912 as *Memphis Blues.* It was among the folk roots that blues continued to thrive in their "country" style, but it was Handy who began to compose the blues or to set down original songs in the classic twelve-bar blues pattern, later having them published as sheet music that could be played by others—which led to their popularization. In his autobiography, *Father of the Blues,* Handy wrote of the way in which he lost the rights to some of his early compositions because he had to sell them to white publishers for a few dollars, since they wanted no dealings with a black song-writer and soon realized that they could make money by exploiting his products.

This was not an uncommon situation, for as Hughes and Meltzer have noted in *Black Magic:*

> Many Negro songwriters have remained anonymous in relation to the major part of their output, particularly in the first quarter of the century when, because of poverty, it was often customary for composers to sell their composi-

tions outright or to permit white publishers or arrangers to put their names on the songs.[22]

During the period when Handy was beginning to set down the blues in a notated form, other events were meshing into an unusual set of circumstances that were to enhance their popularity. A robust, earthy blues singer named Gertrude "Ma" Rainey was touring the southland with her husband, Will Rainey, and his Rabbit Foot Minstrels. What she presented was not a slickly polished music for city dwellers, but a moaning, slurring, shouting music that, dredged from the depths of the heart, dealt with the problems of male-female relationships and was sung in the words of, and reflecting the life style of, the poor southern blacks who flocked to see her. Her audiences were not composed of theatergoers, since blacks ordinarily were not admitted to theaters, but of the soil-bound, long-suffering common people who looked forward to her coming through long weeks of uninterrupted drudgery and crammed into the tents where she performed. When "Ma" was due in town, her fans would ride down on mules from surrounding areas to see her, carrying their lunches with them. Her audience *was* the black underground where the blues remained primarily, even to this day. The rugged flavor of those days when "Ma" performed in the tent shows is poignantly captured in a Sterling Brown poem bearing her name. It can be heard on an original-cast-recording album of an off-Broadway show based on black poetry and entitled *A Hand Is on the Gate,* which includes the classic *Backwater Blues,* recited and sung by Josephine Premice, somewhat theatrically but with feeling.

During her travels through the South, between 1910 and 1912, "Ma" Rainey took under her wing a young girl from Chattanooga, Tennessee, named Bessie Smith.

Though not yet well into her teens, Bessie was well built and had a voice just as big as her body. It has been said that she had no actual style of her own at that time and that, as an urchin, she had made her way singing and dancing on street corners for coins. But "Ma" helped teach her how to sing the blues in the manner that was so popular that soon young Bessie became a star.

At first, Bessie Smith's following was limited to those who attended those tent shows. But on February 14, 1920, three years after the first jazz recordings had been made, a pretty, round-faced singer from Cincinnati, Ohio, made the first blues recording. The date had been secured for Mamie Smith by Perry Bradford, composer of the song she was to record, *That Thing Called Love,* backed by *You Can't Keep a Good Man Down.* Mamie Smith, as the first recorded black blues singer, had been selected only because a white singer, Sophie Tucker, had not been available. That first record was not in the classic twelve-bar blues form, but it did so well on the early Okeh label that later that same year another Bradford composition, *Crazy Blues,* which *was* written in the twelve-bar form, was recorded. Again the response on the part of blacks was unusual. And the first blues record of 1920 ushered in the famous blues era of the twenties, with its "race" records, produced especially for the black audience. No longer were the blues to be merely a folk music improvised on the spur of the moment, as had been the case in "country" blues, they were to become a major popular form, though only among blacks.

Recording opportunists began scouting the country for new blues talent, finding Bessie Smith, who became "Empress of the blues," and a host of others, among them Alberta Hunter, Sippie Wallace, Ida Cox and the horde of blues-singing women named Smith. They recorded a long series of blues records that ranged from the traditional to the bizarre, most of them female laments about problems they had with "no good" men, some with a touch of tenderness but more often humorous, double-edged chiding with sexual connotations. Several songs were composed by black song-writers such as Clarence Williams, who had an office in Tin Pan Alley where he also produced tunes that were to become popular standards, among them *Baby, Won't You Please Come Home?*, *Everybody Loves My Baby* and *Royal Garden Blues*. But others were distorted and contrived ditties with an appeal based on weird titles supposed to authenticate them as the really "low down," as in *Dope Head Blues, Blood Thirsty Blues, Dead Drunk Blues, Monkey Man Blues* and others even stranger. Yet the black public loved them, for at last the "brothers" who had moved North to the proddings of industrial recruiters had found something closely akin to the music they had known "down home."

An old family friend who grew up during the Prohibition and blues period in a West Virginia coal-mining town recalls the way it was: "Every payday we'd bottle up the home brew we'd been getting ready and Mama would send us kids down to the store to get the latest blues records. Everybody else we knew would be there too and we'd carry those records home, stacked in our arms. All the Negroes lived together in that 'company' town and you could go from street to street and hear those blues records blasting out from the open doors. I'll never forget it."

Thus the blues remained the popular music of blacks during the twenties. Simultaneously, however, music was developing in another direction on Broadway. On Broadway black musical comedy had virtually taken over the "Great White Way." But most of the shows, as excellent as their music might have been, were geared to Caucasian tastes and Caucasian ideas about black life, with endless references to "pickaninnies," "coons" and "sunny old plantation days." The Broadway boom is usually traced to the 1921 production of a show called *Shuffle Along*, which was a collaboration among Flournoy Miller, Aubrey Lyles, Noble Sissle and Eubie Blake. After the partners split up, a Miller and Lyles show called *Runnin' Wild* introduced whites to the Charleston. In those days, blacks were accustomed to "taking low," and they tried to swallow these projections of themselves as half-human stereotypes, but they understood full well what was going on. This led Miller and Lyles to issue a joint statement in 1926 calling for *real* black theater, an idea that is being pursued in the current racial renaissance. Thus already in 1926 Miller and Lyles were saying:

> We want to establish in New York, finally, a theater which shall present plays by and of our race, treating us not as mere cartoons of humanity, but in a serious, though sometimes a comedy spirit, as human beings created in the image of God.

Nothing, of course, came of the idea at that time.

In spite of its obvious flaws, however, the black musical comedy of the twenties provided for the emergence of many stars, among them Bert Williams, the "clown prince" of black comics, Florence Mills, the little "blackbird" who died in 1927, still a young woman and at the peak of her career; Bill "Bojangles" Robinson of the magic tapping feet; Ethel Waters, a great dramatic actress as well as one of the finest blues-derived singers of all time; the inimitable Josephine Baker, a "Charleston dancer and comedienne" who became the toast of Paris with her "banana dance." Working in the background were notable song-writers such as Fats Waller, a pudgy pianist-organist who was a radio star of the late thirties and early forties and who collaborated with Andy Razaf to produce the memorable *Ain't Misbehavin'* and *Honeysuckle Rose*; Shelton Brooks, whose *Some of These Days* helped make Sophie Tucker famous; James P. Johnson, one of the greatest of the Harlem stride pianists who wrote the familiar *Charleston, If I Could Be With You* and *Old Fashioned Love.*

Tin Pan Alley was steeped in the essence of the black artists' music, for these were the men who influenced the development of the popular song as we now know it. But the blues, which dealt not only with amorous woes but also with other vicissitudes of black life, as in *Blackwater Blues,* which is a description of a real flood disaster, remained the exclusive property of blacks. Whites, other than record producers and talent scouts, remained ignorant of them, for reasons not hard to find. As E. Simms Campbell has written:

> They did not want to hear lamentations in any form. They wanted something "hot." Knowing nothing of the blues, other than that they were "dirty," they received what they expected.[23]

The coming of the depression in late 1929 was the death of black musical comedy, and never since has the race so dominated the nation's top stages. The lean years wiped out many of Harlem's good-time playgrounds and brought a near halt to the flood of blues records, for the recording companies themselves were "hurtin'."

But the music did not die. Radio, which helped fill the void left by the fading of live entertainment, popularized an early group sound when the Mills Brothers made their national bow in 1931. The Mills Brothers, who were unique in their ability to imitate the sound of instruments with their voices, a reversal of the early jazz approach, went on to set a record for longevity, basing their appeal on a diluted but easy listening type of quartet music of the barbershop variety. In fact, the depression and its aftermath only helped the blues to develop in fresher forms as this music became inextricably interwoven with jazz in its blacker forms. Blues closer to the roots remained popular, as they had all along, in the South and Southwest, though a home-grown composer-guitarist named Huddie Ledbetter went quietly down into history without achieving the public recognition he desired so much.

Ledbetter, who was later known as Leadbelly, was born in Morringsport, Louisiana, on an unknown date, (said to be 1888) sometime before the dawn of the twentieth century. His father was a farmer, and the boy was bewitched by music from childhood. He picked up pointers on the guitar from an uncle, and from his early teens he began playing for Saturday night dance sessions in the backwoods country. Of the milieu in which he grew up, Frederic Ramsey Jr. has written:

> It was a rough crowd. In the North, social workers would probably have intervened. But the 19th century Negro youngsters in the South were allowed to go their way and settle their problems (no one considered them problems, anyway) amongst themselves. They drank, they made love and they got into fights.[24]

That was the way Leadbelly was implicated in the killing of a man. He was convicted and sent to a prison farm. He managed to escape, but he was to spend the greater part of his life in and out of prisons. When free, he was an odd-jobs "bum," roaming the country, getting into more trouble and somehow never managing to break the pattern that had circumscribed his life from earliest years. But he always stayed close to his music and became a master of the difficult twelve-string guitar. He was an itinerant performer, picking up bits of music wherever he went, from the mournful musings of prisoners to the somber strains of those whose prisons had no walls. Somewhere along the way, he became a cohort of the great blues traditionalist Blind Lemon Jefferson, who made some popular recordings during the twenties but died in poverty. But Leadbelly always remained his own man, producing a type of music that is considered quite close to the basic shout and holler and the work songs, which also were prison songs. He *was* the roots, in this respect. During the early forties, the latter years of his life, he became a recording artist. One of his compositions, *The Midnight Special*, has been redone by everyone from neo-folk to jazz artists, and his *The Hesitation Blues* is regarded as a classic. But Leadbelly always yearned for a popular hit that would make him a little money and gain him an acceptance he'd never known in private or public life. When he died in 1949 in New York City, he was a disappointed man, though one of his most appealing tunes, *Irene*, or *Goodnight, Irene,* was to become a nationwide best-seller a year after his death.

The blues did not die; they came bouncing back in the big band-backed shouts of Jimmy Rushing in the forties. And jazz, certainly, followed its own illustrious course as various forces—the country blues, the urban blues and all kinds of jazz—began to merge.

Meanwhile, gospel music remained its own "thing," isolated from the mainstream in the services of Holiness churches and, during the thirties and forties, coming forth with some of its true blues flavor in the compositions of Thomas Dorsey, once known as a bluesman called "Georgia Tom," who wrote gospel tunes that were essentially blues and always bluesy in their essence: *Precious Lord, Take My Hand* and *He Knows How Much You Can Bear*. A very few black performers, such as a "sister" named Rosetta Tharpe, did garner a cultist white following during the forties, but, as Charles Hobson has written in *Downbeat:* "Gospel has no sizable white following; it remains the one music performed almost exclusively by and for black audiences."[25]

This is still true, for the most part, though something did, indeed, happen in 1954. A new sound began to be heard that was still so much a very old sound. It was pure gospel in its flavor, though the lyrics were straight out of the blues "bag." The man who set them forth was a blind former gospel singer from Albany, Georgia, named Ray Charles. The modern soul sound, as basic as its roots might have been, began with the emergence of Ray Charles, whose voice sounded indescribably old, though he was then but a young man in his twenties. His was a rich baritone lyricism into which he injected many African falsetto shout-notes. And there was just so much *feeling* in everything he did, from his 1955 hit, *I Got a Woman,* which black young folks ate up altogether, through his efforts of the past few years when those other than blacks have begun to dig him for all he's worth.

It was through his flexibility and his extraordinary range that Charles was able to break out of the black underground and to establish the black soul sound as a broadly acknowledged force. His recordings of the mid-fifties were primarily rhythm and blues embossed with a healthy portion of gospel stomp. This appealed to some. But it was when he displayed his abilities as a jazz artist on the Impuse recording *Genius + Soul = Jazz,* on which he was featured as an organist as well as a singer doing imaginative versions of the sort of big-band blues that had appealed to jazz enthusiasts, that Charles gained the respect of jazz-loving middle-class blacks who previously had dismissed him as merely another hoarsely shouting R&B man. No black man could resist *I'm Gonna Move to the Outskirts of Town* or a jazzy revamping of the R&B hit *One Mint Julep,* especially when they were done through Quincy Jones arrangements played by the Count Basie band. Charles' ability to transcend the dichotomy of R&B and jazz or bluesy jazz made it possible for him to captivate black music-lovers identified with two separate camps, for, as LeRoi Jones has noted, blues have been the music of the "folk" Negroes, while jazz has been the music of more assimilated or middle-class Negroes.

Having bridged this gap, Ray Charles proceeded toward a different kind of fusion during the very late fifties, when he applied his same basic sound to the melodies of white country and western music. His rendition of *You Are My Sunshine* bears little resemblance to the country original, though the key to his success can be found in those records on which he sticks closer to the white sound, as on Eddy Arnold's *But You Don't Know Me* and *I Can't Stop Loving You.* And once the public had become accustomed to the sound of Ray Charles, it was better able to relate to the later emerging aspects of soul music, as found in an Aretha Franklin, for Ray is not only gospel, he is also blues and jazz. And the sum of all these is soul.

1. LeRoi Jones, *Blues People: Negro Music in White America,* p. 7. Reprinted by permission of William Morrow and Company, Inc. Copyright © 1963 by LeRoi Jones.

2. *Ibid.,* p. 17.

3. Noble Sissle, Introduction, in Perry Bradford, *Born with the Blues* (Oak, 1965), p. 10.

4. Jones, *op. cit.,* p. 4.

5. Lerone Bennett Jr., *Before the Mayflower* (3rd ed.) (Johnson, 1966), p. 37.

6. Ivan Annan, "So This Is Ghana," in *Folk Music of Ghana* (Folkways records, 1964).

7. Melville S. Herskovits, *The Myth of the Negro Past* (Harper and Row, 1941), p. 265.

8. Stearns, *op. cit.*, p. 19.

9. Herskovits, *op. cit.*, p. 265.

10. Stearns, *op. cit.*, p. 70.

11. Lydia Parrish, *Slave Songs of the Georgia Sea Islands* (Folklore, 1965).

12. *The Nation*, May 30, 1867.

13. John A. and Alan Lomax, *Folksong U.S.A.* (Duell, Sloan, Pearce, 1947), p. 335.

14. Bradford, *op. cit.*, p. 9.

15. Richard Wright, Foreword, in Paul Oliver, *The Meaning of the Blues* (Horizon, 1960), p. 9.

16. *The Negro in Music and Art*, ed., Lindsay Patterson, The International Library of Negro Life and History (Publishers Company, under auspices of The Association for the Study of Negro Life and History, 1967), p. xv.

17. Cf. Maud Cuney-Hare, *Negro Musicians and Their Music* (Associated, 1936), pp. 137-139.

18. *Downbeat*, May 7, 1964.

19. Langston Hughes and Milton Meltzer, *Black Magic: A Pictorial History of the Negro in American Entertainment* (Prentice-Hall, 1967), p. 2.

20. E. Simms Campbell, "The Blues," in *The Negro in Music and Art, op. cit.* Cf. *Jazzmen*, eds., Frederick Ramsey and Charles Edward Smith (Harcourt, Brace, 1939).

21. *Pittsburgh Courier*, March 14, 1931.

22. Hughes and Meltzer, *op. cit.*, p. 88.

23. E. Simms Campbell, in *The Negro in Music and Art, op. cit.*

24. Frederick Ramsey, "Leadbelly Last Sessions," on *Leadbelly . . . From Last Sessions* (Folkways record, 1968).

25. *Downbeat*, May 30, 1968.

3

KING OF THE BLUES

HIS BUSINESS card simply states, in the upper left-hand corner: "Blues is King–King is Soul."

To those familiar with the art of Riley E. King, once called "the Beale Street Blues Boy," a name eventually shortened to B. B., the card seems more a statement of truth than a theatrical boast. B. B. King's name is the one most likely to be mentioned by lovers of blues with a contemporary flavor, and he has been recognized, but only within the past several months, as the most influential and most imitated bluesman of the day. Yet he has been around for more than twenty years, ever since he worked his way out of the Mississippi Delta and became a popular disc jockey in Memphis. Subsequently, King went on the road to sing and play on his guitar the same sort of music he had so affectionately sent spinning out over the airwaves from his radio post. During that dimly marked period separating the blues revival of the forties from the rise in popularity of rhythm and blues, he enjoyed some success among blacks. But he has not customarily been a big hit-maker, and one is not likely to see his records gracing the top of any chart.

As has so often been the case with significant music, from the Fourth Symphony of Brahms, which was critically denounced for its "mousy obsequiousness" back in 1886, to the "crude" blues of this century, the art of B. B. King has been contained within the shadowed periphery just on the other side of the spotlight. Jazz-lovers and followers of popular music commonly have dismissed him as "just" a bluesman. On the other hand, he has never been "folksy" enough to be fondled by blues revivalists whose ranks have been dominated by those of a "moldy fig mentality." Charles Keil has used this term to describe the dogged searchers for the "real" blues who, according to Keil, have apparently relied on the dubious criteria of old age, obscurity, correct tutelage, agrarian milieu.[1]

None of the above criteria applies to King. In his forties, he is not yet old, and he has a ruggedly compact body seemingly unaffected by a life of making it, night after night, from one Southern town to another, as well as to South Side Chicago's Regal Theater and the Apollo in Harlem, and playing, until recently, to almost exclusively black audiences on a schedule that might kill a workhorse. King is hardly obscure, for he has been making records since 1950, though it was only in 1965 that he became available on a major label with the sort of modern sound reproduction that does his talents justice. He does come from an agrarian background, but he left home soon after dropping out of school in the tenth grade. The point of greatest similarity seems to be that of "correct tutelage," though there is no definite tie. He never really "studied" music with anybody but recalls listening avidly, as a boy, to the Texas country blues sound of Blind Lemon Jefferson on "race" records during the thirties and of idolizing Sonny Boy Williamson, Lonnie Johnson, Bumble Bee Slim, Big Maceo, Tampa Red and other artists.

There remains something of that old-time Mississippi romp and rout in King's music, but it has been greatly transformed. It is King, in fact, who is widely acknowledged to be the man who "refined" the blues, who honed them into a sophisticated but highly expressive form less alien to ears attuned to modern sounds. He is still as earthy, as "authentic," as they come, singing of the same day-to-day woes and personal tribulations that have marked the blues since their inception, but his approach is so smooth, his fire so controlled that each of his performances comes across a little like a triumph of dramatic as well as of musical art. His sense of taste is so infallible that he is one of the very few around who can cry out in all passion while retaining his "cool." And this is why he is considered a master.

Broad recognition and all that goes with it—the television appearances and invitations to perform in Europe, the magazine articles, the bigger money and longer-term engagements at the "better" clubs—have been a painfully long time in coming, and nobody is more aware of this than B. B. King, who runs his own show and takes care of his own business. He does not hesitate to speak of his unforgettable, but not always pleasant, experiences as "a crusader for the blues."

* * *

It is early March of 1969 and the last treacherous crunches of winter ice have disappeared from Harlem's 125th Street, where the marquee of the Apollo Theater announces in bold letters that B. B. King is co-starring there along with a younger male singing group called the Dells. The title of the current movie attraction is not visible as one approaches, for it has always been the live entertainment and not the films that have attracted the clapping, back-talking audiences to the Apollo, a mecca for black culture that is *really* black.

As is not the case in the better-upholstered theaters further south on the tight little island of Manhattan, it is not difficult to go backstage and see Mr. King. A brief telephone call to the Apollo's public-relations man, Peter Long, or a religiously sworn out statement about being "a real old friend of B's," verified by a call to his dressing room, and you are "in," ushered through the main auditorium where some seem to be dozing through a Suzie Wong-type thing on the screen, tiptoeing gingerly along the dim passageway behind that screen, passing clusters of brightly attired people assumed to be part of the show—including one enormous dark man with an equally enormous natural " 'do," climbing a flight of scarred metal stairs to the second-floor dressing rooms where the usher shouts hoarsely, "Where's B?"

"Out front watchin' the movie," comes the answer from somewhere.

"Just go right in. Make yourself at home. He'll be right with you," the usher advises, then retreats down those scarred stairs.

Though fairly large for a theater dressing room—it contains a sofa, small kitchen table and mismatched chairs, all of which were far from elegant in their long-gone better days—the room seems terribly crowded, simply because there are so many people in it. At the far side from the door, a young man with a carefully slicked-down and waved processed hairstyle is eagerly consuming a take-out fried chicken dinner with a blatant unconcern for anyone else who might be hungry. At one end of the sofa, a twentyish-looking woman sits huddled in her winter coat, though it is quite warm, safe from all the world behind her dark glasses, saying nothing to anybody and looking at nobody. Dave Turner, a singing comedian who once toured with Dinah Washington, straddles a chair backwards and chats with someone who is just getting ready to go out for a bit of whiskey.

"Care for a little taste?" offers a beaming, pot-bellied saxophone player who says he just got back into town after doing a gig with Fats Domino. It is all rather like an informal cabaret where the host has stepped around the corner for a few minutes.

You sit on the sofa while a man who identifies himself as "Bebop," wearing "shades" and beret like any good leftover from Dizzy Gillespie's reign as a style-maker, tells how he used to work as B's valet for several years before shipping out as a seaman. "Here, take a seat in here," he says moving into a smaller but much more crowded room. There are no people here. Instead, there is a peculiar assortment of things: small speaker systems that must go with some of the suitcased equipment scattered about the floor, a valise, pieces of luggage, a rod crammed with coats and suits that takes up most of the breathing space. "Hey! Don't lay that thing on Lu*cille!*" Bebop cautions as a bodyless arm tosses yet another coat into the cramped quarters. He is referring to B. B.'s red electric guitar, reclining in silent regality at one end of her master's cluttered private couch.

There is an intensified rustle of voices from the outer room, and B. B. King, himself, is here. His soft voice filters through the din as he greets everybody, including the silent woman on the sofa: "Well, now, look who's here. What you tryin' to do, get fat?" followed by a warm chuckle. Briefly, he checks out some detail concerning the show with a member of his official entourage, then ambles into his personal cubbyhole.

He is a stocky, dark-skinned man with rounded features set beneath a brand-new "natural," which has replaced his old process, in keeping with the trend toward outer manifestation of an inner racial pride. He wears a straight-cut suit of a subdued blue; the only sign of theatrical flashiness is a reddish-purple tie. On his left hand is a ring with the letters "BB" spelled out back-to-back in small diamonds—the only jewelry he wears. His manner is so gentle as to seem almost apologetic, his warmth and honesty such that he might be an old friend, even on an initial meeting. With what could be a touch of embarrassment, he explains away the messy condition of his quarters. He speaks with the same earthy accents and untutored eloquence of the less-than-middle-class "blues people" to whom he usually sings.

"The thing is, I don't really have a place to live, yet. When I was married, I lived in Los Angeles, but when I was separated from my wife, I didn't want the house because it was no good to me without her, though it was community property. I have a farm in Memphis, but my father lives there and no matter *how* old you get, they still think of you as a little boy. In other words, if I come in a little bit late, they want to know why, so they be checkin' on me like that. After I broke up with my wife, I bought an apartment building in Memphis. Now Memphis, as you know, is not completely integrated—it's comin' along very fine, but it's not there just yet. So I bought this buildin' in a white area. The lady that sold it to me was white and she knew she was sellin' it to a black man, but she knew who I was. But I can't *live* in my apartment buildin' because if I do, I'm likely to lose my tenants there. So therefore I have to still live in motels and hotels, wherever I happen to be."

As the need for love underscores virtually everything he sings, it also is a part of his personal needs:

"I hope one day to maybe find me another lady and, if so, I'll find me another place to live. I think of it this way: If I have a lady that really loves me, or *cares* for me, she will understand my work. I'm not the kind of fellow that demand my wife to stay home. I want my wife to be *with* me. In other words, there's no law against her travelin' with me if she *wants* to. The only thing I *dis*like—this is funny—if I'm married, I don't want my wife to be on the *job* with me all the time. Oh, she can bring me to work and pick me up when I get off, but just to *sit* there like some people do, I don't like, because I don't think it give the public a chance to talk with you, to have fun with you. But I do want my wife or girl friend to *be* with me. I feel secure that way. I'm sayin' this because anyone in show business—man or woman—I hope that it do them some good, because my second wife, I think the main reason for us being separated was because of my travelin'. She couldn't seem to understand that I was travelin' when we got married and she knew about it, because music is my *life; blues* is B. B. King. Yes, and I've been a crusader for it for twenty-one years. Without this, I don't think I could *live* very long—not that I think I'm goin' to live a long time anyway, but I don't think I could live even *that* long if I had to stop playin' or if I couldn't be with the people I love so, the people that have *helped* me so much. . . . I couldn't *live*!"

At the core of his work is one basic desire:

"I try to give them a message. I try *hard*."

As proof that some are interested in hearing his message, he roots around in his valise and brings out a group of clippings, most of them dating from no earlier than mid-1968, from the *New York Times* magazine, *Eye* magazine and the *San Francisco Chronicle,* whose nationally known music critic Ralph Gleason he credits with helping to bring about his new success because "he saw me on the West Coast and wrote about me regularly in his column." But before his recent resurgence, the going was anything but easy, and he cannot erase his difficulties from his mind. There is an unconcealed plaintive note in his voice when he speaks of it.

"All of a sudden, it seem that people remember that I'm still alive and I'm grateful. This is a pretty touchy subject but, you know, for five or six years it seem like the people had completely forgot about B. B. King—

white *or* black. And I was hurt for a long time. It's not that I thought my music should be number one or somethin' like that with the American public, but from about '58 or '59 until a year ago [1968], I knew that a lot of the people was doing the same thing I was doin' or that I *am* doin'. Everybody seemed to get breaks. What I mean by that is either with the press, with the television or radio media, you know, or just with the public. But nobody would ever give me a chance. I tried and I tried and I was very *hurt* about this. I noticed that some people were gettin' a break even soundin' *like* me. I was so very hurt that my singin' or playin' was just a *job* for me, for a while, and I felt friendless when I was on the stage. It *really* hurt, believe me. I've had many people to ask me if I were bitter because a lot of white kids and other people who would play things I had would make a lot of money, but I wasn't bitter. I was just *hurt*, because I thought that if these people thought enough of me to play like me and to do the things that I was doin', why couldn't they give the original a chance?"

Imitative white artists were not the only ones contributing to his pain.

"My *own* people, the black people would *hit*, and the younger ones didn't really have a chance to *know* about me. They had heard stories about blues that made them turn their ears and heads away from it. Now I'm not sayin' that blues is supposed to be praised so much over everything else, but I think it should be *respected! This* is the idea I was fightin' so hard for. I knew the people had heard the stories set upon it, about blues singers not being any good or they was a menace to society and this type of thing. So the children didn't have nothin' to look *up* to, as far as the blues was concerned. So when they saw or heard the name of B. B. King, they say, 'Awwww, that *blues* singer!' And this hurt because I had no defense at all, no more, than to keep tryin' and keep tryin'. And, then, I would think to myself, there are a lot of people that have made a nice comfortable living doin' what I'm doin', and a lot of these people didn't go to college like *I* didn't, but were able, through my blues music that I play—and I don't use dirty lyrics—to make it big. Because I don't sing anythin' dirty, I didn't see anything to be *ashamed* about. But, for a while, I was even ashamed to try and sing my blues to people because I thought they didn't know anythin' about them *any*way and because I thought they would boo me or turn their heads on it. So all this time I went on the stage, I felt friendless. A lot of the time I would be on shows with a lot of rock 'n' roll groups, so I had to *really* work with every ounce of energy I had left to try and generate enough feeling to make them *tolerate* me, which made me work *extra* hard, thinkin' that at any time, the people liable to say or the kids might say, "Aw, we don't want to *hear* that.' And I would go up to my room many nights and I'd think to myself, '*Why*?' And I thought to myself, if Nat King Cole could be a great man in what he was doin', which I admired so much; Frank Sinatra in his field; Mahalia Jackson in hers and since that Aretha and Ray Charles, why couldn't *I*, in what I'm doin', because I don't know anybody else have kept as constant study, working as I have for twenty-one years, in blues."

Part of the blame he places on radio programmers and others dealing in music as a commodity.

"I was talkin' with a fellow the other night and I was tellin' him that when I was a disc jockey back in '48, '49, '50, '51, in Memphis, I learned about the categories they were puttin' music into. If it was a blues tune recorded by one of the white artists, then it would become a *pop* tune. But if it was recorded by a *black* artist, it would be either 'race' music or 'rhythm and blues'—they called it 'rhythm and blues' even back *then.* We were in that category. Now today it's *soul* or 'rhythm and blues' music. But when they come to the thing *I* do its *blues* or 'rhythm and blues.' The thing that's happening now is the underground stations, as we call them, the FM stations, are beginnin' to play *every*thin'. But even a lot of the black-operated stations won't play the blues now. If you think I'm kiddin', sometimes as you travel from city to city, monitor the AM stations and tell me how many Muddy Waters or Jimmy Reeds or T-Bone Walkers or Joe Turners or anybody like *that* you hear. But you turn to the FM stations that supposedly used to be called jazz stations, they'll play it *all!* But the other stations won't. And I'm talking about *black* disc jockeys. I can tell you three cities or maybe four at the most where I know radio stations that are black operated and play blues and even *they* don't play the people I've mentioned to you and it's not because these people don't have hot records out, because Muddy Waters has got a thing out now called *Electric Mud* that's really being played across the country on underground stations, but you check out the AM stations—black *or* white operated—and see how many play him. Check it out.

"I talked to one of my brothers . . . a black . . . not so long ago and asked him why he didn't play blues and he told me that his public didn't like it, it didn't fit his show. People didn't like *that* stuff. It's too 'down-home.' Then I had one brother to tell me—he was on one of those sunup to sundown stations—he said, 'B, you know what? I really play your records. I play you and Bobby Bland, Albert King . . .' and a few others he mentioned. And he said, 'Everyday I have one hour I don't play nothin' but blues.' I said, 'That's beautiful.' I said, 'How long you on the air?' and he said twelve hours. And I said, 'That's very nice. At least you give us an hour.' Since this was a black-operated station beamed to the black audience, I couldn't understand why he had to *segregate* the blues. Why couldn't he just mix it up with everythin' else? Actually, I didn't feel that it was very fair to us. That was almost like being a black man in America the way it *was*! I hope you know what I mean, because I'm not *fightin'* America, but these are some of the things I've felt even when workin' with my own people. Then, too, I know that when I'm introduced to go on the stage—I'm talkin' about playing a black club, a black theater or somethin'—maybe the emcee would say, 'And now, ladeez 'n' gennemen, it's time to get out the chittlins and collard greens . . .' and blah, blah, blah. 'We're bringin' on B. B. King.' And again, I don't think it's fair, because I like all those things—chittlins and pig feet and all—but I know blues singers who don't eat 'em and, even so, it just makes it all seem so small. Again, it's a matter of the music not being *respected*. And I feel very bad about that."

Pausing to answer his constantly ringing telephone with an almost inexhaustible patience, or to peer into the other room to greet a new visitor, always excusing himself with the over-courteous aplomb of a Sunday-school teacher, he goes on to explain the events that, he believes, led up to a change in public attitude toward his music.

"The change started when the Rolling Stones and other English groups started to playin' blues and bringing them back to America—what I call re-importin' the blues. They had a little bit of a different sound, simply by them being white and English, but they were playing them with *soul* in the way they could feel it, and enough so that *I* could feel it, though maybe not as deeply as some of the people I know, because most of them are kids, and when I say that, I mean young people. So then they started goin' into the underground or hippie places and everybody started to listenin'. And so a lot of the white kids–American kids–started to doing research on the blues. And they found that what the Rolling Stones and a lot of the English groups are doin' has been brought from the black people here in America. So then they started listenin' and tryin' to understand what kind of message *we* were tryin' to get over. To me, some of these people are beginnin' to feel a *part* of it. Naturally, they can't feel it as we do, because we've *lived* it. But I make that statement *this* way: You can step on a person's foot. You know it hurt, but you don't know how deeply or how *pain*ful it is. But you *do* know it hurt, because you've had people maybe to step on *your* feet. So that's what's happenin' today with white America wakin' up to us, because the younger people and a lot of the other people don't know how *deep*, how *much*, our pain has been, but they know that we've been hurt, because maybe *they've* been hurt, though they can't measure their pain by ours. But they have a feeling about it and that's why the blues is being played today. They are openin' the door for people that *really* know the blues, that has been carryin' the message for some time and so I think *this* is why B. B. King is beginnin' to be, shall we say, discovered.

"I played a place, not long ago, where I saw a notice in the paper the next day that say, 'B. B. King–New Blues Discovery'–after twenty-one years. But this is what's been happenin'. And another thing. We're beginnin' to be treated among *them* as stars, with *respect*, the same as they would give any other artist.

"I never had a standin' ovation in my life until last year. It first happened at Cafe Au Go Go in New York and the next time it happened was in San Francisco at a place called the Fillmore. When they mentioned my name, everybody stood up. And the next one, that *really* got to me, I was at the disc jockey convention last year and that was the *first* time I'd seen *my* people give me a standing ovation. And I *cried*! Then it happened again with my people—I keep mentionin' *my* people when I should say *black* people, because I feel now that the way I'm beginnin' to be treated, I should call *every*body my people. I say this to let you know between black and white. So it's with the black people I did the *Soul* TV show here [New York City] and that was the first time I've had a standin' ovation on television, for *black* people to stand up and give me an ovation on television. And I cried again.

"But every white college I've played and every underground place, I've *always* had a standin' ovation, not only in the United States, but in Canada and Europe. So I want *my* people—the *black* people—I want them to like me, yes, but if they *don't* like me, I want them to respect this music because I feel this is a part of *our* music.

"Our music, to me, is like one big tree that have many branches. Many people have come up with many different creations, many types of music, like soul music today or rock 'n' roll—all of this came from the spiritual tree. So the blues is a big part of it. I think it's the *basic* part. So I want the *kids* to know about it. More blues singers should be seen on television because we're black, we're a part of society, *we're* Americans *too*! I don't blame the kids, but I blame the people who are out there and can educate the kids to it. The reason I say this is that a lot of the kids might not be fortunate enough to go through school, might be high school dropouts, like I was, but I've made money sufficiently so to somewhat educate myself since I came out of school. If you go to my room now, you'll find many books that I buy and read myself. I don't think I'm an educated man, but I think, shall we say, that I have bettered my condition and I wouldn't have been able to do this were I not doin' what I'm doin'. So it was the little talent I had led me to better my condition, not only that, but to keep twenty-five people on my payroll working, twenty-five people that are paid and take care of their families from this one black blues singer. And I'm very *proud* of that! So there might be some other kids out there who, if they know how it's been with me, might be able to take the same step."

B. B. King's opinions of himself are a strange mixture of abnegation and chest-beating pride, a combination possibly due to the circumstances that have gone into the making of him. Dominating any personal expressions, though, at all times, is an insistence that his music and that of others in his vein be treated with what he believes to be a too frequently denied dignity:

"I don't think that I'm great, that I'm the greatest blues singer or guitarist or anything of that sort. I can't help but feel some thanks for the people who have helped me to make it and to help twenty-five other people to make their livings. I think that's pretty good for someone who came from the Mississippi Delta and today I've been halfway around the world. And someday I hope to go around the other half. In fact, I want my blues to be heard all *over* the world. I don't expect everybody to like it, because I don't like everythin' I hear, but I like music as a whole. I don't like blues only because *I* sing the blues. I don't like spirituals simply because Rev. Franklin or the Dixie Hummingbirds or some of the people I know and like sing them, but I like spirituals by many people. I like pop tunes by many people and even a few light operas, as I like soul music. But in all of this, if a person have a talent, you can try this or something else and stay with what you think is best fitted."

He excuses himself to go down to the stage and to help open the show, doubling as a bandsman, as Bebop explains, in order to earn the extra dollars involved. Then, as the preliminary acts go on, he is back in his dressing room, ready to answer more questions or to proffer opinions. It is brought to his attention that Keil, another King interviewer, has written of this commitment of the blues musician to his art. But when asked whether soul music is just a new name to be affixed to music that springs directly from the blues, King is modestly uncertain:

"I don't know. I think that anything can be done in soul gracefully. I'm not really an authority, you know. I think it's mostly a label, because I remember back when I was a kid in church and in my teen-aged years. People had as much soul back there in church, to me, as I feel they've ever had at any show I've ever gone to. Some of my people were in the Sanctified Church—they called them Holy Rollers and all that—and some were in the Baptist Church. There were some other churches I've been to, but those two denominations I've mentioned are the ones that really had that feelin' I get from listening to a lot of soul singers today. To me, it's a great big mixture of gospel with blues and a good beat. Now that's what I feel and I *feel* it. You know, like, some of the time the artists be on stage and I feel like I'm in church and even want to shout, but speakin' as an historian or somethin' like that, I can't say. But I believe any type of singin' or playin' can have soul. I believe there are types of soul I can't feel as well as others, but I think what make people stand *out* among the crowd, they're the ones who have that certain soulful somethin' that let everybody know, well I'm here, you know, and it speaks for itself and that, to me, *is* soul. Say, for instance, had not Count Basie had *soulful* music, he wouldn't be out there all these years. Nat Cole . . . great . . . Aretha, though Aretha hasn't been out there as long as some of these people, but Ray [Charles] . . . Ray has been out there. All these people, seriously, have soul. I think any outstanding artists out there today *have* soul, because they have that one thing make them stand out above all others."

What are his reactions to his new success as a soul artist?

"I've been on television more since the beginnin' of 1969 than I have in twenty-one years, but do you know that all the years I've been playin' and all the colleges I've been playin' lately, I've only had *one* invitation from *one* black college, and that was in Albany, Georgia. I guess the big schools don't want blues singers or the B. B. King type, evidently, because I never hear from them . . . not *any* of them. Anyway, due to the way I feel about my own people, because black people *have* supported me all these years, I would think that since the students are taught so much, why can't they be taught somethin' about the Negro heritage as a whole, *includin'* the blues. *That's* what I'm thinkin'. Because every black person has, at some time, *had* the blues, even if they didn't *like* them. I've just finished writin' a song with my friend Dave Clark and its about when I first got the blues, startin' off like this, 'When I first got the blues is when they brought me over on a ship and there was many men standing over me and, a lot more, I met people with a whip. *That's* when I first got the blues.'" An ironic chuckle, then he continues, "Another part of it goes, 'I have slept in the ghetto flats, cold and numb. I even heard the rats when they told the bedbugs to give the roaches some. Then everyone wanna know *why* I sing the blues.'"

A smile explodes into a wide grin that bursts out over his face just as he realizes that it is time for him to change clothes in order to make it onstage for his starring stint. "'Scuse me," he says with that benevolent smile. "I have to change my trousers, so if you'll just step into the other room for a moment . . . but if you can't, if you'll just turn your head for a bit. . . ."

Bebop helps him into surprisingly conservative navy blue attire as the crowd in the outer room carries on uproariously. It has been swelled by the appearance of a tall, hefty, bronze-colored young man wearing a luminous green suit, green socks and green alligator shoes. He is Freddy King, a blues guitarist from Chicago. As B. B., who is no relative, passes out through the crowd, he jokes with Freddy about celebrating St. Patrick's Day, then shakes hands with new arrivals, including a gold-toothed woman of matronly proportions and her glowering escort. "I'm lucky," B. B. turns back to explain as he reaches the door. "I have a lot of friends." Then it is show time.

It has been said that there are no audiences quite like those at the Apollo. Considered the most openly critical group to be found in any theater, they have no qualms about condemning a performer with hisses or boos, but when someone on that stage strikes a chord of response within them, they reward him with their jubilant reactions and shouted comments. They are a test of acceptance on a "nitty-gritty" level where there can be no "shuckin' and jivin'." During the Wednesday night amateur shows, which have passed into legend, under the auspices of a lanky former dancer named Honi Coles they have been known to hurl objects at "unready" contestants who are comically "shot" out of the spotlight and yanked off the stage by a hook from the wings. Yet the Apollo crowds are the audiences who also have helped pave the way to an earthly glory for those who wooed them into a sweet and soulful contentment; Ella Fitzgerald and Sarah Vaughan earned their first public hurrahs from them. Perhaps they are so critical because they have witnessed, over the years, practically every great black act to grace a proscenium, from residual vaudevillians such as Dewey "Pigmeat" Markham to rocking contemporary sound-masters. They are living witness of the observation made by several black playwrights that black audiences are seldom mere spectators, simply looking at a play or listening to a singer but, instead, enter into the action on the stage as part of a mutual exchange. Some anthropologists have linked this sort of interaction with the African past when art was regarded as an inseparable part of life that was not to be purchased for a two-dollar ticket. If there is some truth to this, nowhere in modern-day America is it more apparent than at the Apollo.

Dave Turner is finishing up his routine with an expansive imitation of Ray Charles that draws spontaneous applause, but one is not certain whether it is for the absent blind soul hero or the man on stage. At least they do applaud. Then the emcee steps out from the wings and announces B. B. King. At the very mention of his name, expectation becomes audible through hand-clapping and excited cries of "yeah!" Immediately he is identified as someone they deem capable of bringing them gratification.

B. B. strolls into the spotlight, so casually that he might have been just passing through. More than anything, he looks like a black "boy" who made it up North from the Delta on nothing but a hope and a prayer. He plucks a couple of penetrating amplified notes and a deep blue descending arpeggio from Lucille the guitar. So easily, he pulls the audience all the way into himself as the initial murmur builds. Some urge him on: "Yeah! Yeah! Come on, B. B.! Come *on*, B. B.!" And all this is before he has sung the first note. Seeming to sense that they are truly with him, he moves on into one of his most popular numbers, *You Done Lost Your Good Thing Now*, and is instantly transformed from a performer on the stage into a down-hearted man pouring out his pain to a woman who has walked all over his heart. The Reuben Phillips Orchestra falls in behind him as he wails out his mournful ballad of misbegotten love in a musical style that simulates all the inflections of a spoken monologue torn from the depths of the soul.

He begins the phrase at a high falsetto, easing down through a series of flatted blue notes into his mellow mid-range, turning his head to the side, shaking it in disbelief and grimacing at the ingratitude of this invisible woman. Squeals of delight at recognition of this common human plight issue from the audience as he repeats the statement in slightly altered form, building up to a tortured confession.

Women shout out, "No! No! Don't *do* it, B. B.!" Men, seeming to identify completely with the situation, vocally nod their agreement, "Man, do your *thing,* B. B.! All *right*!"

At this, he turns to Lucille and lets her tell the story for herself as he makes the guitar speak with an almost human voice, crying, pleading, giving rise to a deliciously unbearable state of tension by repeating musically simple constructs of bent and sustained notes that are, somehow, hypnotic in their effect. And even Lucille is overcome by the pain as he snatches the guitar from his chest and rips out the last few notes from her one-handedly as he falls back into the shadows to let the band take a chorus while the inflamed audience gets itself together again. When a near calm has come again to the throbbing mass on the darkened side of the footlights, he steps back up front to put in his last "two cents."

Next King switches to a slighty less mournful blues in which he has had a fight with his girl friend and is threatening to go out shopping for somebody else, which prompts one woman from the audience to ask invitingly, "Want me to come witcha?" When he seems to answer her in song, she ricochets with a machinegun volley of chewed-out sound: "*Yeah*-yeah-yeah-yeah-yeah-*yeah*!" And the men continue to prod him with their chants of "*Sing* on! Sing *on*!"

Finally, he tears them up completely with his rendition Leonard and Jane Feather's *How Blue Can You Get.* It is his last New York appearance before he takes off for a short European tour, after which he is scheduled for a long engagement at Art D'Lugoff's Village Gate, a downtown jazz emporium that recently has mixed in quite a bit of blues, in keeping with shifting tastes. But this is now and this is Harlem, and he lets it all hang out on this number that has been preserved on his record, *B. B. King Live at the Regal,* certainly one of the great blues albums of all time. Again there is the response from the audience as he admonishes an "*eeee*-vil" and jealous woman, putting her down with the lyrics as they climax.

"Yeah, *Yeah!* YEEEAAH, Bee-*BEEE!*" from the audience.

It is obvious that B. B. King has not been friendless on that stage, and that those who were listening were not merely tolerating him, even as he walks back into the shadows and the emcee returns to announce, "And *now,* ladeez 'n' gennemen, *star*-time. The *Dells!*"

The band picks up the tempo as five young men in identical fuchsia suits come bounding out onto the stage. This time the audience response is shriller, the clapping more frantic—all of it, perhaps, coming from younger and more hit-attuned persons out there in the darkness. The Dells are sprightly, handsome and flamboyant. They move as one through carefully choreographed dance-steps with their neatly pressed bell-bottoms flapping out over black patent leather dress pumps. Their rich voices meld into perfect harmony as they sing something about "We'll always be together," and their leader tries to conjure up a mood as he speaks directly to the audience, saying: "Have you ever been home sittin' on your couch all alone at night and it be twenty-five below zero outside and you all alone? Now don't that make your love come *down* on you?" The heated response comes back to them, too, for they are good, they are polished and, one hesitates to add the somewhat condescending term, "slick," though it is at the forefront of the mind. For the taste of something else, a more intimate blue sound, a more pungent essence, lingers and cannot be set aside. It lingers throughout the performance and even the long bus ride down through the beckoning and forbidding, spangled, neon-spattered world that is the nighttime circus of Manhattan. Somehow, through the music of B. B. King, it seems that one has been able to push through the tawdry glitter, the faked feelings and artificiality of it all and to move into another dimension where it is possible to reach down and to touch the very core of life.

1. Charles Keil, *Urban Blues* (University of Chicago, 1966).

Other rhythm and blues groups were the Clovers . . .

. . . and the Dominoes, led by Billy Ward, at the piano.

A wiggling, fun-loving singer-guitarist named Chuck Berry wrote a song called *Rock and Roll Music,* setting up a shock wave that has reached into the area of contemporary rock music.

Individual rhythm and blues stars of the 50's also left their mark on what is now called soul music . . .

Sam Cooke

Jackie Wilson

Ruth Brown

Lloyd Price

. . . while a natural truth-talking singer named Dinah Washington became "The Queen" of the blues in the 50's, the first generally popular soul singer of modern times and quite possibly the greatest.

Ray Charles, a blind former gospel singer from Albany, Georgia, known as "The Genius," was the artist who pulled out all stops, bridged all gaps and ushered in the current era of soul music, transforming this black bluesy gospel sound into a general market commodity.

Aretha Franklin, a minister's daugher from Detroit who almost made it as a pop singer in the late 50's, returned in the 60's as the leading soul sister of song, sounding very much the way she used to sound when she sang in church.

Otis Redding became the foremost exponent of what is termed the Memphis sound and dethroned Elvis Presley as the top male vocalist with British fans in late 1967 but died before reaping his glory.

Ebony

James Brown, known as "Soul Brother No. 1," was one of the most popular singing entertainers among blacks for several years before the general public became aware of his talents.

NBC-TV

Dionne Warwick has a polished singing style and has achieved such general popularity that some dismiss her as a soul singer, but beneath that polish she's still a "sister" all the way.

4

RECORDING IN MEMPHIS

As American musicians of another era journeyed to Europe to absorb classical culture at its fountainhead, their foot-patting, finger-popping modern counterparts now go to Memphis to record. It is a far different cultural source that the latter seek to tap, for Memphis, Tennessee, long has cherished its reputation as the home of the blues. Today "pure funk" is being sought in place of high-toned refinement and undiluted gutsiness is desired in lieu of "cultivated" sounds.

Jazz flutist Herbie Mann has packed up his silver whistle and gone to Memphis to wax a set with local lights. The Beatles have long ago expressed a desire to do the same. Dionne Warwick has made the scene, Wilson Pickett is a regular, and in early 1969 there were even rumors that Duke Ellington, the epitome of syncopated polish, was scheduled to make a recording date there.

But why Memphis and why now? After all, it remains, beneath the layers of legend, a medium-sized Southern city of less than a half-million population, far from the money-manipulative towers of Madison Avenue and even farther from the palm-shaded palaces of the West Coast's stucco Nowsvilles. It has been more than fifty years since W. C. Handy immortalized its backstreet life in song and fifteen years since Elvis Presley wriggled his way to fame from its streets. Many of the lauded bluesmen, such as John Lee Hooker, Muddy Waters, Howlin' Wolf and B. B. King, passed through Memphis, but they kept on going, while the town's namesake, Memphis Slim, followed a trajectory that led all the way to Paris. Aretha Franklin was born there, but the music world first heard of her after she had moved, as a child, to Detroit. In all, Memphis hardly presents the characteristics one might expect to find in a center of cultural activity.

And yet it is one. Part of the reason lies in the city's late-blooming resurgence as a capital producer of the highly marketable commodity called soul. In recent years when Motown, the leading producer of soul music in the sixties, began moving several of its artists toward a slicker, pop-oriented format in order to appeal to a more general audience, the music makers of Memphis caught a whiff of an incipient trend and set out to fill the vacuum by supplying the public with music of a raunchier sort—though this is not to say that the Supremes and Temptations can't still get right down with it when they want to. And today, the Memphis music men have had indications that their "noses" were not wrong, for what has been called "the Memphis sound" has been selling, and the name of *this* game is *money*.

Hit records make hit artists, and recording firms will go to any lengths to obtain the special ingredients that will make their products more salable. As Phil Strassberg, personal manager of a popular singing group called Anthony and the Imperials, said in 1967, before the trend had begun to reach its peak:

> Even the TV market is geared to the hit record. Talent has become secondary to this business of having a hit on the charts. If you're on top right now, a record will go on the charts as soon as its released, but if you're not, it's

harder to make it. Momentum is a big thing in keeping it all going.

His group, which made it to the top when it originated *Goin' Out of My Head* and *Hurt So Bad,* had been caught in a hitless dry spell and therefore was relying on nightclub appearances to keep its name before the public. As the story of Anthony and the Imperials shows, above all other things, the recording industry of today is a highly competitive, dog-eat-dog, constantly changing business in which artistry seldom counts if it cannot also show a profit. Memphis artists and those who record with them are coming out well into the black side of the ledger these days, so others have zeroed in on the goodies.

James Cortese, business writer for the *Memphis Commercial Appeal,* a daily newspaper, observed in 1968 that the city's record firms had done twenty million dollars' worth of business in the previous year and expected to gross thirty million in 1968—quite a bit of money for a cotton-picking town of its size. Cortese traced the beginnings of the Memphis boom back to the activities of Sam Phillips, a radio- and television commercial producer considered to be the father of the Memphis recording industry. Phillips, who is no longer personally involved in the business, used his Sun label to make the first records of a singing soul disc jockey named Rufus Thomas in 1953 and of Elvis Presley in 1954.

Today while the Phillips record firm is still very much alive, it has been joined by several others, notably Goldmark, Hi and Stax. It is Stax that holds the key to this dramatic new growth, for Stax is the firm that produced the late Otis Redding. A few months after Redding's death in December, 1967, Robert Shelton of the *New York Times* spelled out his significance:

> Redding was not an innovator of "soul" singing, but was certainly one of its greatest practitioners. He fitted easily into the league of Ray Charles and James Brown as one of the most explosive soul singers of this era. . . . In his final year, Redding symbolized the transfer of leadership in Negro pop music from its long-standing base of popularity in Detroit to the closer-to-the-roots center of Memphis.[1]

Stax, which boasts several soul acts, is alone responsible for more than half of the Memphis recording revenue. Its growth typifies the sort of rapid rise possible within today's record business, which has brought sudden wealth to so many. Like most of these firms, it is white-owned and the bulk of its talent has been black.

Stax's conception goes back to 1956, when a bank teller and country fiddler named Jim Stewart tried producing pop and country records in his "backyard studio," which was actually a garage, after he had been turned down by Sam Phillips. His partner in the home-made enterprise was a disc jockey named Fred Bylar. Later Stewart admitted, "We produced some horrible sounds." Though he had his degree in business administration from Memphis State University and had gotten "about halfway through law school," Stewart ran into difficulty when attempting to put theory to practice. His early efforts achieved only obscurity, and he lost about $10,000. Bylar soon dropped out, but Stewart plodded on. He did gain the support of his sister, Mrs. Estelle Axton, who mortgaged her home so that they might buy a $2,500 Ampex recorder in 1960. They looked for a studio and happened upon a good prospect, a vacant movie theater on McLemore Street in the heart of a Negro neighborhood, which they purchased. The area around the theater was teeming with music and undeveloped or undiscovered talent, though Stewart has said, "We didn't even know what rhythm and blues was then. We just happened to move into a colored neighborhood." In order to support their initially far from lucrative venture, Stewart continued to work at the bank while his sister operated a record store next door to the theater.

Fate already had stepped into the picture through their choice of location, and it was to play an even bigger part in the events that followed. Not too long after they had floundered into business, Rufus Thomas, the same disc jockey who once had been recorded by Phillips, came into the studio with his seventeen-year-old daughter Carla. Stewart and his sister decided to play a long shot by recording Rufus Thomas's version of a song called *Cause I Love You.* It sold thirty thousand records, a figure far exceeding their expectations and the fledgling producers began to have second thoughts about "this music." Thomas later went on to become a nationally known soul figure through his popularization of a dance called *Walkin' the Dog.* His daughter Carla Thomas, later a graduate student in English literature at Washington's Howard University, has become the acknowledged "Queen of Memphis soul."

That was the first break. The next one came in 1961, when a group of white teen-agers who called themselves the Mar-Keys recorded a rock 'n' rollish tune named *Last Night.* A half-million copies of the record sold. Importantly, one of the members of the Mar-Keys was a young guitarist named Steve Cropper, who had come to town from the Ozark Mountains of Missouri. Though Cropper had grown up to the tune of radio's *Grand Ole Opry,* the classic country and western show of all time, he had a keen ear for new sounds and a huge natural talent. An engineering student at Memphis State, Steve began working part-time at the studio, learning the techniques of recording production. Also at this time, a musically gifted sixteen-year-old black high school student named Booker T. Jones began hanging around the studio. Formally trained in piano and possessing the ability to master any instrument he tackled, Booker played with Steve in a studio backup band behind Rufus Thomas. One day Booker was "just messing around" on the organ along with Steve and two other studio musicians when they came up with a catchy little riff Stewart insisted they record. That was possibly the most important snap decision Stewart had ever made in life. The tune, which was so funky that they called it *Green Onions,* sold a million copies in 1962. It firmly established on a national level the combo called Booker T. and the M.G.'s, which in 1967 won a *Billboard* award as the country's top instrumental group, moving Herb Alpert and the Tijuana Brass out of their top spot. Stax was *truly* on its way.

Also in 1962 a public-relations man in Atlanta called Stewart and asked him if he might be interested in recording a band from Macon that was popular on the college circuit in that area. Stewart agreed to give it a try. The Johnny Jenkins band might have been completely forgotten in the years since, had it not been for the man who drove the musicians to Memphis. His name was Otis Redding. Newsman Van Gordon Sauter described the day Otis came to Memphis thus:

> "He was a shy old country boy," Stewart said. "He never said a word. They would say, 'Otis, go get us lunch,' or something like that."
>
> After the band recorded, someone suggested that Otis be given a chance to sing.
>
> "He did one of those Heh, heh baby things," Stewart said. "It was just like Little Richard. I told them the world

didn't need another Little Richard. Then someone suggested he do a slow one. He did *These Arms of Mine.*
"No one flipped over it."[2]

Fortunately, the public reacted differently. People didn't exactly rush right out to buy it, but Redding's first record did catch on gradually, first on the local level and then nationwide. So did Otis, who sang right from the heart, wringing every bit of meaning from a phrase, whether it expressed joy or pain, with a simplicity that was also subtle. Redding always had wanted to be a singer, and he was to make much music during the remaining five years of his life, not only by doing the songs himself, but also by writing songs that others, too, recorded—songs such as *Respect,* which was the vehicle on which Aretha Franklin rode forth to assume her throne. His sound was one of the major factors that helped put Stax, or Stax-Volt, as it was called then, in a position to compete with the biggest and the best of them.

Growth, however, has tended to complicate operations in the converted movie theater on McLemore where the marquee, which has been retained, proclaims that this is Soulsville, U.S.A. The complication has been largely the result of a recent change in the firm's business structure. Until May, 1968, Stax was basically a production company recording the masters for records that were distributed nationally by Atlantic of New York, a giant in the field that has specialized in soul music since the rhythm and blues period of the fifties. Due to this arrangement, Stax was not involved with the full range of activities that are part of the record business. Its main function was to procure artists, to create material for them and to record them with the appropriate musicians, without moving into the area of merchandising. But in early 1968, when Atlantic Records merged with Warner

Brothers-Seven Arts, Stax elected to dissolve its relationship with Atlantic and to go out on its own. In the complex world of big business, the going is extraordinarily difficult for a somewhat small, independent company. Consequently, as a step toward avoiding the imminent pitfalls, Stax allowed itself to be absorbed by Gulf and Western, one of the large conglomerates that includes among its properties Paramount Pictures. However, though owned by a public company with stock on the market, Stax continues to function more or less independently while enjoying the advantage of being able to draw upon the resources of other companies in the Gulf and Western leisure-time division.

This new arrangement has solved many of the problems of being independent, but not all of them. Departments that were previously rudimentary—sales, promotion and publicity—have had to be built up, while whole new departments have been established to work closely with distributors and to lay the groundwork for the setting up of an international department. Furthermore, these changes have had to be accomplished while the company kept up in the most important area, namely, the music itself. New material and new artists are being constantly searched out while established artists are ever pressed to hold on to what they've got in a field where public taste can shift from day to day. Efforts to produce new albums, as well as the singles that are the mainstay of the business, are intense, for all the albums previously produced by Stax became the property of Atlantic on their separation, including all the work of Otis Redding. Yet Stax has many fine artists to work with and their catalogue of talent, though not as large or impressive as that of Motown or Atlantic, still reads like a *Who's Who* of soul: Booker T. and the M.G.'s with Steve Cropper, a star guitarist in his own right; the Staple Singers, a family soul-folk group that still leans heavily toward the gospel area from which it emerged; Johnnie Taylor, whose 1969 hit *Who's Making Love* was a million-seller; Carla Thomas, Albert King, Eddie Floyd, William Bell, Judy Clay and several others. Furthermore, Stax has under contract an exceptionally large proportion of those artists commonly described as possessing "stone" soul. And there lies Stax's ace in the hole, considering current trends.

From a different angle, another important change has taken place at Stax. Color has been added to its top management, in the person of Al Bell, a six-foot-four-inch twenty-nine-year-old former disc jockey who became the firm's executive vice-president early in 1968. This makes Stax one of the very, very few record companies—they number fewer than the fingers on one hand—to have a black man in a top administrative position. Bell's position would not be significant if he were merely one of those showcased "token" Negroes hired to sit out front near the door to keep racial demonstrators off a company's back. He is, instead, very much a part of the scene, for while Jim Stewart, as president, is in charge of the financial end of the company, Bell, who joined Stax in 1965 as promotion director, is the one who works most closely with the artists and is greatly involved in extending the firm's activities.

Bell entered the music business by working as a deejay in Little Rock, Arkansas, while earning his degree as a political science major at Philander Smith College. He started as a "gospel jock," switched to jazz, then rhythm and blues, and once had his own record firm in Washington, D.C., where he picked up the techniques of production while learning to write his own songs. One of his artists there was Eddie Floyd, whom Bell brought to Stax with him as a writer-producer.

"The record business has been just like everything else in America for the black man," says Bell, who looks boyish behind his neat jutting beard and glasses. "He hasn't had exposure. He hasn't had a chance to get in and to *learn* the mechanics of the business. The thing that helped me get into the position where I could handle management and administration is that I've always been an eager beaver, so to speak. When I started fooling around with this end of the business, I wanted to know everything about it. As promotion director at Stax, I traveled around the country, visiting radio stations and trying to make certain our records would be played, but I spent any spare time I could get picking the minds of distributors on the side. Very few black people have had an opportunity to do this. Those who have been in it have mostly been in the promotional end and you don't learn the record business by just going in to see the disc jockey. Only recently have companies begun to hire black guys who could get in there and absorb these things. I think in time we'll see a lot more black people getting into the business if music trends continue as they've been, because the music we're dealing with was given birth by black people and they should have a chance to know something about the way it's handled."

With the assurance of one who has studied his subject in microscopic detail, Bell speaks of the way recent trends have been reflected in sales of Stax products:

"They say the type of product we produce with Negro artists is supposedly Negro-oriented, but when we sell what we've sold on Johnnie Taylor's *Who's Makin' Love,* which is in round figures about one million eight hundred thousand, they say that's an R&B record that has gone pop, meaning that it's a Negro-oriented record that has appealed to the white market. It's almost impossible for a record to make it to a million without developing this biracial appeal. In my experience, with a record that's appealing only to the Negro or black market, the maximum sales you can get—and here I think you've reached a saturation point so far as the black consumer is concerned—is a figure of around three hundred thousand records. There are unusual cases where a record that's bought by black consumers reaches around five hundred thousand, but we base our figure on about two hundred fifty thousand and anything beyond that, we figure that we're now getting to the white consumer's ears."

Is this what happened with Otis Redding?

"Unfortunately, he hadn't really managed to do this before his death—not in *this* country, though he had in Europe and was the most popular male singer in England. Just prior to his death, perhaps the last twelve months, he was beginning to be accepted by the white market [in America] and had considerable sales in some white areas, though we were not doing volume sales in those areas. He had a lot of white fans who would go see him, at that point, who were just beginning to understand what Otis Redding was doing, because Otis Redding was really the soul *messenger* and I think that's when they really began to become oriented as to what soul was. Then Aretha Franklin *really* bridged the gap with what she was doing. But Otis really became a general market artist only after his death, which was with our release at that time, *Dock of the Bay*, which was recorded just four days before he was killed. This was his first million-selling record. He had never had one prior to his death."

What are some of the factors that have helped to shape the current record-buying trend?

"The major buyers of records, *period*, are your teens and young adults, those twenty-five and under. When you talk about your average R&B, pop, underground or progressive rock product, an area in which we are heavily involved, these are the consumers, so we have to look in that direction, for I would say roughly 80 per cent of our records are bought by these people. Now there have been many fads over the years—Elvis Presley, the Beatles and the English sound—but today there isn't a single real superstar out there dominating the field and the kids are beginning to look for something new, which they're finding in this soul music out here now. It's very strong on the college campuses, where a large portion of the albums are sold to these kids, because they don't really have anything else right now that they can turn to and this is the freshest thing around, even though it's been here all these years. The only other thing happening out here right now when you think of a superstar is Tom Jones who is developing a stature of the sort Elvis Presley and the Beatles had, but if you analyze the material he heavily relies upon, you'll find these are the songs classified as soul, so everything seems to be turning toward soul. You also see this influence in other areas. In the past a Hugh Masekela or anyone who might be considered a jazz artist wouldn't have done a tune as commercial as *Grazing in the Grass.* At the same time, a group like Booker T. and the M.G.'s never would have been played on a good- or middle-of-the-road music station, but it's happening now. When you consider that all of this rock and soul music is simply a derivative of Negro gospel and blues coupled with country and western and country spiritual music, you might call what we're producing here *folk* music."

Does he believe the soul explosion is here to stay?

"It will probably reach a peak, because right now, we're growing by leaps and bounds, but even if it levels off, it will still *be* here since black people are here. In some form or another it will probably be here for as long as there's a moon—and if they let any of *us* get up there, we'll have it up there, too."

Bell explains that no matter how strong the trend at this time is toward Stax's type of music, one can hardly be content simply to coast along on the crest of the wave. As is common among those in the very nucleus of the business, Bell and members of his staff, from the clerical aides and secretaries to the musicians and producers, work wicked hours, without vacations and without regard to weekends.

"This business changes so fast that you almost *have* to do that to stay on top of current trends," says Bell. "You can go to bed at night and wake up to find a whole *new* trend is in existence. You have to be able to sense what it is and master it if you're to stay in there, because this business is *very* competitive. It's not like it was maybe ten years ago when there were a few companies putting out a few records. Now there are a number of good companies putting out quite a few good records, so if you want to stay on top, you must constantly beat the bushes to look for that product, meaning the songs, and burn that midnight oil trying to get it together and put it out there."

As might be expected of a proud, brand-new executive veep, Bell eagerly points out that there is a difference between the Stax sound and that generally referred to as the Memphis sound, though there are similarities that set both apart from the industry as a whole.

"In Memphis, we like for the artists to be able to *feel* what's in the lyrics of a song, to live them and *then* to interpret them in their own fashion. Here, when we get a group of musicians together in a studio, there are no written arrangements. The song has been sketched out by the writer or producer and the musicians go over and over it, adding their own ideas, working it over until everybody begins to *feel* it. Once they begin to feel it, then they begin recording it and it's the spontaneity of that whole thing that brings about the Memphis sound, because this thing called soul, as I define it, is based on an emotional experience. Now this is not the way it's done, as a rule, in the average recording session. When an artist is to be recorded, you get a writer who has what might be a good tune. Decisions on material are made by the producer who then selects the arranger he feels can make the proper arrangement for the tune. Then the producer, with the aid of the arranger, tries to find the musicians who can play this work best. They all go into the studio where the band plays it as it has been written and it is recorded. This is, of course, a little bit different from the way we do it in Memphis.

"What we call the Stax sound is based on this same Memphis format but other forces come into play. Number one, we have here what we frequently refer to as a 'freak' studio because it's an old theater building and the floor slopes down and as you look around the walls, you don't see any tuning boards or baffles. It's just open and when we get in there we are subject to acoustics that enable us to get a *pure* sound from all of our instruments. You don't hear electronic sounds. You hear that instrument as it actually sounds."

Whatever the acoustics, the most important distinguishing factor in the Stax sound, as Bell is quick to point out, lies in the group of musicians called Booker T. and the M.G.'s who are, in their lesser-known role, staff writer-producers and the studio band that backs up most Stax artists on recording sessions. This multiplicity of functions fulfilled by one small group in a firm is rare, if not unique, in the industry.

"These guys are heard on 70 per cent of the records that come out of here," says Bell. "Then too, they serve as producers. Booker T. produces William Bell and writes material for him; Steve Cropper produces several artists and is the man who produced Otis Redding. Since Cropper is a self-taught recording engineer, he also mixes his own material. Al Jackson, the drummer, produces Albert King, while Donald "Duck" Dunn is a key contributor to the total sound on electric bass. When horns are added, as they are on many recordings, they are called the Mar-Keys, of which this same group constitutes the rhythm section. Now this is the same group of guys who, every few months, will release an album under their own name of Booker T. and the M.G.'s, though they have been playing, producing and writing all the time for other artists. If these guys were just concentrating on building a career for themselves, I think it would be unbelievable as to how big they could be as recording artists, but they dissipate thousands of their ideas on sessions for other artists. This has amounted to the production of a total of about fifteen to twenty million singles within the past three years and nobody knows how many albums. They are the *real* backbone of our special sound and I think a lot of credit should be given to them."

To hear their music, one might think that each member of the M.G.'s had been cornbread-fed since birth, subsisted on a diet of collard greens and approached his instrument from a barefoot stance, utterly untutored—if one may, for a moment, borrow the overworked clichés of the soul phenomenon. Nothing could be further from the truth, and it is the very disparity in their backgrounds that has been so beneficent musically. As Bell explains:

"You'll find that the leader, Booker T., has his degree in music from Indiana University and is therefore able to add a bit of the academic approach to the playing of music. Mix him with the guitar player, Steve Cropper, who is white and has a basic country music and country pop background. Then take Duck Dunn, also white, who has basically the same kind of background but keeps up with things that are happening in the underground. Take all this and add the drummer Al Jackson, who has a blues and jazz background. Take these guys with all their musical differences, put them in there with that freak studio and add the writing techniques and the philosophy of our writers we've been trying to delevop—which is that in your lyrics, you tell the truth. With these kind of musicians backing us up, we're able to move from a good music tune, through pop, R&B to a country tune. They can play anything they want to play and it comes off sounding like it should because they are accomplished musicians."

But there is another side to Bell's pride in this group, for he adds:

"If you think about where we are, we're in Memphis, Tennessee, in the ghetto. Geographically, this city sits on the banks of the Mississippi River and is bounded on the south by the state of Mississippi, which is only a few minutes away, and on the west by Arkansas, which also is only a few minutes away. But when you look at Booker T. and the M.G.'s, you see four guys, two black and two white, who have been integrated for the past seven years. They were able to do this throughout the school integration battle in Little Rock, Arkansas, the James Meredith crisis at the University of Mississippi and so many other things. And when you look at our company, you see a combine which has been integrated, basically, since its inception—*this* in *Memphis.* I'm very *proud* of this and think that because of this we should be considered a model for other businesses—not just the record business, but for *any* businesses that doubt that black and white people can work together with ideological differences and, at the same time, be productive. We've *proven* that it can be done!"

This spirit of cooperation and go-get-itiveness permeates the firm, but, at the same time, it is quite apparent that the earthy Memphis soul sound, as it is produced in the Stax studios, does not rely on accident or sheer intuitiveness. It is the result of careful calculation that leaves to chance only the individual expressiveness of the artist. However, the deliberation with which the end effect is achieved is so well concealed that the music comes out with just enough strut and swagger to give it a feeling of inborn ease, just a touch of the driving quality of contemporary rock to give it a "now" flavor—but less frantic, less outrageously amplified and technically augmented than so much of what one hears in this era in which records compete for the status of hit on the basis of their decibel readings. This music takes its time and gives the impression of being funky without being phony; catchy, but not gratingly commercial. It is fast enough for dancing and cool enough for foot-patting or leaning back and listening. And so much of this has been coolly thought out beforehand.

The man who most exemplifies this dual-planed approach to the music known as the Memphis sound is Booker T. Jones Jr., leader of the M.G.'s and the one who is heard on the group's recordings playing organ and piano. For this highly trained and quietly businesslike young man of twenty-four, the world could have been dominated by green, purple or polka-dot people, and he still could have found a way to "make it" through music, so broad are his talents. As a child, he didn't come on strong in a genius "bag," but something did seem to be happening with him from a very early age. And as one of the few soul artists to come out of the small Negro middle class, like his Stax stable-mate, Carla Thomas, he was accorded every opportunity to develop his natural gifts.

His mother, Mrs. Lurline Jones, an attractive and articulate former school secretary, admits that her family was musically inclined and that she tried to play the piano in her younger years—"until Booker T. came on the scene and then he was so good, I just left the piano alone."

Mrs. Jones recalls: "I had an old upright piano and when he was very young, only three or four, he would get up there with these two fingers and actually make harmony. A friend of mine who was organist of our church at the time decided that he had talent and that she wanted to teach him piano. This went on for a little while, though there was nothing formal about it. Then one day, I decided that I didn't want that bunglesome piano in my house, so I sold it. Booker's heart was broken. We tried to make up for it by buying him musical toys and, later on, real musical instruments, including another piano. He was so happy that it was evident music was his talent and I never really thought of him doing anything else."

"I could never stop thinking about music or liking it since I can remember," muses Booker T., a dark, dapper, soft-spoken young man who wears his success without self-consciousness or egotism. His formal training began at the age of ten, when his parents bought him a clarinet. By the time he was a sub-teen, attending all-black Booker T. Washington High School, where his father was a science and math teacher, his interests were confirmed. "I used to hang around the band there even before I was old enough to join it. They had a special uniform made for me so I could get in before I was actually old enough to qualify," says Booker. "The teachers there were very helpful to me and besides the clarinet, I learned to play oboe, saxophone, trombone, tuba . . . many instruments." Meanwhile, he also worked out on his own on piano and organ, inspired by the music of Ramsey Lewis who was, in the very late fifties, almost exclusively involved in jazz, and of his idol, Ray Charles, "as an organist even more so than as a singer, particularly on that big band set *Genius + Soul = Jazz* that he cut with Quincy Jones."

By the time he was fourteen, Booker had formed a little combo with a few fellow students, and shortly afterward he went professional. He recalls: "Some friends of my parents had a club and wanted me to play there, with the promise I would be picked up, taken home and well cared for. My parents decided it was all right, so while I was still going to school, I used to work weekends and even some week nights, playing from ten until two. You could say I'm a night owl, for I've been up late almost every night of my life. Then I also kept a paper route in the morning and evening. I'm the sort of person who is always looking for something to do and I liked to stay busy."

During those high school years, the budding musician received an offer to join the Duke Ellington band, but that was where his parents drew the line. "We never insisted that he go on to college," his mother explains, "but we tried to keep it at the back of his mind." When he was sixteen, he became a part-time fixture at Stax studios, and the result of that "loafing around" was collaboration with Steve Cropper, Al Jackson and a drummer named Lewis Steinberg on *Green Onions* and a gold record.

With this spectacular introduction into the professional recording world, Booker might well have stopped at that point in his development, but the same level-headed maturity that marks him today was already manifest. "I knew that it was best not to count on just making it as a popular musician," he says, "for there was no guarantee that popularity would last. I knew that if I went on to college and got a degree, I'd always be able to teach and I figured that if I was capable of producing a hit record at sixteen, I'd still be able to do it at twenty-two . . . even *with* the schooling."

When Booker entered the University of Indiana, with the intention of earning a degree in applied music, he already was a celebrity, smiled at by curious fellow students who had heard his records and sought out by the girls. He did participate in a little campus activity, joining a black fraternity, and those who knew him then remember him as having been "a real regular guy who didn't seem to be carried away with himself." Yet he tackled his studies with the same enthusiasm that had resulted in excellent high school grades.

"Because his father taught at the same school he attended," his mother notes, "he had always thought that the teachers might have been partial to him. At Indiana he proved he really had it by making the Dean's List."

Making it through the University of Indiana, which is nationally known for the comprehensiveness of its music department, was no easy thing. In order to qualify for the particular type of degree he sought, Booker had to learn how to play "just about every instrument there is." But he chose the trombone as his specialty because "you had to have one major instrument and there weren't too many trombone players around." He played in the symphony orchestra and concert band, mastered music theory and the techniques of composition and scored a Bach fugue for full symphony orchestra as one of the requirements for graduation, before presenting his senior recital as a solo trombonist.

During those four years at Indiana, Booker continued to work professionally with the M.G.'s, meeting other members of the group in New York or Chicago for a performance or in Memphis, where they produced several more records. This was not only to earn money, but also to keep his name before the public. He had always been busy, but now he was busier than ever because he had married Willette Armstrong, a pretty co-ed from Gary, Indiana, and two years later there was a little Booker T. the Third. "I had to grow up in a hurry," he explains with a chuckle.

When Booker received his degree in 1966, he faced a future of unlimited possibilities. He might have pursued graduate studies and gone on to teach music theory in a college, a career that he considered. He was offered positions in symphony orchestras, something very few blacks have yet managed to obtain. But Memphis was where his heart was, so he returned to work full-time as a staff musician and producer at Stax.

The greatest challenge in his career came in 1968, when he was asked to compose a musical score for the Jules Dassin film *Uptight,* a controversial cinematic venture dealing with black militancy. For such a film, set in a black ghetto and steeped in racial turbulence, it was necessary that the music reflect the moods of the people it depicted. A black soul musician had to be the man, and Booker T. was the chosen one. "If I hadn't had all that musical training, I never would have been able to do it," he admits. "It's a very complicated technique that involves not only composition but the timing of musical sequences to fit the action on the screen." The former he already possessed, and he picked up pointers on the latter in Hollywood under Quincy Jones, a pioneer black in the area of film scoring. Booker thus became one of the youngest men of any race—André Previn was another—to fulfill such a task. Booker T. and the M.G.'s flew to Paris to cut the film's music track and later recorded the music for an album in Memphis; Booker played organ and piano and sang for the first time on record.

Booker's musical horizons continued to expand in 1969, when he served as musical director of, and was featured along with the M.G.'s and other Stax artists on, a television special, *Getting It All Together,* exploiting the Memphis sound much in the manner that the Detroit sound was presented in the Motown special, *Taking Care of Business,* the previous year. And 1969 also saw Booker voted Best Keyboard Player by rock stars in *Eye* magazine's first annual rock poll (though the readers' choices differed) and the M.G.'s, the top American group.

At an age when most young men are uncertain as to the direction their careers might take, Booker is preparing for his retirement. He does not live lavishly and has purchased two side-by-side comfortable homes in a pleasant Memphis black neighborhood—one for his parents and one for his own family. He notes: "My parents worked hard to get me this far and I'm happy to say I've made it possible for them to retire from their teaching jobs five years early." Though he and the M.G.'s are so tied down with studio work that they seldom make personal appearances, Booker's income from royalties and producing and as a staff man is quite substantial. But he isn't "blowing his bread," as has often been the case with those who had early success. He is investing in real estate, already having bought or constructed several apartment buildings. One doubts that he will ever be "up tight."

Booker's greatest fan remains his mother, who keeps a bulging scrapbook of Bookerania, stuffed with everything from a complete set of his elementary school report cards to press clippings and citations. The book is inscribed: "Dedicated to my son, Booker T. Jones Jr." And the introduction reads: "This book is compiled with the hope that someday some lad may scan its pages and become inspired to follow the lead of the person or persons depicted within its covers."

As Booker T. Jones has been a key force within the M.G.'s, so Steve Cropper, coming from the other side of the racial fence, has brought special gifts to the group. A twenty-seven-year-old white who plays guitar with such deep feeling and exceptional skill that his music transcends the barriers of color, Steve Cropper is the man the Beatles admired so much they wanted to come all the way to Memphis to cut a set with him.

When Steve was a child in Missouri, his parents, a pair of school teachers, were fond of the country and western sounds that were the dominant music of the Ozarks area in which they lived. This was the first influence on Steve's life, but when he was nine, the family moved to Memphis, and there, within a few years, he was exposed to another sound, for the fifties marked the great rhythm and blues era and saw the phenomenon of the soul disc jockey come into prominence. While other white teens were listening to Elvis Presley, Steve turned toward the originators of this black sound. He listened to Rufus Thomas spin out black blues sounds over radio station WDIA and quickly became a fan of artists such as Chuck Berry, Bo Diddley, Ray Charles, the Platters and the Five Royals. He liked what he heard and absorbed the style of it.

When he was about fifteen, Steve bought a guitar for eighteen dollars and began picking out the tunes for himself, scorning formal training after taking a few lessons. "I had enough lessons to learn the chords," he notes, "but I was too impatient to go through too much training . . . maybe because I was so late starting. I was more interested in playing actual tunes than ditties like *Little Brown Jug.*"

Steve was not the only white youth in Memphis who liked a soulful touch in his music, and he soon helped organize a little combo called the Mar-Keys. One of the members of that group was a pudgy, red-headed bass player named Donald Dunn but called "Duck," because of his penchant for injecting a little bit of humor into everything he did. Steve and Duck had known each other since they were in the fourth grade and were "like brothers." Several years later, in 1964, Duck was to become the bass player for the M.G.'s.

One of the boys in the group knew Mrs. Estelle Axton who, by 1960, had taken a step into the recording business. As a result, the Mar-Keys made a record of their tune *Last Night,* which soared to number three in the nation. Later the group dissolved, the members going their separate ways, though the name was to be carried on later by a Stax instrumental recording group. Steve, however, as has been noted, stuck with the firm after abandoning his course as a mechanical engineering student at Memphis State University and soon became one of the company's chief recording engineers, fulfilling a function that is his today, as well as becoming a recording artist with the M.G.'s

It is a mark of Cropper's high level of artistry, which he has developed on his own, that he possesses such a complete musical compatibility with the formally trained Booker T. Jones. When the two men perform together, the organ and guitar seem to be conversing, while Steve's solo work is so clean and his improvisations so imaginative in their frequently understated funkiness that he is considered both by fans and by other musicians to be one of the best electric guitarists in the business. The public knows him primarily in this role, but his skills as a producer and writer of songs are equally impressive.

Cropper is the man who produced Otis Redding, working more closely with him than anybody else, supplying the technical know-how the untutored soul master lacked, collaborating on songs with him and making certain that the right musicians were chosen for his sessions so that the final sound recaptured the same feeling Redding had intended to project. Cropper fondly recalls his late friend and colleague, saying, "Otis was just fantastic, a pure man and a good man that you felt good to be around. He was one of the greatest people anyone would ever want to work with, and he *always* worked. He was always anxious to try new things and to cooperate on anything you asked him to do. Many times we'd stay up all night long, working out new songs. The thing is that he really didn't know how big he was." One of their sessions resulted in Redding's memorable *Dock of the Bay,* with its strange premonition of the way he was to die when his private plane crashed into a Wisconsin lake.

Cropper remains, according to the charts, one of the nation's top-selling producers. And as a composer, he has written, by his count, nearly a thousand songs, 250 of which have been recorded. By early 1969, twenty-six of Steve's songs had made the charts at one time or another, and he had earned four gold records as a songwriter, for *Dock of the Bay; Green Onions,* a collaborative effort with the other M.G.'s; *Midnight Hour,* which has been recorded in at least seventy versions, the most popular of which is the one done by Wilson Pickett; and *See-Saw,* which was a smash hit for Aretha Franklin. When one considers Cropper's accomplishments and the quality of his work, it is difficult for anyone, even the most hard-core exponent of black exclusiveness, to deny that a white man might have soul.

Respect for the white soul artist is even more significantly expressed by Al Jackson Jr., the M.G.'s drummer who got his start in music at the age of twelve by performing with his father's jazz and blues band, itself a popular unit throughout the Southwest during the fifties. Al first met Steve when the two were young pre-M.G. professionals making gigs around Memphis, and the friendship that ensued goes beyond the recording studio into their private lives. Of Cropper, Jackson openly states, "Some people might be startled that guys like Steve and Duck can play real soul music, but when it comes to this soul thing, people have to remember that whites, particularly in this area, have their own kind of soul roots in country and western music, while we as blacks have ours in blues, gospel, R&B or whatever you want to call it. When you get a white guy who is flexible enough to blend the feelings from those two different kinds of music and to come up with his own thing, then you have something that is really formidable!"

Such are a few of the people who have helped to create an enthusiasm for the Memphis sound and to light the fuse of the soul explosion, but in the recording industry, even more than in most popular arts, everything depends on a joint effort. Every person in the recording industry, even those on the lowest rung of the ladder, has to put in his little bit in the hope of sharing in the riches looming so tantalizingly in the near distance.

In few places does one find the sort of constant bustle and interminable thump of sound to be encountered at a record firm that houses its studios in the same building. This is the way it is at Stax, where visitors and staff alike must enter by the back door leading in from a sometimes muddy parking lot. The old movie theater has come a long way from its earlier days; the plant has reached out in all directions to swallow up the record store that lured some of its future artists to its doors, a laundry and several surrounding establishments. Smiling, bronze-hued receptionists greet you at the doors, and you are seated in a comfortable anteroom until properly fetched by whomever you wish to see. Most likely it is Deanie Parker, a diminutive twenty-three-year-old former singer who serves as director of promotion. Just as often, it is her secretary, yet another smiling young woman who escorts one through labyrinthine, windowless passages flanked by paneled offices furnished in the most modern style. Thick carpeting conspires with the paneling to absorb the sound of footsteps that would, even without the carpeting, be inaudible because of the rhythmic thooms, thumps, whirs and plinks coming from all directions—new tunes being tried out in the studio or played back in the control room.

A tall, dark, bald-headed but youthful looking man passes by, striding confidently along in an iridescent purplish suit. He is escorting a brown-skinned girl in a fuzzy fake-fur jacket and an orange-red wig, walking along beside him with such an air of overdone grandeur that one knows immediately she is a singing hopeful in search of an audition. The man is Isaac Hayes, a songwriter and singer who has collaborated with David Porter to create some of the greatest soul hits of the sixties, among them *Soul Man* and *Hold On, I'm Comin'*, which made the team of Sam Moore and Dave Prater into the nation's top soul duo. Other people pass by, most of them with faces lit by an unconcealed appetite for the next moment—which might be the really *big* one. They all smile or nod politely to whomever it is that crosses their paths. And it is easy to see that all of this cannot be dismissed as mere southern hospitality; for these are all young people, some yet so young as to display the acne insignia of adolescence, and all of them seem to be infused with the excitement and anticipation that pervades the very atmosphere in which they move. This is their day and they know it. And you feel happy that this day has finally come; for almost all of them are black and beautiful in the hope they bear so conspicuously.

Deanie Parker is hard at work in her own windowless, paneled office, tending to some of her duties, which include editing and publishing a monthly magazine called *Stax Fax,* which is issued free-of-charge to publications and writers specializing in popular music; analyzing copies of clippings supplied by a nationwide service in order to determine whether the firm's artists are getting their share of publicity; writing and sending out press releases of her own; arranging interviews by telephone; ironing out the personal problems of artists; arranging for benefit performances that might eke out some much-needed press coverage; setting up special "days" and "programs" to promote the Stax sound; thinking up ideas for album covers and new types of records that might be attempted. Somehow she manages to find time to send personal thank-you notes to everybody who writes anything about any Stax artist anywhere and bubbles over with eagerness at the approach of a newcomer who just might be able to spread the name of the firm for which she works. She conducts a personalized tour of the place, going down yet more twisting passages, around carpeted corners and through a door where a lone red-headed man sits near the lowest point of a dramatically sloping floor, wearing a broad-brimmed cowboy hat and bobbing his head, with beard and locks that know no cutting off point, to his own solitary thoooooomms.

This is the main studio, and the single thoomer is Duck Dunn, who has arrived early for a recording session set for 10:00 A.M. In quiet respect for artistry at work, no matter how weird it might seem in its rough form, Deanie closes the door and goes around still another corner to a room where there sits an almost pitifully battered baby grand piano, so incongruous among its spanking new companion fixtures. This is the office of Porter and Hayes, and Deanie Parker explains that the names of all the artists who have passed through Stax are scratched somewhere on that piano. Some such as those of Sam and Dave and Carla Thomas are well known, but one scrounges through the memory to find a connective point of identification for many of the others. Deanie Parker recalls the way in which she, as a Memphis teen-ager with singing aspirations, first arrived at Stax, so certain she was going to knock the whole world dead with her talent. "I knew I was so great I even came in here with my own band. I cut a record and I don't know what happened to that thing and don't *want* to know. But soon afterward I began working here. It was really something, then. You had to do everything and I even wrote songs, though I had never written a song before in my life. You wrote a song about just *any*thing that you felt. I know one morning I was getting out of a taxicab, coming to work, and I was feeling so depressed I went right in to that beat-up piano and put it all into a song." Her efforts as a composer were not entirely crude, for she still draws royalty checks for her songs, and one of them, *Give Me Enough to Keep Me Going,* is one of the popular recorded numbers of Carla Thomas.

It is well past ten o'clock, now, and a wave of activity is building up in the studio. Up a flight of stairs in the walled-off second level that is the control room, Ron Capone, the recording engineer who says he is a very, *very* distant relative of the notorious Al Capone, fiddles with some dials on the control board. He obligingly offers a highly condensed five-minute course in the recording process, explaining the way in which several instrumental tracks are cut for a musical background long before the vocalist's track is added to it. With its still-new eight-track recording equipment, Stax can select the best segments of all the instrumental and vocal takes, adding instruments or taking them out when the producer voices his choice, in order to produce a final product that has all of the composite sounds in proper balance. Horns can be injected or removed, strings can be added when wished, and a mistake made by one musician on an otherwise good take can be replaced by a perfect segment from another take. The method by which these various takes and sounds are brought into the desired balance is called mixing, which is a standard procedure in the recording industry. Except for live performances, as when Albert King was recorded at the Fillmore Auditorium in San Francisco, the solo artist is not even present when the background is recorded.

This is the day when tracks are to be recorded for a new release by Johnnie Taylor, the former gospel artist who replaced the late Sam Cooke in a gospel group called the Soul Stirrers. He is not anywhere to be seen.

Downstairs in the sloping studio, other musicians gradually wander in to join the still-bobbing Duck Dunn. Steve Cropper arrives, lean and handsome with keen features that have led one writer to compare his looks to those of a Spanish dancer. He nods silently to Duck and immediately goes about tuning his guitar, bending close to the speaker in his amplification system. He seems to shut the whole world out from him, and there is only the promise of the music he plans to make. A stubby young man with a tan cherubic face comes in carrying a guitar of his own, chatting with a slender, long-haired brown girl called Betty Crutcher: Raymond Jackson, a staff writer.

It is now well past eleven o'clock, but there seems to be no set time schedule. A few riffs ram against each other as the musicians try out ideas of their own, listening, for the moment, only to themselves. A compact, curly-headed young man works out extended phrases and gospelish passages on an electric piano. He turns out to be a writer-producer from Motown who isn't supposed to be there but has come to sit in with some friends, namelessly.

A sudden getting-down-to-business attitude seems to take hold of all those in the studio as the set producer, Don Davis, arrives. A short-haired, terribly worried looking tan man, Don Davis has been with the company less than six months and already has produced Johnnie Taylor's golden hit *Who's Making Love*. Burdened by the degree of this initial success and obviously pressed to maintain its momentum, Davis seems sullen, is unsmiling and appears not to have enjoyed a single night's rest since he arrived in Memphis as a previously independent producer.

He sits down at an uneven-legged ivory-colored piano, made even more uncertain in its stance by the sloping floor, and puffs nervously at a cigarette, fingering out chords for a new song called *Because Your Love Is Gone*.

Cropper listens carefully, noting that the tune is possibly in 7/4 time, and states, "I like anything different. Yes. It's fresh." Davis continues to pluck away at the piano, his expression on a face bearing at least one day's growth of beard growing more harried with each phrase. Al Jackson, whose ebullience is so great as to place him beyond the pale of worry, wanders in, steps up to the tiny platform where his drums have been set up and works over the accompanying licks as Davis flusters away at the piano and Steve joins in. The nameless pride of Motown injects his own statements while Duck Dunn bobs away, hitting a few wrong notes but quickly correcting them and never repeating his errors. Raymond Jackson plunks away on his own guitar and begins to mouth out the melody. Only occasionally do any of the men present glance at a sheet of paper on which the basic chords are sketched out. It is all very informal, all of it taking place in that sloping studio where momentarily abandoned instruments are scattered and empty pop cans bearing the traces of cigarette ashes adorn all flat surfaces. Motown's joy states that he believes that the greatest soul musicians play, like him, by ear: "They have a freedom to create their own fields as compared to those who read music. They go by this *sounds* right, rather than this *is* right." And he adds, "You can see this in fantastic people like Ray Charles and Stevie Wonder who are blind and can't even *see* to read music, and yet they can *play* it."

Then they get into the song. There is the heavy, pulsating amplified bass sound thooming away almost outrageously to underscore the sharp guitar whanging in voice imitation, the deliberately undersung statements of songwriter Homer Banks, who will not be the final singer but is so much into the groove that everybody weaves and rolls back and forth. The only important thing seems to be that they are enjoying what they are doing. Don

Davis, who is gradually unwinding, shouts out chords that might be misinterpreted at each point of muddiness, "Make that an F sharp diminished . . . make that a G," even getting so deeply into his own thing that he laughs a little and cries out to the others, "I think I got the best groove in here," since his playing will not be heard on any of the tracks. "I just want yah'll to know what I'm doing here."

Ron Capone comes down the stairs and into the studio, constantly arranging and rearranging microphones for each instrument and peering inside the yawning top of the piano where one of those ever present microphones is located. All sorts of people wander in and out, digging what they hear and shaking their heads in tempo to it. Eddie Floyd, whose hit *Knock on Wood* was recorded in much the same way, passes through, a tall, square-faced young man who reacts to the gospel flavor in the tune, seeming to tie it in with his own past as a singer with a gospel group called the Falcons. Constantly, new personal statements are injected, and when they are striking enough to draw a response from Davis, he yells out, "Keep that *in*!" They go over the number, over and over and over again. The total result is never quite the same, and each element begins to jell. Then Don indicates to Ron Capone that they are ready to make some takes. At this point, Al Jackson sets the pace from his drum domain, chanting in the proper meter, "One, two . . . one, two, three, four," as everything seems to fall into place and chaos becomes cohesiveness. Over and over they record the tracks. Again none is exactly the same as the one recorded before. And eventually they have exhausted all readily explorable possibilities.

More people wander in and out and Booker T. slides onto the set, with the unstudied ease of a black panther, going up to Steve Cropper in order to check on the control room schedule because he wants to mix a set he has produced and wants to put in his bid early for a technical facility that is always being used by *some*body.

The musicians at hand and Davis move into another tune and someone shouts out, "What's the name of this thing?" Davis answers in a hoarse voice, "*I Had a Fight.*" There is something about it that reminds one of those good soul-cleansing, sanctified Sunday morning services, and a spirit of unbridled jubilation takes hold of everyone in that room as all heads begin to bob as one and all feet become part of a single exultant stomp. It is good and everybody knows it, and it has not been a matter of work but more a manifestation of personal expression.

It has all been going on for several hours now, though nobody seems to have noticed it, and the phones are ringing madly in all the offices as Al Jackson tersely explains, "Wives." He runs up the steps to catch a few minutes of mixing with Capone on an Albert King set he is producing, and after hearing one particularly good track, he advises Capone, "Let's just put it down and don't try to funk it up too much. Those are the ones that really make it."

From the temporarily abandoned studio, one of the secretaries shouts up through the control window to Capone that he has a visitor. An energetic preschool-age little girl half-slides and runs down the studio floor and up the stairs to the control room, followed by a plump young woman who obviously is her mother.

"That's Ron's wife," Al Jackson explains. "She came down here and brought the little girl to be with him. We get home so seldom that some of them do that, sometimes."

Within a few minutes, Don Davis is in the control room, along with Ron's wife, hearing again the tracks just cut and giving advice on what should be done with it all. Again, he puffs nervously on a cigarette, his rather youthful face folding into a prematurely old visage as he listens over and over again, cautiously but finally proffering each opinion. When he leaves the room, Capone explains, "Don is a slow worker, but he thinks everything out and gets his thing together. He's one of the great producers."

It has been less than a half-hour, but all the musicians are back in the studio and Don Davis is back in command. They begin reworking a number, and Davis halts it all to demand, though not harshly, "Raymond . . . give me more volume and I want to hear the bridge with vibrato on electric piano and Steve let me hear you at the bridge doing the same thing you played before." The music is dissected in his hands as he suggests the ways it might be reassembled in better form: "Raymond, sustain your chords since Steve is doing the same thing you're doing anyway. You ready to cut it? All right!"

The work goes on and on and on in the studio. But work progresses elsewhere, also. Some artist is always arriving in town for some reason or another. It is said that Sam and Dave will be in to cut a set that Saturday night, less than twenty-four hours away, and that Albert King happens to be passing through town, right at the moment. Albert King is the musician Albert Goldman has called, in the *New York Times*, ". . . the greatest black musician of the decade." Goldman heralded King's "transmutation of country blues into city surrealism." In *Life* magazine, Goldman also has called King "the last great figure in the history of American country blues," going on to describe his style:

> A fusion of the ancient Mississippi "bottleneck" style (the fret finger sheathed with glass or metal tubing) and the sighing, swooning, "psychedelic" sound of the Hawaiian

steel guitar, King's blue note is so "nasty," so cruelly inciting, that after a quarter of an hour under its spell, one itches for a bottle to break and a face to cut.

Goldman notes that King has helped to stimulate the blues appetites of young Americans following "the 'Death of the Hippie,' the exodus from the Haight-Ashbury, the murder of Linda Fitzpatrick and Groovy"—the last of which murders shocked the gentle "flower people" into a recognition of reality. The handle Goldman applies to King is "The Biggest, Baddest Bluesman."[3]

While one would hesitate to endorse such a setting-apart of one artist from all others—such sweeping judgments are so often arbitrary and unnecessary, unfair to others—Albert King does stand as one of the finest blues guitarists and vocal interpreters of the time. His bigger-than-life countrified sound not only has caught on among post-hippies but also has found more than a nodding favor among their more affluent, modish counterparts within the establishment, for as Richard Goldstein has written in *Vogue* magazine: "Bluesboppers everywhere are searching the mud bayous of American music for a soul guru. And they have finally found him in Albert King, B. B. King's half-brother and a dazzling musician in his own right." Goldstein, too, delves into King's style, noting:

> This husky, yet humorous approach to blues is not unusual among black performers, yet to white audiences—who often approach blues as a litany to be recited with utter sanctimony—King's casual assertion is potent novelty.[4]

That's the way his music goes down, so often, with his newfound audiences, but for Albert King, as a black bluesman, fad and fashion are not so important as the music itself and the afterglow of knowing that people *really* have enjoyed what he has done. This type of thinking is inseparable from the tradition of the blues in which music of this sort has been played and sung to give pleasure to others at informal gatherings, as well as to make money. And though money and recognition have come to King of late, he remains a creature of two worlds, playing to large audiences of young whites in the North while retaining a longer-standing popularity among blacks and some whites in the South. And when he goes to a city such as Chicago to perform for the long-haired "in crowd" at a North Side psychedelic circus, he goes, after the show, down to the South Side to spend the night at a black motel. Like so many other "new discoveries" in this soul-hungry age, King has not altered his general pattern of life to any great extent, in spite of fame. Perhaps it is, indeed, his simple approach to things both ordinary and extraordinary that has made him such a hit with those unaccustomed to the unaffected.

On a visit to Memphis, Albert King walks into an office looking like a true man mountain, all six feet four inches and 250 pounds of him. His blackness is as impressive as his stature, and regardless of his oversized tailored suit, he looks like a friendly farmer in his Sunday best, with his diamond stickpin giving him a touch of the aura of a small-time gambler from a riverfront town. Considering the stories that have been told, one searches (trying not to appear obvious) for some physical similarities between him and B. B. King, for the question as to whether or not they are half-brothers remains unanswered. It all depends on which source one consults. Material from B. B.'s camp has said "no," while that from Albert's camp has said "yes." Any considerate human being would hesitate to ask another a direct question about such a relationship. But though Albert is large and B. B.

is almost small, it does seem a bit strange that two of the top blues artists of the day—possibly *the* greatest two—both come from Mississippi by way of Memphis and its environs, have the same last name and, as singers, accompany themselves on guitars that B. B. calls Lucille and Albert calls Lucy. There are even striking similarities in their styles, though B. B.'s is more urbane, more influenced by jazz. Yet out of a sense of taste, one lets the question hang.

Albert settles his huge frame on a chair as he explains that he has just played the Fillmore East in New York and will be returning to Manhattan to tape the musical background for a cigarette commercial. This "country" looking gent doing commercials? It sounds like *too* much. But he sits there without presenting any walls of reservation and simply talks about the way he happened to become what he is.

"Kids nowadays got a good education and can read up on how to do things," he begins in an untransmuted drawl, "but when I got started, there wasn't anybody to help you. If you wanted to get a band together, you'd just pick up on whoever could make a sound. I got to seventh grade. I had to work. My mother was a widow. Wish she was livin' now. She wouldn't have to worry 'bout a *thing*. That's the *truth*!"

Briefly he explains that he was born in Indianola, Mississippi, a town sporting so many barn-like clubs for weekending black folks seeking relief from the drudgery of day-to-day plantation work that it might well be called the nightlife capital of the Delta. As a child, he moved to Forest City, Arkansas, which is about seventy-five miles from Memphis. He recalls musical impressions of those days.

"I used to hear the blues, you know. Like, I was a little *bitty* boy when I used to listen to a blues singer called

Dorothy Dailey [a man]. Back in *those* days, now, Lonnie Johnson used to play the guitar and Mercer D. was a piano player then. He kept time with his feet; he played the bass with one hand, played the lead with the other and sang and they would record him. If you listen to him, he really gets your attention, because he's a man who really played from the *heart,* you know what I mean? I got his album at home and the only place I know to get it is in St. Louis. Paid seven dollars for it. Back then, I had the same feelin' that the kids got now. I wanted the *natural* thing . . . anything that was for *real.* Then I dug it, but if it *wasn't* for real, I wouldn't listen."

Though he enjoyed listening to music, he did not try to play it until he was in his early teens.

"I paid a dollar and a quarter for my first guitar." The word is pronounced with the emphasis on the first syllable: *gui*tar. "Bought it in Forest City on the streets from another boy. He'd paid seventy-five cents for it. He wanted to go to the show with his girl and tried to get me to loan him a dollar, but I wouldn't do that. I didn't *have* no girl, but I had the money and I wanted the guitar. We settled on a dollar and a quarter for it.

"Every night I was through with work, I'd come home and play that *gui*tar. That one wore out on me and I kept it, so when I made me some money, I had my dollar and a quarter *gui*tar refinished, refretted, bought me a case for it and it's at home now."

During that period and until recent years, King worked part-time as a musician, making his living primarily as a bulldozer operator. When he speaks, he seems almost as proud of his record as a good laborer as of his musical reputation.

"I've been workin' since I was nine years old—farms, mostly—and then when I got up to size, I started doin' construction work. I helped build the dam in Grenada, Mississippi. I was a young boy. I put the last load of dirt on top of that levee. But when I was startin' to playin', I left Forest City and went to Little Rock, Arkansas. Everybody was leavin' this part, goin' up there because work was good at the time—about '48 or '49. I bought me another *gui*tar in Little Rock, Arkansas, with an amplifier. I was workin' on the levee then, drivin' a bulldozer. I started practicin' on that *gui*tar and I'd keep people up half the night. They'd be hollerin' out, '*Turn* that thing off, you *so*-and-so! Don't you *never* go to sleep? I wish that thing would get *tore* up!' So I made up my mind I wanted to get up a band. That's when I went to Oceola [Arkansas] to work. I started me a little band up there, the In the Groove band. I didn't know but two songs to play, but I'd play them two—speed 'em up and slow 'em down."

Oceola, which is nearly seventy miles from Memphis, is, in Albert King's estimation, "just across the river." Therefore he often made it into the big city with his little band. Nostalgia comes over him and he smiles a big gold-toothed smile when he recalls the Memphis of the late forties with its famous Beale Street.

"It was wild and woolly! We played in Beale Street Park over there. *Beale* Street." He seems to fondle the word in his mind. "That's where you could find anyone in the world you look for . . . walk up and down Beale. If you don't see him to*day*, you'd see him to*mor*row or to*night*. Beale Street was a *mon*ster! *Yep*! Aw, them was the *days*, though. They had the One Minute Cafe. You go in there with fifteen cents or a quarter and get a meal so big you couldn't *eat* it all. Don't *leave* it, though, to go get the salt. If the salt's up there on the counter, you holler for somebody to *throw* it to you, 'cause when you come back, wouldn't be *noth*in' on your plate. That's *right*! I remember from when I was a little boy they've taken *many* a plate from me."

In general life was difficult then, but it seemed less complicated.

"Wages was cheap, everything was cheap, but it was accepted. The people was . . . well . . . they wasn't understanding the way they are now, but you could do 'most anything to make fifty cents. Like, if you had yourself a day job and was makin' thirty dollars a week or thirty-five, you had a *good* job."

His band began to gain a toehold in the Arkansas area near Memphis, particularly Oceola, and he recalls:

"The Memphis bands would come up there to play when I had my little band. Course, when *they* played, I couldn' play because there wouldn't be nobody there to *lis*ten to me. I had to close up and go listen to *them*. I started from that, but I kept on pushin', kept on pushin'. I'd work through the days and play on weekends . . . sometimes during the week. We did pretty good. I worked myself up to fourteen . . . fifteen dollars a night. This was like in '54 and '55. By then, I knew more than two songs, but I wasn't *too* strong. I knew 'bout five or six. They'd be mostly somebody else's tunes. I'd like 'em, learn 'em, sing 'em, play 'em. I was playin' sittin' down, then." A hearty laugh. "I'd a missed the whole *guit*ar if I'd tried to play standin' up!"

Like so many itinerant workers, King sometimes jumps from one period of time to another, just as the laborers had to move almost constantly in order to make a decent living. But he unbegrudgingly struggles to place things into a rudimentary chronological order.

"I left Oceola and went to South Bend, Indiana, in '62. I left there and went to Gary, Indiana. Started workin' at a service station. Didn't stay *too* long, maybe six or eight months. About in '62 or '63, I recorded a record with the Parrot Record Company, *Lonesome in My Bedroom.* Didn't get no money out of it, but the record did pretty good, so I began to be recognized by the other musicians. Muddy Waters and all of them was already up there in Chicago. When I'd go in a place and *really* want to let them know I was there, I'd go in at the door and tell them, 'Let me see Muddy Waters,' and they'd say, 'What's your name?' I'd tell them and they'd go tell Muddy and he'd say over the mike, 'We got Albert King in the house . . . *Lonesome in My Bedroom*!' I'd go 'round and sit in with *all* them bands for nothin' just to get myself known, but I was *hap*py.

"When I was in Gary, I got to know Jimmy Reed. He was a disc jockey then. I'd be with Jimmy and he'd sing a bit and I'd sing a bit and we'd go over to Chicago and play, too. This was them little *small* joints where folks be callin' each other bad names from way 'cross the room and someone like to throw a wine bottle at you. I remember there was a place in Gary where we was playin' one night and the joint was *jump*in' and the boss man's old lady, she was *fine*! So I got stuck on her and she kinda went for me, but this dude kept *watchin'* me. Well, we was up there playin' that night and a dude got outside and got up on a bench and shot *through* the window and shot another man in the mouth. Well, I thought it was this man shootin' at *me* and I went *out* the back door! Jimmy Reed was up there talkin' about 'Don't be shootin' while *I'm* singin',' but I was *gone!*"

This was the period when King recorded a few songs that attained popularity among R&B followers. Some were on the Veejay label, produced in Chicago.

"I did *Baby You Don't Have to Go* with Jimmy Reed. Then, too, I played drums behind the Spaniels—that's what I *really* had started out to do before gettin' to the *guitar*. And I had a group called the Dutones—*Shake a Tail Feather*. If you remember a group called the Tabs—they did *Kill That Roach*—well, I got their lead singer playin' guitar with me now."

At some time during these years, and one cannot be certain as to exactly when, according to his account, King left the Chicago area and returned to Oceola, Arkansas.

"Now this is when I really got a pretty good band together and started bookin' the dates 'cause then I figured if I could get some money, I could go to Memphis and hire me some musicians. It was a good idea. I had some fellas play with me much as four years because I've always been known to *pay* my sidemen. I never did try to *cheat* them. I got up as high as seven pieces in my band, with three horns. We played white clubs through the Arkansas area. That was the way we made our money. We'd play for Negroes like on Sunday night, maybe. I got my group to go on, but it cost me a lot of money and a lot of headaches. *Lawd!* I don't wanna go through that no *more*. Musician get up and quit on you so you got to sweet talk him, 'I'm gonna give *you* some more money, but don't you tell *him!*' I have *paid* my dues."

It was in the early sixties that King began to achieve a notable regional popularity as a blues band leader and singer in the Southwest.

"I really started makin' it when I came back to St. Louis. This was after I'd gone back to Arkansas and stayed only 'bout two weeks and then I went back to St. Louis and formed a little three-piece band—drums, bass, piano and myself. I went to playin' in the taverns, so this label called Bobbin recorded a few of my things and they did good so I built my band with St. Louis musicians. Right now, if you go to St. Louis and ask who got the best band, they say Albert King. I built a *storm* of a band and I just cut them down here in the last year and a half 'cause I didn't need them after I started doin' shows. But *now* I got to add some horns *back* in my band. That just shows you how things go and change."

It was this St. Louis band that recorded his regional and "race" hits, among them: *Blues at Sunrise, Let's Have a Natural Ball, Ooh-ee, Baby,* and *Traveling to California.*

Though one writer has indelicately referred to him as "a B. B. King come lately," Albert, too, has clearly been around for a long time. In fact, he has only begun to gain a considerable national reputation within the past two years, and his success, which has come to crest in the past year, dates from the release of his critically acclaimed record *Live Wire: Blues Power.* Why, then, the charge? King credits one person with the shaping of his success:

"I've been with this company now about five years and this is where I got my greatest results. Al Bell, *he's* the cause of it all. Now I play with folks like Jimi Hendrix and Janis Joplin . . . she's a hard worker, nice people."

Late afternoon has eased into early evening and Al Jackson Jr., the M.G. drummer who produces Albert King's records, has joined his older professional charge. There is a marked contrast between the suave, business-like manner of Jackson and the uninhibited countriness of King. It is not simply a generation or so of living that separates the over-forty bluesman from the under-thirty producer-musician. It is a different process of maturation stemming from a shifting social climate that makes it easier for the young to regard themselves with respect and to evaluate their talents from a different point of reference. Yet there is a strange affinity between the two men, and their opinions, though expressed in disparate language, are more alike than not alike. They move into an impromptu symposium on soul and its relationship to the white mainstream, while the author injects an occasional question or comment:

K. Now, you got some of these white blues players who are good, such as Elvin Bishop and . . . and what is this other kid's name?

J: Eric Clapton.

K: Yeah. Eric Clapton. . . . Is it Herbie Cotton and who's this *guit*ar player with Big Brother and the Holding Company, or used to be with them . . . and what's that guy's name with the Electric Flag?

J: You're probably thinking of Mike Bloomfield.

K: *Yeah! Mike* Bloomfield. Now Mike can come so close to B. B. [King] it's pa*the*tic! This is the *truth!* Now, those are about the only ones I know who are really *good.* Oh, you got some white boys out there playin' bass and drums that're outa *sight!* Those boys, they down *with* it! I ain't lyin'. You just take that bass player Jimi Hendrix got. *Jee*sus *Christ* Ahmighty! Now one little small under*es*timated group was on the show with us a couple a nights out West, but, anyway, there was this boy playin' *two* sets a drums!

G: *Two* sets of drums?

K: In a *swim*min' suit!! *Two* sets a drums this cat was playin'.

J: You double your tam-tams, use two bass drums and sit in the middle of them.

G: Have you ever tried that sort of thing?

J: No.

K: But he can *play!* He can *really* play. And you got some white boys can play harmonica. I ain't lyin'. We had one here, didn't we? What was that kid's name? He wanted to go out on the Coast with me but *I* couldn't take him out there. But let me tell you, honey, we got some *tapes* back there with him playin'. He choked that harp [harmonica] to *death!* I ran across another young white boy in Detroit, Michigan. Here I'm up on the stage playin' and he was down there on the floor, sittin' there with his girl, playin' his harp, so I called him up on the stage and we had a jam session from *way* back.

G: Listening to the M.G.'s recording in the studio, I found it difficult if not impossible to distinguish a white sound from what was supposedly a black sound.

K: That's what I was gonna say. You have to watch *Steve.* I swear to *God,* you have to watch him. He can hear you play somethin' two, three times and he *got* it, ain't he, Al?

J: That's right.

K: And when you find one of them country and western players that can switch and come on down and play some *deep* blues, man, you got a *bad* baby!! We had a saxophone player here and I don't care what you been eatin', but when they turned him loose, you can listen because he's just that *bad!*

J: The tenor player you're talking about was born and reared in Mississippi. He plays tenor, guitar and fiddle. His name is Gene Parker. He played around town for years and he worked with us here at the studio for years and, for some reason, he felt he wasn't getting anywhere, so he just went back down to Mississippi and started farming again.

K: Farmin'? That's a *shame,* because I sure wanted him with me.

J: You know, the first time I met him was after I had known Albert King for years, though I hadn't worked with him. But Gene Parker invited me to his home and he was playing nothing but Albert King and B. B. King albums. He was still a tenor player, but he studied guitar from those albums. Originally, he was a country fiddler and that's the way I believe it came about, because country music is the white man's folk root, but once a cat has lived the life, then he's also been exposed to *our* type of soul. *Then* you've got a combination that is hard to beat.

It's my belief that soul comes from a cat's *folk* roots, regardless of *what* color he might be. He has his *own* soul. But in today's white market, the general market that uses the term soul, they think of Negroes only. But on the basis of the statements we've made here, I'd say that soul has no *color*. It's a matter of exposure. A white kid is taught one thing about racism and once he's ex*posed* to another race, he finds it's not like what Mama and Dad told him. And when it comes to music, it's a known fact that music is an international language. Musicians can get together regardless of *what* color they are. They have one thing in common. That's their life, their music. Now we might go separate ways once we leave the bandstand, but when we're on the bandstand, we're together. The word soul is being used too loosely today, because I don't think any one performer has an absolute definition of soul. Everyone has his own belief about it, but it's a difficult word to define.

G: Some people have used the term soul to describe what is natural and expressive, something that isn't just put on.

K: You can't beat *that* soul. That *is* soul!

J: It's so basic. You're being yourself and doing your own thing, as they say.

K: It's like if I'm up on that stage playin', I can tell just as good when I play somethin' that the people ain't diggin' too much. I don't play it long. I cut it off. And I can tell what*ever* song it might be or who*ever's* in the house, I can tell if they feel it when I get started playin' it.

G: I've seen you perform before white audiences and, in comparison to black audiences, there seems to be little overt reaction, little movement and they don't seem to let go as much.

K: Not while you're playin', but they show it after you finish. They give you that much respect. They sit there and listen. Just like one girl out in San Francisco one night when I was playin' the blues and she sat there and cried. And the same thing happened another night in Chicago. I had got me two or three little nips of wine and

I was feelin' pretty good, you know, and I come down just as nicely on the blues. Really, I was thinkin' about home. I was *tired,* you know. And I came down just as nicely on Lucy and this girl stood there and cried and said, "I don't know what kind of fingers you got." I looked at my hands and looked at her and said, "Well I ain't got nothin' but *fin*gers!" They didn't want me to walk off the bandstand and that's why I say this had to be a soulful thing. They felt it. *I* felt it. I felt good behind the reaction I got from them because I knew *they* felt it.

J: This same sort of thing has happened to us [the M.G.'s] as in San Francisco. The majority of the audience was white, but the reception was beautiful because what happens is that *any* audience, regardless of what color they might be, is composed of individuals. You might play some numbers that appeal to some and others that will appeal to others. Usually, they'll give you the courtesy of listening and applauding. But somehow, down on the program, you hit that *one* tune that hits *every*body. It goes beyond race and age and this is what soul is about. Now what's happened today—and I'm not putting the blues down—but you take today's market. Why is it that so many white kids are digging the blues? But you take that same age group among black kids and you find they don't really dig it in the same way because they've been exposed to it all their lives. The blues *is* them. Years ago when these whites were kids, their parents didn't let them listen to the black radio stations. They only listened to the pop stations. But now even the pop stations are playing black music and they're exposed to it and they like it because it's different from what *they've* been hearing. The more whites who listen to it, the more white musicians are learning to play that way.

K: They *have* to, because it's so powerful. It's just like I say in my album *Blues Power,* now if you just take the time to listen to the blues, every word that is said, this thing has happened to somebody somewhere that *you* know . . . if it didn't happen to *you.* Instead of talkin' about it, you *sing* it and you *got* to sing it with feelin', because I can sit here and just say that if you have an old man who whoop you everyday and he take your money and you work hard or, say, when you get down sick and you got four or five kids and he go on off and marry somebody else, I just get to thinkin' about it because maybe you a friend, but I'm thinkin' about what I saw happen to you. So I can place myself in the same position and I can feel how *you* would be feelin', because I'd feel the same way if somebody was to do *me* that way. And this is what I be thinkin' about at the back of my mind although I'm singin'.

G: This is merely a matter of personal conjecture, but it seems to me that many young whites might be turning toward this type of music and the open approach to life that it presents because so much of what they have witnessed in their own environment seems artificial and contrived. But here, in this music, they find something that is real and reassuringly human in its honesty.

J: That is true. Why paint a dirty picture with beautiful colors . . .

K: 'Cause *some*body's goin' to look under that color and see the *real* thing.

J: That's right. So why tell me a *lie*. Give me credit for having the five senses I was born with . . .

K: Don't be jivin'.

J: Give me the truth and then I can adjust to it and I can fight my way through the battle . . . lying to me with color and all that, making me live a false life. Give me the *truth* and I can make it through this world, *then.*

K: This is why you see so many hippies, because this is what they call doin' their own *thing*.

J: They rebel against society.

K: That's right. Now don't get me wrong. They're master-minded people. They're not *dumb.*

J: They're educated people. Anybody who faces reality must identify with them at heart.

K: When I play for them, I can't do nothin' *but* let myself go. They don't demand that I have on no shined shoes or no tie. I *be* clean. I could wear a suit, but I'd look like a *fool* out there with a suit on. I go out there on that stage and they accept me as I *am.* I could pull off my shoes and walk out on that stage barefoot, as long as I play and give 'em a good show.

J: Because *what* do they buy—the clothes or the individual? Have you got to *dress* everything up for it to be accepted? Can't it be accepted in the raw? If it can't be accepted in the raw, then it's not worth being accepted *any*way. Then you're making it all phony. You're taking away the true identity. But some of us started out with one gift in life that we should be *proud* of, and that *is* being *black,* because the day we were born into this world, the *truth* was *slapped* into our faces!

K: That's *right!*

J: We *know* what we had to go through in order to make it through life because the day that they took us home from the hospital and we first opened our eyes, we could *see* that shack we were living in and that big, fine house across the road and we *knew* that something was wrong!

K: You'd *have* to know, because if everythin' was fine and equalized, *you* might have been born in one of them big fine white houses.

J: *And,* at the same time, you wonder *why* does that kid who's born in that big fine white house . . . why is it that every chance he gets, he comes over there to that shack to play with that *black* kid. The true meaning and the *real* meaning of love are in that shack where there's a family together. As the old saying goes, the family that prays together *stays* together, and the same thing can be seen in the young people of today and their reactions. The ghetto is there for a *reason,* and it will never *leave,* no matter how much you paint it up and clean it up, it's *still* there! You can't *change* that!

It is now quite late. The sounds continue to issue from the studio, which is being used on an around-the-clock basis. Despite the tardy hour, a tiny, somewhat wilted cluster of youngsters is seated in the lobby, waiting for who-knows-what, in their crumpled shirts, wrinkled trousers and shoes run over at the heels.

"Are you a singer?" you ask them without a note of discomforting challenge.

"No, I'm a song-*writer*," the answer comes as the spark of hope burns on and on, beyond the limits of the night.

1. *Memphis Commercial Appeal,* March 3, 1968. © 1968 by The New York Times Company. Reprinted by permission.

2. *Chicago Daily News,* March 2, 1968.

3. *Life,* March 28, 1969.

4. *Vogue,* December, 1968.

5

NINA SIMONE: HIGH PRIESTESS OF SOUL

To HER fans, she often seems a wily sorceress, disarming them of their common human defenses and luring them into forbidden portions of the self where the pain and raw ecstasy of intense emotion must be confronted without recourse to subterfuge.

She casts her spell through the fluid but frequently complex patterns of the notes she etches on her piano and with the distinctive sound of her richly reedy voice. This voice of hers is not the finely honed tool of a trained singer, but it possesses something those other voices lack —an earthy naturalness, the compelling coarseness of a homemade instrument that once was whittled by hand in the fields and now is played with consummate artistry.

Yet the secret of her special brand of black magic lies beyond her sound, in the message that always lurks there somewhere in the lyrics of her songs and in the way they are projected. She speaks not only of love between man and woman but the black man's pain and passion whipped to a swelling rage, filling the sung phrases with her own spirit of rebellion. Always when she does it, she is so real and comes on so strong that she can make the unready squirm in the heat of the truth. She never permits her audiences simply to enjoy what she is doing in bland comfort. She forces them to feel more deeply and to react on a cerebral as well as on a visceral level. With the seventh sense of any good sorceress, she senses when they are not so reacting, and she chides them from the stage with an admonishing, "You're not giving me a *thing* tonight!"

At such times, she is like a domineering mother whipping a surly and recalcitrant child until it realizes that it had *better* follow where she is leading. When her audiences do not obey, the embarrassment of failure is theirs, not hers. And when they enter obligingly and even eagerly into the extraterrestrial structure she is creating, they are rewarded with an aesthetic experience that is both powerful and beautiful.

For Nina Simone, the "high priestess of soul," music is not only an art, but an expression of life in *all* its verities. Such is her potency that many shy away from it, preferring to indulge themselves in forms of expression that can be appreciated without overt effort. But to those who put forth that little bit of personal mental and emotional exertion necessary for any understanding of her, she stands as a goddess, a singular musician and one of the great artists of her time.

More than any popular performer of the day, Nina Simone is an eclectic, a one-woman summation of musical confluence. Though soul is the convenient label under which she is currently classified, there can be detected in her singing, playing and choice of material the mark of all the major streams that have gone into the making of modern music. Her pianism is heavily laced with the classical techniques she learned as a student at Julliard in New York and at the Curtis Institute of Music in Philadelphia, where she studied with Vladimir Sokoloff. And yet the touches of Bachian counterpoint have mingled with the improvisatory approach of jazz and the modulations of the blues.

As a singer, she is a stylist who plays with and around the melody while manipulating the words to create a tone-portrait of dramatic intensity. Her songs are not only sung but enacted through facial and bodily expressions, and when her exaltation can no longer be contained, she jumps up from the piano and moves rhythmically about the stage in a nameless dance of joy.

Her repertoire reflects her experience as a cocktail and supper club performer during the fifties, including the introspective ballads dear to the tête-à-tête set, but it ranges all the way from old American tunes of tradition and folk music of other countries, such as the African chant of *Flo Me La*, to the most contemporary of protest songs, many of which she has written herself. She has even dipped into the well of rock and is one of the few performers around who can make a Bob Dylan composition sound good to both blacks and whites.

All of this is underscored by her deep alignment with her initial baptism into music as a child gospel pianist and organist. Many influences contribute to her style, but the inflammatory rhythms and insistence of gospel music are the key to her artistry, as she herself stresses. In Nina Simone's opinion, the feeling in her music springs from this elemental source and there are times when she goes directly back to these roots to mesmerize her listeners with a rendition of the old baptismal chant *Take Me to the Water* and its conjunct, a tambourine-accented *I'm Goin' Back Home*.

Because of her exceptional range, Nina Simone appeals almost as much to those conditioned by classical music who have some affinity for her beat but do not possess sufficient ethnic empathy to respond to a Muddy Waters or an Otis Redding as she does to those whose preference is for sophisticated folk music or modern jazz. Possibly, it is her complexity that has led her to become the darling both of intellectual black militants who find some echo of their ideology in her music and of those whose brilliant twists of mind have been extolled by the establishment, such as the essayist-novelist James Baldwin and the late Lorraine Hansberry, the award-winning black playwright whose career was cut tragically short when she died of cancer in 1965 at the age of thirty-four. This palatable convolution might be the special quality that led the late Langston Hughes, poet laureate of black people, to say of Nina Simone in 1962: "She is strange. . . . She is far out and at the same time common. . . . She is a club member, a colored girl, an Afro-American, a homey from down home. . . . She is unique. You either like her or you don't. If you don't, you won't. If you do—wheee-ouuueu! You do!"[1]

This might be considered the definitive statement of where she is and always has been, and, it might be noted, that the respect accorded her by others has often been returned on her part. She is the one who early acknowledged the multi-talented composer-performer Oscar Brown Jr. to be a genius (we'll get to him later), and she is the one who set to music and recorded Langston Hughes's *Backlash Blues*, a folksy indictment of bigotry.

It cannot be ignored that while Nina Simone, too, has been folksy, she has not been one readily embraced by the hard-core "folk" who take their blues undiluted, nor even by lovers of "stone" soul music. Her eclecticism has tended to set her apart from many whose background she shares. Yet she has never allowed her pursuit of acclaim to supersede a basic integrity linked to her black roots. All of this is to be found in her music. And as art is an expression of life, the art of Nina Simone has been an expression of her own exposure to life.

It was in the almost infinitesimally small town of Tryon, North Carolina, that Nina Simone first bellowed out to the world her outrage at the personal violation of birth during the mid-thirties, at a time when the depression had become a fact of life and not a transient inconvenience to be rationalized away. It was not exactly the best time and place for a potential prodigy to be born into a poor family of uncompromising religious leanings. A little later on in this chapter, Nina Simone speaks for herself of the musical influences in her early life, but it might be noted here that this sixth child of eight children—four boys and four girls—revealed that she had exceptional gifts at a very young age and proceeded to develop them within the context of her environment, which was one of gospel expression presided over by her mother, a housekeeper by day and a minister at all other times. Her father, who was a handyman, shared this religiosity.

Her name was Eunice Waymon back then, and from the age of three she began to accompany her minister-mother as a musician at the lusty, shouting revival meetings she gave in nearby towns. As a child, Eunice played and sang with two sisters in a trio called The Waymon Sisters. Though talent scouts were not likely to be frequenting a place such as Tryon, she did attract the attention of one well-to-do woman, following a performance at a Tryon theater. This early patron sought the young Eunice out backstage and, upon learning that the seven-year-old never had had a music lesson in her life, offered to pay for formal training.

By the time she was eight, Eunice had commenced taking piano lessons from a local teacher, Mrs. Lawrence Mazzanovich. Soon afterward, she gained the distinction of being the brightest little girl in town, but she was colored, and this led to some hang-ups, especially when she was called upon to perform at recitals given by her teacher. When interviewed by John S. Wilson for a story published in the *New York Times* in late 1967, Nina Simone recalled:

> I hated those recitals. At the first one in the white library, there was a big hassle about where my mother and father

> sat. That hurt me. Mis' Mazzie (her teacher) never knew how tense I was and how scared those white people made me. I had to go across the tracks. I was split in half. I loved Bach but the music was never a joy, never a pleasure. Only years later, when I stopped studying and went back to improvising, I realized she had trained my fingers. When I think of what she did for me, I have to look past what I hated about the white people. She loved that music. That was all she was concerned about.[2]

When the support of her early patron was discontinued, Eunice's teacher continued her lessons free-of-charge. She even helped to establish a "Eunice Waymon Fund," wherein contributions were solicited after public performances. As a result of this effort, Eunice was able to attend a boarding high school in Asheville, North Carolina, graduating as valedictorian of her class. There was even a little money left over at the end of high school, and she was able to move north to New York and Julliard, where she studied piano and theory. Later, her family moved to Philadelphia to be closer to her. When her support from this private fund was depleted, after two years at Julliard, young Eunice moved in with her family in Philadelphia and earned her way by giving private piano lessons and serving as an accompanist at a vocal studio. Meanwhile, she continued her studies, at the Curtis Institute. The friends she met there turned her mind to new areas of musical expression through jazz and popular forms. When, in the early fifties, she was out of work and out of money, she sought employment as a cocktail pianist in the resort area of Atlantic City. The going was far from easy, but, finally, she did land one job. However, the owner of the club insisted that she sing as well as play. She had never sung before professionally, but the ninety dollars a week at hand meant the difference between starvation and survival. She sang, but only because she had to, reaching back to her church upbringing to draw upon the ready source of spirituals and church songs. The people loved it.

By this time, Eunice also had been introduced to the work of the late Billie Holiday. A seed had been planted that was to bear significant fruit. During the mid-fifties, she worked small clubs on the Eastern seaboard while continuing her work as a teacher and studio accompanist. By 1959, the seeds planted so long ago and in so many places had begun to germinate, and a new artist named Nina Simone was catapulted into the national spotlight with her recording of *I Loves You Porgy*, a Gershwin composition transformed by Holiday. Eunice Waymon had been pushed into the background; Nina Simone had taken her place. The name "Nina" had been chosen because it meant "little one"—which is what she had been called as a child, and "Simone" because it was euphonically compatible. There was more than one reason for changing her name. First, her family was so deeply identified with the church that it would not have been acceptable for one of their number to be known to be on the nightclub circuit, and, second, as a teacher she had to steer clear of the taint of any bawdy influences that might discredit her in the eyes of the parents of her students.

Porgy was Nina Simone's first real hit, and it led, even as early as 1959, one critic to state that she might be "the greatest singer to evolve in the last decade and perhaps the greatest singer today." That writer, Sidney Lazard of the *Chicago Sun-Times*, went on to observe:

> Her every song is like the revelation of a beautiful, exciting secret. And those who listen fill up with an undisguised happiness, tempered only by the knowledge that it will all end too soon. . . . If I seem to have gone overboard in my admiration for Miss Simone, it's because I honestly believe that the greatest compliments could only be understatements of her talent.[3]

This was at the beginning of Nina Simone's reign as a supper club singer in an era that produced her now-out-of-print Bethlehem recording: *Nina Simone—Jazz As Played in an Exclusive Side Street Club.* During those days and on into the early sixties, so much emphasis was placed on her position as a songstress for the elite—with write-ups in magazines catering to those of tired tastes who sought fresh stimulation—that it came as somewhat of a shock to the black public when she reentered their sphere of consciousness as a purveyor of protest songs in the mid sixties. Previously, she had enjoyed a respectable following among those in the black underside of society, but it was not until her recorded composition *Mississippi Goddam!* was widely broadcasted with its "beep-beep" deletions of a so-called offensive word that blacks were informed of her inner status as a true "soul sister" who had been with them all along, regardless of her sophisticated trappings. If she had been anything other than an essentially black woman, they knew, she never could have written a song of such bitter fury.

Mississippi Goddam! which marks a milestone in modern protest music, was written by Nina in late 1963, just after four little girls were killed in the bombing of a church in Birmingham, Alabama, and in the same year in which Medgar Evers, the thirty-seven-year-old field secretary for the National Association for the Advancement of Colored People in Mississippi, was shot in front of his home in the capital city, Jackson. So it was that she wrote those memorable lyrics, accentuated by a furiously galloping piano, that went:

Alabama's got me so upset;
Tennessee made me lose my rest;
And everybody knows about Mississippi—God*dam!*[4]

Thus Nina Simone established herself as the leading popular singer of black protest, for she had given voice to the stifled rage of her compatriots of the skin. This reputation was consolidated in 1966, when she wrote and recorded a song entitled *Four Women*, based on the varying life styles and attitudes of four black women as linked to their skin colorings. *Four Women*, indeed, struck a note of response in black women who heard it, for never had anyone expressed so eloquently and so openly the life that had been their burden for centuries: a rejection of their own blackness, reinforced by the "fair-skinned, blue-eyed blonde" standards of the larger society that led them to believe that their full lips, ample noses and rounded features could never be considered beautiful and that their kinky hair was a crown of shame. It is a turning against this long-standing sort of self-destructive thinking and a rejection of *white* beauty standards that has led increasing numbers of black women to adopt the "natural" hairstyle within the past three years and to accentuate their Negroid features as a manifestation of self-pride. And as psychiatrists William H. Grier and Price M. Cobbs have said in their book *Black Rage*, this sort of action on the part of the black woman is "psychologically redemptive."

Nina Simone, who has herself abandoned the straight-haired image of her supper club days to wear a natural hairstyle, had it all there in *Four Women*—and a lot more, too. I recall that when it was released, one reviewer (whose name I'll be kind enough to omit) wrote of it that he liked the music but thought it had been squandered on "trite" lyrics. When I, for one, read this, I realized that he had no idea whatsoever as to what the song meant. I merely chalked it up as another of the seemingly endless misevaluations of black art by white critics who either do not understand it or insist on judging it by standards that are not always applicable to black culture and the subsociety that creates it. As a black woman myself, I know that I am not the only one who can be moved to the point of tears or whipped into a state of personal outrage by a hearing of this song, for each one of its four concise verses is a complete chapter of our history and our peculiar psychological reactions to it.

There is the black, woolly-headed "Aunt Sarah" of the first verse, whose monumental strength has been drained into the unrelenting struggle to endure pain; the "high yellow," straight-haired "Safronia" of the second verse, who is the racially mongrelized product of a rich white man's forcible seduction of a black woman—which was the case throughout the dark night of slavery and the continually troubled dawn that has followed; the pretty, tan-hued "Sweet Thing" of the third verse, who has sought a fleeting self-acceptance in the transient encounters of prostitution while using her inviting body to buy survival. Then there is the unruly, loud-talking, no-shit-taking "Peaches" of the final verse, who comes closest to where so many black women of today stand, regardless of age:

My skin is brown, my manner is tough
I'll kill the first mother I see
My life has been rough
I'm awfully bitter these days because my parents were slaves,
What do they call me? My name is "Peaches."[5]

If Nina Simone had not written anything other than *Four Women*, she would still have a claim to greatness, so far as blacks are concerned, for this song stands as one of the most powerful and moving social documents set to music to come out of the black man's heritage.

But she did not stop there. She has included protest songs, hers and others, in her recordings and performances. One more recent number is *I Wish That I Knew How It Would Feel to Be Free,* composed by the jazz pianist and lecturer Billy Taylor, with its resounding final lines:

> *Say it clear, say it loud,*
> *I am* black *and I am* proud!

Another moment of musical significance transpired in April, 1968, when Nina Simone was scheduled for a sold-out performance at the Westbury Music Fair on Long Island. Two nights before her show, Dr. Martin Luther King Jr. was assassinated in Memphis, Tennessee. Gene Taylor, her bass player at the time, wrote, out of his own disbelief and heartbreak at this tragic event, a poignant, somewhat bitter song called *Why?,* subtitled *The King of Love Is Dead.* It was completed less than twenty-four hours before the concert at which Miss Simone sang it for the first time, pouring into it her own sorrow and sense of horror. This stirring performance was recorded live and is presented on her album *'Nuff Said!.* Then, too, Nina Simone concluded the concert with Thomas A. Dorsey's gospel classic *Precious Lord, Take My Hand.* Her reasons for doing so are expressed in the lyrics of this modern spiritual that is so profound in its simplicity.

So it was that in a time of such pain, such bitterness and despair so deep that it is doubtful any non-black in this country will ever be able to comprehend it, Nina Simone turned again to that "old ship of Zion" that has offered sustenance to black people from the days when they cowered hopelessly in their slave cabins, hungering for death as a release from the ordeal of life, to today's times when so many have turned away from the church through an inability to reconcile its pious axioms to the brutal reality of contemporary civilized barbarism, though even they hesitate to profane this institution of "the Lord," and possibly to an undefined tomorrow that we dare not contemplate. But this might have been expected, for Nina Simone always has reflected in her music the prevailing mood of black people, from the fifties, when she tried to track down an only reluctantly forthcoming acceptance by whites on their own standards, and into the sixties, when her utterance has been one of protest. And it should be noted that one of her latest records is entitled *Revolution.*

But Nina Simone is also a highly articulate woman, as capable of expressing herself through words as music, especially when she is speaking as a "black soul sister" rapping to another.

* * *

Nina Simone is a slender, dark-browned-skinned woman who carries herself with an ever present self-protective chip on her shoulder, as though telling the world, through her very stance, that it had better not mess with her. This shield of what might be called hostility is not directed exclusively toward whites, for members of the working black press have sometimes pegged her as a difficult number. Yet others have lauded her for being "so nice and so cooperative." Much of the reaction experienced might depend on the way in which she is approached and the mood she happens to be in at the time. She is at her best, though, when met at the midtown Manhattan offices of Stroud Productions, the management and booking firm presided over by Andrew Stroud, a former police detective who has been her husband of nearly eight years. There all appointments for interviews are carefully checked, confirmed and reconfirmed by a secretary with a crisp, "white-sounding" voice, though she turns out to be black. Andy Stroud, a stocky, good-looking fortyish man with an easy-going manner and out-going personality, takes a personal interest in setting up his wife's appointments and speaks of his desire to build the firm's production activities to the point where Nina Simone, its mainstay at present, will be able to take long vacations and to devote more of her time to composition and doing just what she feels like doing, particularly taking care of their six-year-old daughter, Lisa Celeste.

It is early afternoon of a brisk mid-winter day when Miss Simone arrives after a drive into the city from her suburban Mount Vernon home. She is wearing a fitted lightweight tweed maxi-coat that sweeps nearly to the floor. Beneath it is an above-the-knee-but-not-quite-mini-dress of semi-mod design, set off by beads, a bit of jewelry and a headband clasping her natural above her brow. From the moment she enters, there can be no question as to whether or not she is the star, but her manner is not overbearing. "Guarded" might be more the term one would use for her approach, and it is easy to overlook the reserve when one considers all the rebuffs and frustrations she must have encountered as a black girl from the South who had nerve enough to come north to the roughest city in the world, armed with nothing but a formidable talent and a whole lot of guts and, above all, the nerve really to *make* it.

"Now what is *this* for?" she demands brusquely with an unsmiling glance at the prospective interviewer, triggering with this affected iciness the first twinges of uncertainty. The project is explained in brief, and she flatly states, "Please make your questions as much to the point as possible," as she eases gracefully into a black leather armchair, one of several pieces of functionally elegant furniture adorning the red-carpeted office facing onto

Fifth Avenue. She interrupts her unyieldingly hard gaze to indulge in a short affectionate exchange with her husband, as he rummages through stacks of papers on his oversized desk. But as soon as she has finished with him, the wall goes up again. She sits there staring the enemy that is the world straight in the eye and almost daring it to bat an eyelash back at her.

The first timidly proffered questions, interspersed with a few nervous smiles intended to reaffirm good intentions, draw blunt "yes" and "no" answers leading to nowhere. But gradually the wall of ice begins to thaw, and she begins to speak from her true self. There are even several broad smiles, so unexpected as to be dazzling, and a spontaneous laughter that is almost musical. Then one realizes that she is no ogre, no pillar of glacial arrogance, but an artist who might have good reason to distrust those who prey upon celebrities. Similarly, she seems to understand that this is no voracious beast seated before her but simply a lover of music who greatly admires those who are masters of it. She is questioned about her use of protest material as compared to the more conventional songs of her earlier career. Has this switch been a deliberate one?

"I suppose one might say that because, for the first six or seven years of my career, I mostly played nightclubs and supper clubs, but during all those years, I had quite a vast repertoire. So when I was in supper clubs and nightclubs, I simply played the things that were applicable to those particular places. That was for about six or seven of the fifteen years I've been in show business—since 1953. But now that my people have decided that we're going to take over the world," a knowingly affectionate and not at all condescending laugh, "I'm going to have to do my part."

The original Supremes (left to right, lead singer Diana Ross, Mary Wilson and Florence Ballard) first made the world aware of the Motown sound, a considerable factor in the development of popular soul music in the early 60's, and became headliners of a formidable stable of talent in Detroit, among the artists . . .

Moto

The Temptations

Smokey Robinson (2nd from right) and the Miracles

Motown

Motown

Martha Reeves (center) and the Vandellas

The Four Tops

Motown

Stevie Wonder

Motown

Motown

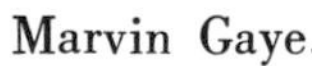

Marvin Gaye.

Stax

Booker T. Jones . . .

Stax

. . . and the M.G.'s (left to right, Steve Cropper, Al Jackson Jr. and Donald "Duck" Dunn) are the most successful racially integrated soul instrumental group. They are greatly responsible for creation of the Memphis sound, having provided musical backgrounds for artists such as . . .

Stax

. . . Carla Thomas, "Queen of Memphis soul," who is shown performing with Atlantic aritsts Sam (Moore) and Dave (Prater), the nation's top soul duo whose biggest hits have been written by . . .

Stax

. . . Isaac Hayes (left) and David Porter.

Sta

Above all, soul music is a big business, and for the outstanding artist there are considerable rewards, such as the gold record Stax executive vice-president Al Bell is shown presenting to Johnnie Taylor for his million-plus seller *Who's Making Love?*

Ebony

But in another area of the soul spectrum there are those who concentrate on conveying messages of social importance through their music, foremost among them the gifted singer-actor-composer Oscar Brown Jr. . . .

RCA Records

. . . and the formidably talented Nina Simone, whose utterances of protest in song have led her to become the acknowledged musical voice of the black revolution.

From there on, the interview falls into a compatible groove, with G being the author and S being the artist of the chapter.

G: You know, it seems to me that what you do in music is like preaching. You're telling the truth and spreading the word, the way Baldwin has done it in writing, but you're using music to do it.

S: That's right. Um-hummmm. I was told by H. Rap Brown once—and I was *highly* complimented—that I was the singer of the black revolution because there is no other singer who sings real protest songs about the race situation that *I* know of. Oh, of course, a lot of guys are doing it *now,* it's become a popular thing, but I mean to really *mean* it and to try to give inspiration to my people—I think I'm the only one. I *like* it! I like the idea.

G: I think you really began to get through to all of us when you did *Mississippi Goddam!* So many of us felt the same way.

S: Yes, I can understand that, but I'd like to clear up one thing. I hope the day comes when I'll be able to sing more *love* songs, when the *need* is not quite so urgent to sing protest songs. But, for now, I don't mind.

G: Because of the sort of material you use, it seems that you might be the sort of person who believes that the artist should reflect the time in which he or she lives.

S: It *has* to be that way, my friend. I *live* that. There's no other *purpose,* so far as I'm concerned, *for* us except to reflect the times, the situations around us and the things that we're able to say through our art, the things that millions of people *can't* say. I think that's the *function* of an artist and, of course, those of us who are lucky leave a legacy so that when we're dead, we *also* live on. That's people like Billie Holiday and I hope that I will be that lucky, but meanwhile, the function, so far as I'm concerned, is to reflect the times, what*ever* that might be.

G: I guess that means the unfortunate state in which so many things are today—racially and otherwise, I mean.

S: Yes, but in many ways, it's a good time to be alive. I feel more alive than I *ever* have and this is true for many of the black people. Let's face it. It's a struggle and a big fight, but I would rather be fighting for something that I know is going to make a better person out of me and to make me *feel* like I'm alive, more than to be like we *used* to be—just accepting and going along.

G: Yes, and you probably remember, as I do, the way we'd see our people walking down the street looking so downtrodden and with their eyes averted from others. Now it seems that this image is being replaced by one of defiance and courage. I remember seeing you perform in Chicago shortly after the assassination of Dr. King and you seemed to project this same sort of image of defiance and courage. I believe that you let your true feelings come through that night, but, at the same time, your range of materials is so great that you seem to be expressing, simultaneously, the universality of human feelings. Is this also what you attempt to do through your music?

S: Yes, I am. Music is one of the great forces in the world and ever since I can remember, I've loved music and I've been interested in all *kinds* of music. From the beginning, I've been *singing* all kinds of music and I want to continue to do that. Of course, again, the most important thing *these* days is to make certain that I make some *statement* on the stage about how we feel as a *race*. That's more important than *any*thing. But I love *all* music from all lands.

G: I think I've read somewhere that your training in classical music was your earliest major influence.

S: Let me clear *that* whole thing up. When I was three years old, I played by ear. I traveled with my mother, who gave revivals, so I was playing gospel and jazz and blues for about five years before I started to play classical music. I started studying music when I was eight, but before then, I was playing what was real *swinging*, I mean like what they have in the Holy Roller churches. So I want to clear that up because some people think that I first studied classical music and switched to jazz. I played for *revivals* and I was *colored* long before *that!* I played by ear all the music that was around me, which was all these things. *Then* I studied and *then* when I got into the nightclubs, I simply called upon all of these schools that I had known before—the classical, the gospel, the blues and jazz.

G: I can detect that gospel influence in your music in general and particularly in numbers such as *Take Me to the Water.*

S: Yes [*with an exceptionally broad smile*]. You *know* where *that* comes from! My Mama had us *all* baptized, way, *way* before. Some of my most *fantastic* experiences—experiences that really shake me, now that I think of them—happened in the church when we'd have these revival meetings. I'd be playiNnNnNnNnNng, *boy!* I'd *really* be playing. I *loved* it! Folks would be shoutin' all *over* the place. Now *that's* my *back*ground!

G: I can feel that in your music. Would you say that this gospel background supplied one of the key elements in your musical style?

S: Yes! [*She breaks into a rhythmic chant of words repeated for effect of the sort black ministers employ while delivering their sermons.*] That's the power! That's the *pow*er! *That's* the *pow*er! And I'm grateful . . . I'm grateful.

G: It seems to me that this fire, this intensity to be found in gospel music has been carried over, in great part, into the area they now call soul music.

S: Right!

G: It even sounds very much the same.

S: It *is* the same. [*A shared burst of hearty laughter at mutual recognition of a black phenomenon.*] It is the same, I mean *real*ly! [*The last word, "really," commonly used by blacks for emphasis, is always shot out quickly with a heavy accent on the first syllable.*] The more you *listen* now to the radio—there are about five or six groups I can point out that came *straight* out of the church, I mean *real*ly, I mean the *feeling*. It's the *same!* But they just call it *soul* music. [*Another laugh.*] It bridges that gap. You know my people . . . my parents have a way of looking at it—I always give them a hard time about it because I have never believed in the separation of gospel music and the blues. Gospel music and the blues have always been the same. It's just that Mama and them were so *religious* that they wouldn't allow you to play boogie-woogie in the house, but would allow you to use the same boogie-woogie *beat* to play a gospel tune. [*She cracks up at this.*] I just don't agree with this attitude because our music *crosses* all those lines. Negro music has *always* crossed all those lines and I'm kind of glad of it. Now they're just calling it soul music. And have you heard any of the gospel music lately? *Whew!* Some of it is so bluesy it's not even funny. *Whew!* You'd just think you were listening to . . . and it's *all* soul music. I just think that we make a mistake, we as a people, in separating it. It's all the same.

G: But this music is the way that we have expressed ourselves ever since we've been here.

S: *Real*ly!

G: And I'm happy to see people taking a pride in it instead of pushing it into the background.

S: Oh, it *is* time. It's *after* time. Oh-*Lord!*

G: Getting back to your own music, I've read somewhere that in your early years you listened to the late Billie Holiday and were influenced by her style.

S: That's not exactly right. I knew who she was, but I never heard her sing at all until 1953 when I came to New York. I was just a *country* girl [*a light chuckle*], you have to understand. I came from North Carolina and the music I knew was the gospel music and the blues music that we did in church. Mama didn't even *allow* me on the other side of town where "the sinners was." [*A bigger chuckle.*] And there was the classical music. But when I came north in 1953, I met someone who introduced me to most of Billie Holiday's records, at which time I fell *so* in love with her that I learned *Porgy,* which was my first hit. So I didn't do any *studying* of her when I was small. I didn't even *know* the woman, but I think I was just about in my late teens when I heard her.

G: Do you recall listening to or favoring any particular blues or jazz artists when you were a child?

S: No. In the first place, we had no record player. We had a piano and we all played it, and a radio. Oh yes, there was Buddy Johnson and his sister or his daughter—I think his sister—Ella Johnson, Ivory Joe Hunter and Bull-moose Jackson. I was in my teens then in Asheville, North Carolina. These people I listened to and we used to dance to them, you know. "When I lost my baby, I almost lost my mind" [*she sings the first line of a popular jazz-blues song of that time*], that and the Ink Spots were around then. Those were the people I *heard,* but I wasn't *playing* any of that music. I was playing *gospel.* I didn't know how to play *that* and I didn't even try. Boogie-woogie, though, I tried a lot of that because there was a boogie-woogie pianist around I liked at the time. I can't remember who it was, but I *do* remember *After Hours.*

G: Yeah. That was *the* song. You know, one thing that has impressed me is how so much of our music forms a continuous stream, moving from one generation to the next without losing its basic characteristics.

S: Isn't it *won*derful? Some of the same songs, the same source. And I'm so glad. [*She breaks into another chant.*] *Oh,* I'm so glad! *Oh,* I'm so *glad* we haven't changed things. We can't *help* it though. [*A knowing laugh.*] My mother told me when I was a kid, she said, "I gave all my children back to God," she said, and what she meant was that there is a *thing* inside of us. We've had it since before . . . our forefathers, our ancestors from Africa. There's a *thing* that we have that makes the essence of us and I don't think it has anything to do with a *choice.* We're just the way we *are,* as a people. *Who* invents slang?

G: Everybody's saying "*maa*aan" now.

S: *We* came up with that. [*Mutual smiles.*]

G: And what about the use of words in speech to lend a certain rhythm to a sentence?

S: *Rhy*thm! [*She sings out the word.*] It's the truth, *real*ly! It goes all the way *through* us.

G: And the way we move?

S: It's the *truth! Rhythm!*

G: And I don't need any anthropolgist to tell me these things. I just call it black soul.

S: *Real*ly. Yes it *is!*

G: But what is your opinion of some of the new music being created by young white artists?

S: You mean rock?

G: Yes.

S: Well, I'll tell you. Some of these white kids are trying very, very hard to imitate colored people and they're doing it very well. Some of them actually have got some real fire and I don't know what *price* they're paying for it, in the sense that I don't know how much drugs they have to take; I don't know how far out they have to go in their heads, but some of the music that comes out of some of these rock groups has got some real *fire*. It's like, they're trying so *hard* to *get* that soul that *I* think some of them have got a *hold* of it, yes I do. Like I said, I don't know the price they're paying, because most of the kids I know about who really sing good hard *rock,* which is the equivalent, so far as I'm concerned, of Holy Roller *revival* music, most of them are hooked on drugs and I mean really *out* there, and that's a big price to pay to sound colored. Most of it is *junk,* but a lot of them are good and there's *one* guy I'd like to speak of who's not like us at all and doesn't try to sound colored. But he has his *own* thing, and I respect him and I really admire him, and that's Bob Dylan. The man is his *own* man, has his own *statement* to make and makes it. He's a universal poet. He's not trying to be white *or* colored. The man is just a great *poet*. And I admire him very much.

G: I certainly can agree with that and do respect *all* who are developing their own things, but what about these young white soloists and groups who seem to pop up overnight and, before you know it, there they are on the Ed Sullivan Show or some other television show, doing a song originated by a black artist or group that has never even *been* on television.

S: Oh, I resent *that!* I *deeply* resent that. It makes me very bitter and very mad and it has for *years,* but I like to think that, you know, *our* music is leading the parade now, all over the *world,* so it really doesn't mean too much, as far as I'm concerned. I mean, I still *resent* it, but I think it's just a matter of time before we take over television too, I mean just take it *all* over, I really do.

G. But meanwhile, what can be done to help some of the young black groups and artists get a wider exposure?

S: We have to work on that. I don't know how because I know that, say, a little group will get up a hit-tune album and then some white group comes along and takes the dress, the songs, the style and the next thing you know they're featured on television. Now, we have to put an *end* to that. I don't know *how.* This might sound contradictory to what I said before about us not having to worry about them, because we *do* have to worry about them, because if you get a hundred white groups like that and they get exposure, they have actually gotten the advantages that a hundred *black* groups could have gotten who created the music. I don't know *how* to put an end to that, but the young black kids have *got* to get the advantages. They've got to stop the white ones from stealing our stuff, getting the money and then influencing a thousand other white kids to think these were *their* ideas. That's *also* what they do. They *sing* the songs and then white kids who don't know any better think they *did* them. I know we're slowly moving along, but I know that with all this fighting and all going on, especially in the colleges, I think the young kids'll get it all together.

G: Do you think that this spirit of rebellion and demand for change to be found among young people of both races might lead them to alter white attitudes in general and to influence the establishment for the better?

S: I have no idea, because, I'm going to tell you the

truth, I distrust the establishment *so* much and so *deep*ly that I don't even *think* in terms of their giving us our rights. I don't even *think* about that. All I think about is this, and this is the essence of me, what I want for the rest of my life. I read it in a book, I don't recall which one, some black book. It's a four-line poem and it said: "Brothers, brothers everywhere . . . and not a *one* for sale." And I think that says the *whole* thing.

G: Amen!

1. *New York Post,* June 29, 1962.

2. *New York Times,* December 31, 1967. © 1967 by The New York Times Company. Reprinted by permission.

3. *Chicago Sun-Times,* December 12, 1959. Reprinted by permission.

4. *Mississippi Goddam!* (Rolls-Royce record, 1963).

5. *Four Women* (Rolls-Royce record, 1966).

6

ARETHA FRANKLIN: SISTER SOUL

SHE SINGS of life, of love and of the terrible thrill-driven torment of lust with an uncompromising honesty of feeling that leads one to believe that every twisted note, every conjugated cadence and imploring lyric, has been ripped from the bowels of her very own soul. She *feels,* and so she is, and thus she sings. To hear her is not to be entertained; it is to undergo a baptism of emotion that leaves one weak and yet fulfilled, as in the aftermath of good sex. This is the soulful side of Aretha Franklin that springs from a sheer sensuality, baked down in the brimstone expressiveness of her Baptist upbringing. But there is more to it than that: a fine sense of musicianship that leads her to place her rhythmic accents in all the right places; a fundamental knowledge of the blues as a pianist as well as a singer; a dramatic instinct on which to build her shrieked and wailed climaxes. She is truly "somethin' else."

At the age of twenty-seven, Aretha Franklin is the top recording artist of her time, the standard-bearer of the soul phenomenon and a young woman who has already staked out a major claim on immortality in black music. She is the consolidated Bessie Smith–Billie Holiday–Dinah Washington of the day and sells so many records, having come along at just the right moment, that she makes more money than all three of her progenitors combined ever did. Hers is the power, the glory and most certainly the cash. She has done it all without ceasing to sound as black as she did in the beginning, though she is flexible enough to move from the more familiar medium of popular soul into stylings closer to jazz and, when she feels like it, all the way back into the gospel vein where she served her apprenticeship. While she does it all, she manages to sound exactly like herself and nobody else. That's genius.

This is where she stands today, and it all seems like a second coming, deeply desired, vaguely sensed and yet totally unexpected by fans who dug her, though hardly so exuberantly, on her earlier outing as an obviously gifted but somewhat uncertain late-teen. She was better-than-good even then, though her basic sound was muffled in all sorts of stringy, torch-like trappings. But nobody might have guessed that she would come to all of *this.*

The first time I went to see Aretha Franklin perform in person, I managed to miss her completely. The year was 1963 and the event was a "cabaret" in Pittsburgh—the sort of affair for which a private civic or social organization takes over a big white nightspot for just one night and sells tickets at five dollars a head for a B.Y.O.B. (bring your own bottle) party featuring a black entertainer such as Jackie Wilson or Lloyd Price who does not ordinarily play such clubs. Customarily this has been one of the few ways in which black soul artists of a less than hit-making status have managed to appear "live" before their followers in the hinterlands—meaning anything beyond the Apollo in New York, the Howard in Washington and the Regal in Chicago. Most often the cabarets are held on the club's off-nights, such as Sunday, as this one was.

Aretha was to be the star of the evening—which was the only reason one might be prepared to pay five dollars to sit and drink one's own whiskey. Though she was hardly at the top of the heap, she was a big enough drawing card, especially among young people who could sense the real Aretha beneath the overdone arrangements on her recordings of *Skylark, Today I Sing the Blues, Try a Little Tenderness* and *Without the One You Love.* But that night it just so happened that she came late, played one set and left early—long before I arrived with a group of gospel-singing buddies who had admired her from before the time she "went commercial." Nothing remained but a vacant seat before a piano, and we were left with the house band's black substitute of the night, who played music that sounded good enough but could hardly compensate for the long-gone Aretha. Well, that was that, and most of us simply said we'd know better the next time and come early, before she had a chance to escape.

We didn't hear too much about her during the next couple of years and almost put her out of our minds, though our fondness for her music was only dormant, not dead. And then she bounced back bigger than ever, in 1967. Aretha came on strong with a greatly revamped version of an Otis Redding song called *Respect* that not only was irresistible in its sound but had a special meaning for black folks. The spirit of rebellion that had begun to sweep the nation with the Watts rebellion of 1965 had begun to crest with major racial uprising in Newark and Detroit. H. Rap Brown had replaced Stokely Carmichael as head of the militant Student Non-Violent Coordinating Committee. "Black power" was all the rage, and a great many blacks had begun to tire of things as they were, after 350 years of waiting, and were letting the whole world know that they intended to take matters into their own hands if nothing was done. Newspapers, periodicals and television commentators pondered the question of "Why?" as Aretha Franklin spelled it all out in one word, *R-E-S-P-E-C-T!* Black folks adopted the song as their new "national anthem" in what David Llorens of *Ebony* magazine has called "the summer of 'Retha, Rap and Revolt!" Word of the song went out through the nation's black belts as her old fans were reactivated and new ones added to the chorus of acclaim: "You heard this new thing 'Retha's got out? *Maaaaaaaan, it's* outa *sight!*"

So it was that the second time I went to see her, in the summer of 1967, everything was quite different. There were no disappointments.

It had been an ordinary evening so far as the noisy, star-crowded events called jazz festivals are concerned. Some considerate deity seemingly had answered the promoter's prayer that it wouldn't rain as more than thirty-five thousand fans huddled in the stands or rocked their folding chairs in the grass of Downing Stadium on Randall's Island, a little bit of New York rising in the East River within walking distance of Harlem. In a relaxed atmosphere suggestive of an evening picnic, people elbowed their way through clusters of competitors for a dwindling supply of hot dogs and beer, grumbled about defects in the sound system, talked loudly during acts that were not their favorites and, above all, awaited the top-billed performers in a show heavily steeped in gospel-flavored funk. They were pleased enough, but some singer or instrumentalist had yet to unleash their full capacity to enjoy. Then the moment came when a full-bodied young woman with chocolate-brown face offset by a pink brocade gown came onto the stage to be greeted by a chorus of expectant shouts, cheers and applause that soon became frenzied hand-clapping and foot-tapping. It was the sort of unbridled response that is accorded only a star, a favorite, an entertainer possessing the uncommon ability to electrify an audience.

It was the "new" Aretha Franklin who set off all this human thunder and lightning. It was a resounding "amen" to all the words and emotions she had projected in her later records that were becoming automatic hits almost as fast as she could produce them. A new dimension had been added to her precocious but uneven career as this onetime gospel singer had returned from near obscurity to achieve a new level of popularity as "sister soul herself." This time she had not straggled in reluctantly and left early; she had arrived in style in the chauffeur-driven black Cadillac limousine that she demands in each city where she plays, perhaps as a reaction to all those years when she played the gospel circuit, making it from town to town on a bus with other blacks who were shut out of Southern hotels and hesitated to stop at restaurants where they might not be served. And all her success had happened in less than one year.

Under a contract negotiated with Atlantic Records in late 1966, Aretha Franklin had released three consecutive million-selling singles. Her first album on that label, *I Never Loved a Man the Way I Love You,* had quickly become a certified million-seller, and a second album, *Aretha Arrives,* had nosed its way up right behind it. The National Association of Radio Announcers had given her three awards as the top female vocalist who produced the top single record and top album for the year. While she had been recognized by *Record World, Billboard* and *Cashbox* magazines as a leading artist among mainstream arbiters of public taste, she had held on to the "thing" she'd had for blacks by virtually taking over *Jet* magazine's Soul Brothers Top 20 Tunes poll, week after week.

All this sudden adulation might have overwhelmed some, but not Aretha, who had endured the bitter experience of almost making it, once before, only to become a comet that had apparently burned out too soon.

In the rush of this fresh success, many tried to seek her out for interviews, seldom drawing too much from her. For Aretha Franklin is a singer, not a talker, and, as her younger sister Carolyn has confided, "Aretha's really very shy. She's *so* shy she won't even dance except around a few close friends, but on stage she'll dance when something moves her." This reticence commonly has been mistaken for hostility or indifference, for she is quite aware of where she has been and where she *is*.

After stealing the show that night on Randall's Island, drawing an ovation even greater than that given one of her idols, Ray Charles, she went on to Atlanta to receive a special citation from Dr. Martin Luther King's Southern Christian Leadership Conference. That citation, too, had something to do with "respect," the sort she had now achieved for herself and the sort her song symbolized to others. Later I caught up with her in Detroit, where she makes her home. An interview had been set at her minister-father's home, a well-kept brick mansion on a tree-shaded street in one of the city's better black residential areas. She arrived wearing a turban that matched her simple but elegant beige dress of French design and readily admitted that clothes are one of her passions, though she has a tendency to be plump and has to watch her diet. For a while she sat at the ivory and gold baby grand piano, fingering out a new song she was working on and crooning softly to herself. Then, when she began to talk, it was not as a celebrity but as a shy young woman who holds a great deal within herself, letting it out only in song.

"I don't feel very different," she said with a quietness that belied her ebullience in song. "People ask for my autograph now and that's real nice, but I don't think it puts you up on any pedestal. You can't get carried away with it." She was quick to acknowledge the ups and downs that came in the wake of her earlier exposure in 1961, when the star-maker John Hammond had said she had "the best voice I've come across in twenty years," signing her to an exclusive contract with Columbia Records. Though some of her recordings from that period gained critical favor, she failed to break into the top money-making level of the big hits, and, after a while, her public following began to fade. "Things were kinda hungry then," she said of the interim years, adding, "I might just be twenty-five, but I'm an old woman in disguise . . . twenty-five goin' on sixty-five."

Much of the flavor to be found in her music is linked with her early background. She was born in Memphis, Tennessee, one of three daughters and two sons of her Baptist father, the Rev. C. L. Franklin, and a musically gifted mother who left the family when Aretha was six and died a few years later. Her childhood thus left scars of the kind that do not heal.

Though the family moved from Memphis to Buffalo, New York, and later to Detroit, the South left an imprint on Aretha's speech, with its slight drawl and softened endings on words. When Aretha was "about eight or nine," she began to teach herself how to play the piano by listening to Eddie Heywood records, "just bangin', not playin', but findin' a little somethin' here and there." Her father noticed her efforts and engaged a piano teacher whose approach was scorned by the young Aretha. "When she'd come, I'd hide," she recalled. "I tried for maybe a week, but I just couldn't take it. She had all those little baby books and I wanted to go directly to the tunes."

This first failure was overcome, shortly afterward, by the arrival of James Cleveland, now the nation's best-selling singer-composer recording in the gospel vein. When he came to live with the family, he befriended

Aretha, who remembered, "He showed me some real nice chords and I liked his deep, deep sound. There's a whole lot of earthiness in the way he sings and what he was feelin', I was feelin', but I just didn't know how to put it across. The more I watched him, the more I got out of it." Cleveland helped Aretha, her older sister Erma (now a recording artist in her own right) and two other girls form a gospel group that appeared at local churches but lasted only eight months, because "we were too busy fussin' and fightin'." Though it was short-lived, the group did enable Aretha to get her first public experience as a singer and sometime pianist. Another gospel artist who left a deep impression on Aretha was Clara Ward, who was known on the church circuit before popularizing gospel music in nightclubs. "I wasn't really that conscious of the gospel sound," Aretha explained, "but I liked all Miss Ward's records. I learned how to play 'em because I thought one day she might decide she didn't want to play anymore and I'd be ready."

The Franklin household was a fertile field for the development of musical talent—a statement that is attested to by the fact that all three sisters are now recording artists in the pop-blues style. Because of her father's prominence as an evangelist, Aretha came to know most of the top gospel artists, including Mahalia Jackson. But the tie between so many types of music is so strong that people's paths are always crossing, regardless of the type of music with which they are identified. So it was that artists such as B. B. King, Arthur Prysock, Dorothy Donegan and the late Dinah Washington also were Franklin houseguests. She met Lou Rawls when he was an unknown singer with gospel's Pilgrim Travelers and became a friend of the late Sam Cooke when he appeared at her father's church with the famous Soul Stirrers. She remembered Cooke as being "just beautiful, a sort of person who stood out among *many* people."

Along with Sam Cooke, James Cleveland and Clara Ward, one of the celebrities who impressed Aretha tremendously with "the way he could just sit down and play" was the blind jazz pianist Art Tatum. "I just canceled that out for me and knew I could never do that, but he left a strong impression on me as a pianist and a person." But Aretha credited her father above all others with having the greatest artistic influence on her in his singing style and fusion of rhythm with words in preaching. "Most of what I learned vocally came from him," she readily admitted. "He gave me a sense of timing in music and timing is important in everything."

Before entering her teens, Aretha became a member of the youth choir at New Bethel Baptist Church, which Rev. Franklin pastors in the heart of Detroit's black ghetto. Occasionally she was soloist, and during four important years of her adolescence she toured the country with his evangelistic troupe. During one of those tours she recorded her version of *Never Grow Old* and *Precious Lord, Take My Hand,* which are still regarded as gospel classics and established her reputation as a child singer. However, at the time, she had no dreams of becoming a star or an entertainer of any sort—which has led to her current status as a reluctant celebrity. All along her primary ambition was to become "just a housewife."

It didn't turn out that way.

When Aretha was eighteen, yet another friend, Major "Mule" Holly, bassist for jazz pianist Teddy Wilson, convinced her that she had a certain basic style that could be commercially salable if applied to jazz or popular music. Though rumors persist that the religiously oriented elder Franklin opposed his daughter's pursuit of a secular career, he actually escorted her to New York City when she made her first demonstration records to be presented to commercial firms. His opinion has been that "one should make his own life and take care of his own business. If she feels she can do what she is doing as successfully as she does it, I have nothing against it. I like most kinds of music myself." It is true, however, that in his congregation there was "at first a quiet and subdued resentment, but now they acclaim her in loud terms."

For Aretha, the experience of being thrust into a different milieu was, if not traumatic, somewhat difficult. As she attended classes in New York that were intended to polish her as a performer and a personality, she was confronted with the problems that face most fledgling entertainers. But these problems were complicated by her inner shyness and personal conflicts. She became ensnarled in hassles with booking agents and managers that earned her a reputation for being difficult to handle. As the first glimmer of success began to vanish, she retreated into silence, returning to Detroit and a personal life she has tried to seclude from the public, though not always successfully. In 1963, she did appear at the Newport Jazz Festival and the Lower Ohio Jazz Festival. In subsequent years she played Bermuda, the Bahamas and Puerto Rico. Yet the plum of a major success had not come her way. There was some enthusiasm for a European tour, but her husband and manager Ted White contends, "Her earnings wouldn't have made it possible to take along the musicians who could back her up and show off her talents in the best way. Even in this country, you have to work for practically nothing if you don't have a hit, so she just worked less."

White, who described himself as having been a small-time promoter before his marriage to Aretha, believes that his wife's limited success in her previous outing was partly due to the fact that her Columbia recordings were not geared to the rhythm and blues or rock 'n' roll market and, therefore, received limited jukebox and radio attention. A five-year contract with a one-year option precluded any drastic change in approach. "We waited out those years," says White, "but when the time came to move, we were ready. We knew we had something to offer."

When a change did become possible, Ted and Aretha got a helping hand from Jimmy Bishop, a Philadelphia deejay, and his wife, Louise, who had access to the interested ear of Jerry Wexler, vice-president of Atlantic Records. A new contract resulted, and since that momentous day Aretha has been waxing hit after hit. If there is any key to her resurgence, Wexler believes it is based on the magnitude of her talent as a singer, pianist and prolific song-writer.

"I'd say that she's a musical genius comparable to that other great musical genius, Ray Charles," says the bearded recording executive who has specialized in soul artists for more than fifteen years, having been involved with Wilson Pickett, Solomon Burke, Ruth Brown and Ray Charles. He believes that many parallels can be drawn between Aretha and Ray Charles. "Both play a terrific gospel piano, which is one of the greatest assets one can have today," he states. "Since they have this broader talent, they can bring to a recording session a total conception of the music and thus contribute much more than the average artist." According to Wexler, Aretha's recordings evolve out of "head arrangements." She sets the tone for the whole session. Afterward, strings and other instrumental effects are built around what she has done as singer and pianist. Though it is generally unknown to much of the public, on most of her first Atlantic hits, through a process known as over-dubbing, she was backed by a vocal group consisting of herself and her two sisters. On other recordings, a girl vocal group called the Sweet Inspirations shared the spotlight.

For some soul artists, the sound might be a mere artifice, but for Aretha Franklin, it is an element deeply embedded in herself. She has never learned how to be pretentious enough to build a false image and sincerely identifies with people on all levels who hear her music. "Everybody who's livin' has problems and desires just as I do," she said that day in Detroit. "When the fellow on the corner has somethin' botherin' him, he feels the same way I do. When we cry, we all gonna cry tears, and when we laugh, we all have to smile." She was not eager to project herself as a new queen of the blues and asserted, "The queen of the blues was and still is Dinah Washington." Though her scheduled future engagements included some of the nation's top nightclubs, she expressed a preference for one-nighters, the bane of many performers but more suited to her rather withdrawn personality. "I dig playin' at night and leavin' in the mornin'," she said. "When I'm not workin', I like to come in the house and sit down and be very quiet. Sometimes nobody even knows I'm home. I don't care too much about goin' out. By the time I get home, I've had enough of nightclubs."

The home of which she spoke was a sixty-thousand-dollar colonial-type brick residence in an integrated section of Detroit that had become a haven for middle-class Negroes. "I just want a big comfortable house where we can lock the door and have a lot of family fun." Part of that family fun includes cooking favorite foods, such as chittlins, "with maybe some hot water cornbread and greens or ham."

Since that day in 1967, she has moved into her home with her husband and her three sons. Yet the greater her success, the louder the rumors of marital problems have become. In spite of the occasional stories and items in gossip columns, it should be noted that no matter what is going on in her home, it is nobody else's business, for any problems she might happen to have are common to others. The only difference is that she is famous, and the public often demands more than what it is rightfully due from the famous. At any rate, controversy is nothing new for Aretha, who wanted to be "just a housewife." Back in 1963, she provoked quite a storm when she appeared before an audience in Philadelphia though eight months pregnant. The shadows of scandal that enshrouded her at that time were fanned by the fact that her secret marriage to Ted White had not yet been revealed.

To those who might question anything she does on stage or off, she supplies a single answer: "I must do what is real to me in all ways. It might bug some and offend others, but this is what I must live by, the truth, so long as it doesn't impose on others."

No answer could be more soulful than that.

7

A CONSIDERATION

COMMONLY, THE term soul music is applied to the popular songs of today, as performed by some of the artists we have discussed here. Somewhat less frequently, the definition is extended to include the urban blues of a B. B. King and the rougher city blues of a Muddy Waters. Too seldom, though, is it realized that many of the characteristics that distinguish popular soul music of today from the rhythm and blues hits of the fifties have been drawn from the field of jazz—the more elaborate instrumental backings and the basic rhythm section's implementation by horns; more complex call and response patterns that are both sung and played; use of more daring improvisations and offbeat tempos.

The development is a natural one, for jazz, which is primarily an instrumental music as compared to the vocal emphasis in the popular stream, always has had its *own* soulful side. Throughout the years, it has been impossible to separate jazz from its roots, no matter how far out it has gone, for the blues feeling always has been apparent in the brassy big band sound of a Count Basie and in the convoluted, delicately shaded statements of a Modern Jazz Quartet, and it remains quite recognizable in the sometimes startling innovations of an Archie Shepp, whose growling tenor saxophone has a most familiar sound.

Furthermore, the very term "soul" is no new thing to jazz. A decade ago, buffs used it to describe the music of pianist Horace Silver, a former church organist from Norwalk, Connecticut, whose jazz hits, such as *Senor Blues* and *Sister Sadie,* were called "funky," a word which formerly had a more odorous meaning among blacks. Silver's approach was (and is) fiery, while most of his compositions remained extended variations on the blues. This was during the period when another young pianist named Les McCann came barreling out of the West, playing unaltered gospelish tunes under such titles as *The Truth, The Shout, A Little 3/4 for God and Co.* and *Fish This Week but Next Week Chitlings.* Critics, in general, dismissed McCann's style as being trite and pretentious in its churchiness, though fans, and particularly black fans, were captivated by it, judging it all from the more fundamental criterion of music being good if it "moves" one. Soulful certainly was the word for the music of Jimmy Smith, who towered over an era of fleet-footed, nimble-fingered organists. As jazz had moved out in new directions with the emergence of "Bird" and bebop in the late forties and the "birth of the cool" in the early fifties, another branch of its tree had turned again to the roots.

The year 1965 might be regarded as the time when soul jazz converged completely with popular music, for that was when a Chicago pianist named Ramsey Lewis picked up a catchy hit tune called *The "In" Crowd* from a jukebox, followed the basic line as it had been sung by Dobie Gray in the original, altered it with a bit of the jazz feeling and set in motion a trend that is still gaining momentum. Increasingly, jazz artists, and not always those commonly linked with the soul "bag," have been recording jazzed-up versions of hit tunes. Count Basie has recorded an entire album of Beatle tunes, tenor saxophonist Stanley Turrentine commonly draws from this sort of material, and it is no longer considered unusual.

"Jazz ought to move in any direction it wants to move," the accomplished composer-arranger Oliver Nelson has said. And it has been doing exactly that. Not the least of these directions is toward soul music.

8

JAZZ IS ALIVE AND WELL AND IN NEW YORK

DAMN! ALL this soul business has just about driven jazz clean *off* the radio!

You know, I used to follow all them cats a few years back when I was blowin' tenor and dreamin' of the day I'd be able to cut Sonny Rollins, but then everybody started gettin' so far *out*. *Wow!* I couldn't even find where they were *at*! I guess I'm just not enjoyin' the kind of music they're playin' now the way I used to *really* dig things.

You can't sell these kids no jazz these days. All they want is rock and soul. The closest thing they'll buy is some of them real funked up things like Ramsey Lewis does, and lots of them're just hit tunes turned around. Jazz was the music of my generation when I was coming up ten years ago, when we'd get those stacks of Miles sides and just lay back cool and listen. But these kids today don't dig that kind of sound. They want something more frantic and you have to be able to dance to it.

John Coltrane's death marked the end, at least temporarily, of the religious fervor, the messianic certainty, which constituted the vitality of jazz as we have known it. We must look elsewhere for that fervor.

The above remarks, the last of which is taken from Michael Zwerin's "Jazz Journal,"[1] while the others are casual comments from devoted jazz buffs, indicate that this music called jazz might be in almost as much trouble as God when it comes to suffering death throes. There is some evidence to substantiate their dismal viewpoint. Those who remember Chicago of the previous decade, when Ahmad Jamal was playing the Pershing, the Sutherland Lounge billed top artists and live music of a high caliber could be heard in many a South Side club, point to the deep silence that has come in recent years. In Cleveland, Pittsburgh, Detroit, Kansas City and other fairly large cities, most live music is confined to loud and not always listenable organ trios geared to overcome the din of bar talk. In New York, there are some who point to the passing of Birdland as the "jazz corner of the world," to the death of the Five Spot where Monk used to bob and weave close to his moody pianoisms, to the fate of the short-lived Jazz Gallery where Gil Evans appeared with his full orchestra of the proportions he'd used on his finest recorded collaborations with Miles Davis. Radio seems to be one of the most telling indicators of the dire state of jazz. Throughout the country, it is rare to hear jazz on AM stations, while even on the less "commercial" FM outlets music that is presented as jazz is usually limited to the softer, subdued or more popular types—Cannonball Adderley's soul hits of the sixties or sweet ballads, Ramsey's rollicking romps through popville, the smooth stylings of Kenny Burrell or Wes Montgomery cutting loose. Seldom do you encounter the really *hard* stuff—Art Blakey or the still adventuresome Miles of today, the jazz classics left by Charlie Parker and Bud Powell. Almost never will you hear the futuristic sounds of an Ornette Coleman, Archie Shepp, Cecil Taylor or Albert Ayler. Even the great Coltrane seems to have disappeared from the airwaves, though there is a belated and primarily mouthed appreciation of his legacy.

Where have all the truly imaginative and excitingly improvised sounds we once knew gone? Has the substantial audience of less than a decade ago settled down to middle-class monotony and forgotten the music once so beloved? Can music really make it today only if it duplicates the less subtle or cerebral modes of pop, rock and soul? Has the temper of the times become such that few are willing to pause and listen to music that requires a certain amount of attention? Is jazz *really* dead?

While some have said so, there are others who can as effectively show that quite the reverse is true. They point to the fact that jazz is very much with us and has been integrated into types of usage previously unknown to it. There are the movie sound tracks that now commonly use jazz music to create a mood reflecting modern life. The days of domination by Europeans such as Dmitri Tiomkin, Bronislau Kaper and Miklos Rozsa are gone. Among the respected jazzmen who have of late composed movie scores are Lalo Schifrin and Quincy Jones, while the avant-garde alto saxophonist Marion Brown has been engaged to create an original score for a French film directed by Marcel Camus, of *Black Orpheus* renown. Equally jazz music has found its way into the backgrounds for television dramas. Schifrin is to be heard here, too, along with Oliver Nelson, one of the most highly respected composer-arrangers of the age. One of the most interesting ideas proposed by those who say jazz lives is that all these divergent types of music—rock, soul and jazz—are moving closer together, borrowing elements from each other in such a way that might eventually lead to the emergence of new types of music.

Foremost among exponents of the jazz-is-*far*-from-dead attitude is Billy Taylor, a long-established pianist-composer-arranger-lecturer-leader who has devoted much of his distinguished career to the task of stimulating an interest in jazz. As well as a string of music instruction books, Taylor has written articles for *Esquire* and the *Saturday Review.* A member of the board of nearly every major organization involved with jazz, he has lectured at colleges throughout the country and was the founding father of WLIB–FM, "the voice of jazz in New York," which he serves as both a deejay and program director. A solid musician who formerly played with Ben Webster, Dizzy Gillespie, Slam Stewart, Don Redman and others, before forming his own group, Taylor has spent much of the past four years working as head of Jazzmobile, an ambulatory civic project that carries top jazz artists into the streets of Harlem and other ghetto neighborhoods to give free concerts. In 1968, these activities were extended to include Jazz Interactions, a program set up through an eleven-thousand-dollar grant from the New York State Council on the Arts to present jazz concerts to children in schools throughout the city.

Billy Taylor draws from his considerable background and observations of public reactions to substantiate his opinion that there is, indeed, a very bright future for jazz. Slender, bespectacled and looking about half of his forty-eight years, he speaks on the subject with such ready authority that one musician admirer has said of him, "That cat's so articulate it ain't even funny!" And he is. One of the factors he cites in the prevailing "death of jazz" controversy is that so many fail to recognize the extreme range of this music.

T: Many people think of jazz as a very small kind of music that appeals to a minority. This is not true. There are all kinds of jazz—that which sounds like classical music, some that sounds like rock 'n' roll and another kind of jazz that sounds like soul music. All these different elements are part of the same overall family. The trouble in the past has been that many have tried to narrow it down: only *this* is jazz. This is a mistake, for, certainly, Ella Fitzgerald is a jazz singer, Sarah Vaughan is a jazz singer and Aretha Franklin is a jazz singer, yet their approaches are different as is always the case because jazz is a personal expression. Even though there are stylistic differences which occur every five or ten years, as in the swing period or the bebop period, you'll find many people who are within that time structure who don't conform to what was popular in that era. Thelonious Monk was a great player and one of the inventors of bebop, yet his music was *not* bebop. His music *is* Thelonious *Monk*. Another fine player of another time, Fats Waller, epitomized the music of the twenties, the ragtime kind of piano, the stride piano. Yet he played what he did, which was completely different from the music of Willie "The Lion" Smith or James P. Johnson, despite the fact that he was very much a part of these times. So I re*sist* the idea of saying jazz is any one thing. Jazz is *many* things and I believe it is *this* that makes it so durable.

It is not correct to consider it only a connoisseur's music. Listen to the great improvisations of Jimmy Smith or Richard "Groove" Holmes [soul-jazz organists] and then on another level, in some cases a more intellectual level, the fan*tas*tic imagination of a John Coltrane, musicians who have a completely different point of view. This is *all* jazz. Ornette Coleman plays *his* kind of jazz and Cannonball Adderley plays *his,* but it's the kind of a difference you would find in, say, the way people speak. One man speaks and you can understand him because he's using language it's easy to relate to. Another man speaks and you have to kind of think about what he's saying and ask, "Now wait a minute. What do you *mean* by that?" And you have to go into it from a different point of view. This is true of music.

G: Why do some link the so-called demise of jazz or its vital forcefulness to the death of John Coltrane?

T: There's always someone who wants to capitalize on the fact that attention is centered on a great artist. When

John Coltrane died, many people who didn't even listen to his music or know about him suddenly began to talk about how great he was. When he was living and available for people to listen to him, many of these *same* people were not interested. Now jazz is in *some* respects a connoisseur's art because many aspects of jazz relate to the metaphysical or the psyche. So there's a kind of jazz that would appeal to your intellect—something that has nothing to do with "soul" per se—but to say that's the *only* kind of jazz is a big mistake. In this period as well as those past, there has always been someone to say, "Well, jazz is dead. It's not as popular as it used to be." In the twenties, black musicians were working all downtown and on Broadway and it was called the Jazz Age and when that passed, in the thirties, and swing came along, they said, "Well, swing *isn't* jazz." In the forties they said bebop *wasn't* jazz, and in each case they would say jazz is dead. It is no more true now than it was then.

Actually, jazz is undergoing many changes. You'll find it in the movies and on television. This is functional music and they're not using it just because they happen to have Quincy Jones available. This means they feel it reaches or *touches* a lot of people and if Quincy Jones is used, it is because they feel the jazz he will write for an important movie will add a *dimension* to that movie. We've realized this sort of thing for a long time here in New York because our audience is a very responsive one. We promote live jazz concerts, records, every aspect of jazz and, as a result, we have *free* jazz concerts in schools, in museums and libraries and many places where you ordinarily don't look for it. You know, some people think that jazz can only be played effectively in nightclubs. Nothing could be further from the truth. So we're activists here. We try to get jazz right to the people with the Jazzmobile. It was the idea of the Harlem Cultural Council and we function as a community project. We find that when we can get directly to the people in this way, we have no problem, but when someone is *interpreting* what we're doing, then it becomes a problem. That's when you have someone saying, "You should only listen to Coltrane," or someone else. *Malarkey!* Nobody in concert music says you should like only Beethoven or Debussy. If you like music, you like *music*.

This is the line of thinking we follow in programming here at the station. We present the kinds of music we feel to be relevant to the kinds of audiences we're playing to, so we play, historically, things that cover a long span. We go all the way back to "Jelly Roll" Morton and some of the old ragtime players and we come all the way up to the present and Cecil Taylor, Archie Shepp and some of the others who are representing *their* aspect of contemporary culture and are representing it very well.

G: Since some of these experimentalists are those whom many jazz fans find difficult to understand at the present, does it seem likely that the audience will grow to appreciate them once they begin really to listen to them, as was the case with bebop?

T: I'm certain they will. I'm not sure which aspects of these experimentations will be lasting on the part of the great innovators who are with us now—the Cecil Taylors and the Albert Aylers among the younger men and older men like Sun Ra who have for *years* been looking for new ways of expression. *All* of these people are making such a valid contribution to the overall fabric of jazz that only time will tell. But they certainly have an audience, as we can attest here at the station. We get requests for more of their music and we hear in the music of other musicians elements of their experiments. It's a matter of growth, of redirecting the attention of the audience in hearing and being open to new things as well as retaining the heritage of the older things.

G. But what about potential fans who live in places other than New York where this sort of music never is played on radio? What can be done to expand their tastes and why does such a narrow approach typify most broadcasting?

T: It's very difficult in other places where you have a smaller numerical group to draw on and you are in competition with other radio stations. It's a difficult thing for a program director to say arbitrarily, "I will educate my audience," because radio is, unfortunately, a business. Theoretically it belongs to the people, but realistically it belongs to whoever is running that particular station. You have to consider what your competition is doing and you have to play the kind of music that will keep you on the air. But they should try to keep *some* jazz on the air instead of following the example of one radio station in Chicago that switched over from a complete jazz format to a completely popular format because the top management thought it couldn't compete with the rock 'n' roll and soul stations in the area. I think that sort of thing is wrong, but the owners will say it's *their* ball game, their money that has been invested and the station has to pay back that investment. So it's strictly business and has nothing to do with artistic standards. If it weren't this way, if they were programming artistically, I think you'd have an entirely different type of programming on the air.

G: Is it true that rock and commercial soul have just about squeezed jazz off the air?

T: In many cities this is true because there are not enough imaginative people in those areas to recognize the fact that there is a large jazz audience and many others who *could* like it if they only had a chance to *hear* it. I have found indications of this during my experiences playing for children in the schools. My group is one of several that are used. It's a lecture series and we do an hour-long concert for children whose ages range from kindergarten to high school. The consensus of opinion is that these are rock 'n' roll fans and that nothing else will touch them, that they'll be bored stiff unless you give them lots of rock and that's *all.* That's the way the radio stations view it all over the country. Now we find that this is *not* true, because we go in and we present jazz. We don't play *down* to them. We play according to the age and attention span, for you can't play a long, involved composition for a six-year-old, but you *can* for a high school student and he will remain interested. At any rate, we do this, we go into the schools to present these concerts and we just don't have enough time, enough money or enough musicians to do as *many* as we're *asked* to do. We are doing approximately fifty or sixty concerts this year; Jazz Interactions is doing fifty or sixty of these concerts for young audiences with possibly twenty or thirty of them being jazz concerts. That's all in this area [Manhattan] and we haven't even *scratched* the surface of what we could do.

Actually, it does more for me than it does for the audiences, because I learn so *much* from young people. We tend to underestimate their capacity, not only for learning, but for enjoying sophisticated things. Young people—and I don't mean young people *just* in the ghetto areas, because we play at all kinds of schools, but young people *period*—are much more rhythmically sophisticated, as a result of rock 'n' roll and soul being played so much, than their parents. This is apparent during our concerts when we involve them in the performance by having them clap their hands and do various physical things to indicate where *they* feel the music and it's *tremendous!* If I asked a group of five or six hundred adults to clap on a certain beat, I would have bedlam and it would not make any kind of sense at all. But the kids are as *one*. You really get a good solid beat when you tell them, "Look, I want you to clap your hands now in *this* soulful fashion," and they've got it and *gone!*

G: Does it seem that rock and soul are moving toward jazz and vice versa?

T: That's exactly the way I see it. The better rock artists are incorporating elements of jazz into their music and jazz also is being influenced by rock and its innovations. In a series we've done for the *Captain Kangaroo* television show, we've used this approach. I try to trace the music to its African origins, then the early ragtime influence and the New Orleans kind of jazz and the contemporary forms with the interaction that is going on with music coming from other places—people hearing jazz and then giving it a little something of their own. For example, there was the bossa nova. People in Brazil heard jazz, said, "Oh, that's beautiful and harmonic and lively and if we put *our* beat to it, it'll sound like *this*." And then when it came up here, something else happened to it.

In the final analysis, you get to what's happening with the kids today where they go as far as they can in terms of volume, in terms of just soul from *their* point of view, and then they begin to realize that there are other things going on and that they can incorporate them. So they learn to play in a little different fashion. They begin to *listen* to jazz musicians and they come up with some exciting things. By the same token, jazz musicians listen to what the kids do and are influenced by it, like Eddie Harris and Cannonball who come up with little things in their music that are drawn *directly* from what the kids have done. This sort of interaction is one of the *healthy* things that's happening today. It's possible for exciting new concepts to develop from this sort of interaction. I don't know where it's going, but certainly every person is aware of what the other is doing and is drawing what he can *from* it!

1. *Village Voice*, December 19, 1968.

9

REQUIEM FOR TRANE: ANOTHER KIND OF SOUL

The death of John Coltrane, the saxophonist and jazz experimentalist, in 1967, is said to have marked the end of an era, for he became in the final decade of his life a dominant musical force. His essential message was in his music, but there is another that he expressed with his total being—a belief in the universality of music and a concern for the human condition. He was, indeed, another kind of man with another kind of soul.

IN THE days, not so long ago, when he played, he stood before his audiences like an earnest black knight intent on blowing away evil spirits with an unrelenting sound that seared the consciousness of those who had come to listen. Horn in hand—most often tenor saxophone, but occasionally soprano sax—he gave freely of his complex musical "thing" to anyone willing to accept it. For those who did not understand his music, he tried ever a little harder, but even they could not dissuade him from his quest as he reached for the sonic stratosphere, rising to fantastic peaks of intensity.

And, suddenly, the sound was no more.

John William Coltrane, known to friends and fans alike as "Trane," was dead at the age of forty, victim of a liver ailment that had steadily sapped his strength during the last months of life. A giant had been silenced.

In the general scheme of events where art, and particularly black art, must take a back seat to wars, rebellions and celebrity weddings, his death in a Huntington, Long Island, hospital on July 17, 1967, was briefly noted—if at all. But later it was said that a whole phase of jazz died with this man who reached out beyond the constricting barriers of time, rhythm and harmony. He led where others might follow and go further out on their own. After his death, those who realized his significance as a man and a musician entertained a shadow of belief that he might still be "cooking" away in some celestial combo.

As those who did appreciate his music paused in the void he left, many tried to evaluate what had been lost. Measured by any standards, the contribution of John Coltrane must be considered unusual. Conception for him was so interwoven with act that he became one of the most prolific and extensively recorded of modern artists, leaving behind forty albums in print, not to mention countless sessions on which he did not appear as leader. They contain a vast store of original compositions, the later ones in an experimental "free" form. But he produced this huge quantity without compromising his artistic standards, never bowing to the bids of commercialism. Though he disdained calling the music he played "jazz," objecting to the term as being too confining, jazz was the foundation of the musical architecture he created, rooted in rhythm, sustained by inspired improvisation of the most daring sort. Discontented with the patterns into which this music had fallen before his arrival on the scene, he sought to expand its horizons, never willing to rest too long on any plateau of expression. He abandoned the song as a necessary point of departure and opened up the music, enabling it to move in all directions, filling the spaces with incredible flurries of notes not always related to any set pattern or form. As his voice called out for a new freedom, others were impelled to answer their own inner voices, and he became the acknowledged spiritual father of the avant-garde in jazz. Like "Bird," the late Charlie Parker, he, too, soared, and left the scene a little different from how he found it.

Yet the importance of John Coltrane exceeds his prominence as a musician. He was known to be a gentle and deeply religious man who had succeeded in finding a path to personal truth while making his way through the dusky evening world. The aura that surrounded him was steeped not in drugs, drink and debauchery but in a sincere concern for the human condition. This, too, was unusual for a man who had to live the late-hour life, described by one musician as being a matter of "always hustling, living out of suitcases, paying two rents, trying to get the leeches off you and wondering where your next gig's coming from." Though a leading exponent of a music still unjustifiably linked with the early brothels where it was played, Coltrane apparently saw through the surface of things and went on to seek a higher meaning. *A Love Supreme,* an extended four-part jazz "prayer" without words that became one of his most famous recorded works, grew out of his nonsectarian spirituality and was dedicated to the God in which he believed. In his dedication of that album, he referred to a spiritual awakening he had experienced in 1957, which was followed by a period of irresolution and, later, reaffirmation of faith. In his words:

> I do perceive and have been duly re-informed of His omnipotence, and of our need for, and dependence on Him. At this time I would like to tell you that no matter what . . . it is with God. He is gracious and merciful. His way

is in love, through which we all are. It is truly—a love supreme.[1]

It was not a "jive" thing. If it had been, those who knew him best would not so frequently speak of him as being a "sweet man, the one cat who never put anybody down." They would not so openly describe him as being "almost a saint."

Coltrane best stated his philosophy in the last extensive interview conducted with him, which appeared in *Jazz and Pop* magazine. He simply said: "I know that there are bad forces, forces put here that bring suffering to others and misery to the world, but I want to be the force which is truly for good." As a mature person, he arrived at this conclusion only after he had been through his "changes" and "paid his dues."

Born in Hamlet, North Carolina, on September 23, 1926, Coltrane was the son of a tailor who played several musical instruments as a hobby. The family later moved to Philadelphia, where his mother still lives. After young John's father died, when he was twelve, his relationship with his mother became exceptionally close, possibly because he was an only child. The spiritual strain that later was to become so apparent might have been linked to the fact that both his grandfathers were ministers. But while the traditional family mode of expression had been that of the spoken word, it was to be music for John, who studied E-flat alto horn, clarinet and saxophone in high school. However, music was not to become a dominant force in his life until he reached the age of eighteen. It was then that he undertook serious studies at Granoff Studios and the Ornstein School of Music. After fulfilling military duties with a U.S. Navy band in Hawaii, Coltrane returned to the mainland in 1947 to serve his musical apprenticeship as a sideman in the bands of Eddie

"Cleanhead" Vinson and Dizzy Gillespie, working later in small groups led by Earl Bostic and Johnny Hodges,

The first major break in his career came in 1955, when the relatively obscure Coltrane joined the Miles Davis Quintet, a group that was destined to become one of the most outstanding of the post-bop era. Even in that early stage of his development, the style for which he was to become known was beginning to be evident: his way of playing blistering barrages of notes, even more startling when contrasted with the economical Davis approach. In those days, critic John S. Wilson wrote of Coltrane that "he often plays his tenor sax as if he were determined to blow it apart, but his desperate attacks almost invariably lead nowhere." Unlike the improvisations of Charlie Parker, whose ingenious constructions were variations based on the chords underlying familiar melodies and variations on those variations, Coltrane's eruptions of 16th, 32nd and seemingly undefinable notes sometimes appeared to bear little or no relationship to anything else that was going on in the music, though this was just the beginning of where he was to go. Furthermore, his tone was not "sweet," in the terms of a tenor saxman such as the late Ike Quebec. Later, Coltrane himself admitted, "When they first heard me with Miles, they didn't like it." But eventually his surging passion and strange kind of lyricism began to reach those who had scoffed at this wild new man. A very few hailed him as an individualistic and influential musical personality.

In the latter part of 1957, Coltrane worked with Thelonious Monk at the old Five Spot in New York, rejoining Miles Davis the following year. The reputation he acquired by performing with that other giant of jazz provided the impetus that led to an initial acclaim when he branched out on his own and recorded works that have now become classics in their genre. He achieved a droning, hypnotic Indian sound when he turned to the neglected soprano saxophone for a singular interpretation of *My Favorite Things,* which is found on the Atlantic record of 1960 that first turned the public onto him. His lovely composition *Naima,* which was included in the album *Giant Steps* from that period, eventually found its way into the general jazz repertoire. By this time, his method of imposing torrential explosions of notes on basic changes had been dubbed "sheets of sound." Coltrane was a force to be reckoned with.

The year 1961 marked the beginning of Coltrane's ascension to the position of the most influential jazz musician of his time. Settling down to a group composed of himself on tenor and soprano saxophones, McCoy Tyner on piano, Jimmy Garrison on bass and Elvin Jones on drums, he created some of the most remarkable music of the sixties. Occasionally a second bassist, another reedman, such as the late Eric Dolphy, or a big-band backing was added, but Tyner, Garrison and Jones were the three key men in the unit that was with Coltrane in 1965 when he made an unprecedented sweep of the annual *Downbeat* magazine readers' poll, being voted top tenor saxophonist and Jazzman of the Year, elected to the Hall of Fame and honored by having his *A Love Supreme* named Record of the Year.

The Coltrane quartet of that period, the most popular unit he ever led, has been most vividly described by Jimmy Garrison, who was associated with the leader longer than any other single musician, remaining even after 1965 when Trane's desire to experiment led to a shifting in personnel that resulted in McCoy Tyner's and Elvin Jones's going out on their own.

One night, within a month after Coltrane's death, I met Garrison in a small East Side Manhattan bistro where he was accompanying a nondescript cocktailish singer-pianist whose job was to provide an unobtrusive background for intimate discussions. With a touch of nostalgia, he recalled the way it had been. Garrison had joined the Coltrane group after working with Ornette Coleman, who had not then been recognized as the great innovator he is. "It was at a time when Trane was just coming into his own," said Garrison, "a time when he was searching for the right combination of people to produce a sound that only he could hear." In the group that finally was assembled, a rare sort of musical empathy flourished. "Things were just unbelievable. We'd get on the bandstand and everything would build to such an intensity that everything else would disappear and there would just be the music."

Amazingly, the group that played with such an uncommon unity never had an actual rehearsal. The music unfolded spontaneously, with each man building his own ideas on a general pattern set forth by the leader. "Many of the times when we went in for a record date, it was the first time we'd seen the music," Garrison explained. "Often there was *no* written music. He'd just announce what key we'd be playing in, or that we'd be playing in twelve tones and we'd take it from there. I remember one time when he announced a certain number and I said, 'Man, I've never heard *that* before.' He answered, 'Well, you'll be hearing it now,' and we proceeded to play it. It was really a unique band, but he gave you confidence by giving you responsibility. He was a genius."

In live performances, the group also acquired a reputation for the length of some of its renditions. The habit of extending a single number, *My Favorite Things,* for example, to twenty-five minutes or more drew criticism from some, particularly those unaccustomed to atonal sounds interspersed with harsh bleats and shrieks. According to Garrison, this grew out of Coltrane's deep desire to communicate and to share. "He wanted people to like what he was doing. If they didn't, he wouldn't bust it over their heads, but just hoped that eventually they would understand. Sometimes he thought maybe he hadn't gotten his thing together enough to really put it across to them, but he felt that if he stayed up there on the bandstand long enough, he was at least giving to the people."

Like all great innovators, Coltrane was frequently misunderstood. The harshness of his sound, at times, the forcefulness and intensity he projected were misinterpreted as expressions of rage. Actually, the reverse was more likely true. As Garrison said, "There was a love that he emitted that is rare to find, a thing you recognized immediately on meeting him. He lived the way of the things he wrote or said. There was something sainted about him. This force he had became a part of the band. There was never any malice. We were like four brothers in the deepest sense of the word. We had respect for each other, a love for each other." When the end did come for that notable band, it was not due to inner strife, but because "Trane had started hearing other voices, other ways of doing things. He was the sort of man who was always learning, always practicing, even between sets. He was one big piece of music and he knew there had to be more roads to cover."

Coltrane's desire to cover new territory and to scale restraining barriers led him to assemble an eleven-piece unit in 1965 to record *Ascension,* a thirty-eight-minute free form improvisation that was hailed by one critic as "possibly the most powerful human sound ever recorded." Here all customary forms were set aside and all that went with them in order that all concentration might be applied to the music itself, springing from each of the eleven men as it was felt and thought, meshing into a tour de force of free sound. In his liner notes for that album, critic A. B. Spellman quoted tenor saxophonist Archie Shepp, who played on that set, thus:

> It achieves a certain kind of unity; it starts at a high level of intensity with the horns playing high and the other pieces playing low. This gets a quality of like male and female voices. It builds in intensity through all the solo passages, brass and reeds, until it gets to the final section where the rhythm section takes over and brings it back down to the level it started at.[2]

Spellman aptly adds, "By that time your nervous system has been dissected, overhauled and reassembled."

This drive toward the new also resulted in Coltrane's forming another quintet, markedly more avant-garde, featuring Pharoah Sanders as a second tenor saxophonist, Rashied Ali on drums, Garrison on bass and Trane's wife, the former Alice McLeod, of Detroit, on piano. Many of his fans from the earlier periods recoiled at the seeming chaos of his new sound, but he continued to forge ahead, for, as his associate later explained, "He felt every man must live his own life and find his own path to himself."

This searching nature was carried over from his music into his personal life. During his later years, he delved into Eastern religions, studying yoga, the Bhagavad Gita, sacred Hindu text and the Torah. He was known to be a health food advocate who drank "mostly a lot of carrot juice," ate meat only infrequently and found great pleasure in his family life, as was demonstrated in an eight millimeter home movie showing him romping in the grass of his back yard with his three small sons. Successful enough to be able to work as often as he liked, Coltrane would hurry home after he'd completed a night's work, tarrying in the clubs only when another master such as Sonny Rollins, the tenor sax colossus, was in town.

The sanctuary of John Coltrane was a large, comfortable modern house situated on three acres of land near Deer Park, Long Island, within driving distance of the mashing crowds of Manhattan. There it was that he spent the happy moments with his wife, three sons and one stepdaughter. Aside from music and spiritualism, he had few compelling interests, but he did personally furnish his favorite part of the house, a sprawling living room done in bright colors that seemed to echo his celebration of life. Even after his death, his touch remained in that room with the piano where he sketched his music. On it sat the tenor sax that was the musical nucleus of his life, an alto sax that he was exploring and an unstrung Indian sitar, reflecting his manifest affinity for music of the East. On a leather bench beneath the piano sat another tenor sax, as though awaiting his breath to give it animation. His musical catholicity was apparent in a set of drums, on which he was practicing not too long before his death, the flute he played on his last record date, a set of bagpipes, a small African horn.

"He was a humble man who didn't have the personality one would expect of a musician," reminisces his wife. "He was a healthy energetic man who liked to get out early in the morning and be in bed by ten or eleven o'clock." She points to his importance as a teacher, saying, "The best part was when I joined the band, after McCoy quit. We could travel together and we went to Japan and made a couple trips to California. He was very patient with me, because I hadn't played or even practiced in almost two years and I was blowin' some wrong chords. But he showed me how to build the sort of impact he wanted. He always made you feel you could do it yourself if you really tried. One point he made above all others, and that was 'Don't ever play *down* to anyone. Play just what you feel yourself.' He didn't believe in just playing what people might want to hear."

She describes him as "a man with a universal concept," for he liked to draw an analogy between his horn and mankind, explaining that one group might represent the upper register, another the mid-range and yet another the deeper notes, but that it took all to make the whole. Because of this desire for human unity and his exposure to a world in which things were more often bitter than sweet, he had a great concern for "the plight of his people." During the last months of his life he expressed a desire to go to Africa, "to check everything out." He was also concerned with the plight of musicians, the conditions under which they had to work and the way in which their music was received. "He was disturbed because the type of music he played was confined to nightclubs," says Mrs. Coltrane. "It was music for listening, not for drinking in all the places where there's so much buying and selling. Maybe the concert hall would have been the place for his music, but we had thought of setting up a center that would be like a church—we wouldn't call it a church, because it might frighten people away and they might wonder what kind of church it was, but it would be a church in that it would be a place for music and meditation, and maybe someone would feel like praying. It would bring others a kind of fellowship based on music, because he thought music was a single universal force and that there could be no dividing lines or categories. That's why he disliked the term 'jazz.' "

But the end came too quickly for John Coltrane to fulfill all his dreams of universalizing music. He never did set up his "church," and he never went to Africa. He spent his last days stretched out on a couch in his living room, listening to tapes of the new music he had created. Quiet, as always, he never let anyone know how ill he was.

"Maybe I didn't know how bad he felt because he wouldn't tell me," says his wife. "I used to leave him alone when I thought he wanted to be alone. I was busy with the kids and I didn't want to bother him, to get in his way or to bug him."

Mrs. Coltrane readily contradicts any rumors that her husband died of the destructive forces that have cut down so many jazz musicians in their prime. He had been under medical treatment for at least two months before his death and seldom performed in public during the last six months of life. Sporadically, he had complained of feeling tired after playing, of being tired of working, of the nightclub life and all it entailed. Nobody knew exactly how tired he was. Nobody knows what dread disease he might have thought he had, but he rejected his physician's suggestion that he have an operation and refused to be hospitalized until his last day, when it had become impossible for him to take even soup.

"It was on a Sunday," his wife recalls, "and he was such a strong man that he walked out the door himself. He was walking slow, but he made it. And then he went down so fast. He was such a beautiful man and I guess those kind of people don't stay here too long. They come here and do their work and then they leave."

There are some indications that Coltrane had suspected his own imminent death: casual statements about "if I ever play again" and "if I have to leave you," a stealthy, abruptly concluded telephone call concerning insurance, the fact that he made seven record sessions during his last year while his usual output was two or three discs a year. For his wife there are only thoughts of "all my life I have to live without him, though I know it is his invisible hand that has brought me through."

But though the man Coltrane is dead, his valuable musical legacy lives on, not only in the recorded sounds he left behind, but in the marginal world of New York's East Village where the eager young exponents of free music lurch toward their own aesthetic horizons. Their music has been described by some, such as Nat Hentoff, as "black, angry and hard to understand." It, too, is marked by a stark breaking away from the old conceptions of melody, harmony and form with the inclusion of sounds other than those customarily produced on musical instruments. Where Coltrane led, others are reaching ever further out.

One of the front runners and an heir to the Coltrane mantle has been Archie Shepp, a tenor saxophonist who is also a highly articulate spokesman with an academic background in playwriting.

"He was a bridge," Shepp says of Coltrane, "the most accomplished and comprehensive of the so-called post-bebop musicians to make an extension into what is called the avant-garde. I met him at the time when I was still a student at Goddard College and he took the time to talk to me. It was time for that sort of thing, for the younger men to begin to have that sort of exchange with their elders. He was one of the few of the older men to demonstrate a sense of responsibility toward those coming behind him. He provided a positive image that was greatly needed and stood against the destructive forces that might have claimed so many. Having suffered and seen so much himself, he tried to see that others coming along wouldn't have to go through all that.

"Perhaps many didn't understand his music—the sort of thing he was doing in his last two years, not the earlier things for which he was known best—and they might not understand the music we are creating now, but it is truly a reflection of our times, as much as the spirituals were of their time, or Leadbelly. Trane's music exemplified his feeling for what *is* and he accomplished a great deal for the short time he was with us—much more than most do in a lifetime. He left the scene a little different and I believe John's death has drawn us, as musicians, closer together, has brought us closer to a kind of unity. This is the way we must assess a great man."

1. From impulse! Album A-95 A Love Supreme / John Coltrane © 1964 ABC-Paramount Records, Inc. All rights reserved. Used by permission.

2. A. B. Spellman notes. From impulse! Album A-77 Ascension / John Coltrane © 1965 ABC-Paramount Records, Inc. All rights reserved. Used by permission.

10

THE SHAPE OF SOUL TO COME

FROM MY window overlooking a main street on Chicago's South Side, it is possible to overhear the sounds of contemporary black life. In the morning and the evening and throughout the noise-riddled day, they are always there.

This night a random cluster of young girls has passed by below. One was warbling operatic fragments in an incongruous mocking style when one of her companions blasted back at her: "Oh, *shut* ya *fuckin' mouf!*"

There is the eerie sound of a young man who passes by this place each day at just past dawn and near midnight, playing a flute, blowing from it breathy bits of old Miles things and particles of popular tunes.

One overheated spring evening when the windows were open very wide, something *very* strange came drifting into my own private pad. It was the muted sound of one of Bach's suites for unaccompanied cello, flowing from the apartment building across the street and into mine. And juxtaposed against it was the high falsetto chant of several youths, strolling down the boulevard and breaking into three-part harmony on an unfamiliar melody that seemed catchy enough to be recorded by *somebody*.

A whistler now and then . . . an undulating hummmm . . . a foot-borne transistor radio . . . a broadcast bellowing from an open car. But seldom silence.

In between those bursts of music, there is the mechanical roar of buses, the churn of cars all mixing with occasional laughter, the rubbery bounce of children with their balls or the splat-splat of ropes brushing against the pavement as little girls jump double-dutch to the affectionately derisive chant of little boys lapsing into improvised exchanges:

"I don't *want* you to come over here an' play with me."

"Don' need to play. Somebody *else*'ll play."

"You just best not *mess* with me or I'll come over there and tear you 'part!"

"How *you* gonna tear anybody 'part. All you got's a mouf so big you sound like a alligator."

"I don' mind you calling me *that* . . . what's a *all*igator?"

There is the sound of older youths, spewing out their own profane lingo loudly enough to announce to the world their defiance of custom as they amble along to the rhythm of their own heel-taps in a continual parade. A black woman in brightly colored ankle-length garb strolls down the street while eating a take-out sundae from a paper cup. There are the hat-wearers and the Afro-sporters moving alongside sedately striding junior executives swinging attaché cases at their sides, looking *very* important as they lean forward with a confident gait that proclaims to all that they are *surely* going somewhere. This latter group does not sing or shout in the streets, though they walk with a certain lilt. But their presence never imposes a sense of inhibition on the part of the others. They are merely a different thing and perhaps not *really* to the core.

All of this is part of the usual sound and scene in the ghetto. Though it has more than its share of ugliness and dirt, there seems to be something very special about it.

Certainly there are all the frightening reports of break-ins, of women being beaten in the streets and of purses being snatched, while the grating, terror-striking sirens of fire engines are an everyday affair, ever racing toward some new disaster in the making. Last week I left town for one day and returned to find that my apartment had been burglarized by smart thieves who carried off the goods in my last decent suitcase, while a few nights later a teen-aged boy came stumbling up the steps, sobbing hysterically as he fulfilled his mission of telling the woman across the hall that her son had been shot in a gang squabble.

These are the trials of urban black life. They are not simply tales or newspaper accounts that can be regarded with the easy indifference of distance; they are an axiom of existence, for beneath the color and the flair of it all, it is hard, sometimes damned near impossible, to survive. Yet there is something that keeps one going, keeps one hanging on. It is not merely because there is no place to run (the suburbs are closed, if you please, until further notice), for often, in spite of the hardships, there is no actual desire to run at all, though the problems are to be encountered even in the better parts of the ghetto—which is where I live—since these enclaves of the elite among the unfortunate are never more than a stone's throw from the hard and bitter core of the black bottom.

That holding force, that vital and sometimes dangerously uncontainable spirit that embues everything about it, cannot be easily dismissed; for who would readily forsake a certain intensity that is, in itself, an affirmation of life for an escape into numbness. Who would willingly exchange an imposed awareness for the dubious rewards of an anesthetized state of being. As it is, all prisoners of the black world who dare to regard themselves or life honestly must continually confront these unpredictable life forces. Perhaps and perhaps not, it causes one to remain a little more alive, though it is just as likely to drive one to the outermost limits of escape from that which is unbearable. Few willingly walk into discomfort or flirt with disaster, though to do so might mean encountering life as it really is and not being deluded by some pretty facade. Some do, some don't and some simply cannot accept the ultimate challenge of that journey. Perhaps this line of demarcation tells us what soul is all about. In the final summing up, it cannot be restricted by race or region but merely by human feeling and the expression of that feeling. Possibly this is why soul music and so much of what it represents have been adopted by others.

Often, these days, one hears bluesy, soulful sounds that are so appealing that it should not be important that the artists are not black. Ideally, the music might be simply enjoyed for what it is, though that is not the case, for as long as the embattled black is denied full access to the fruits of his creations in *any* area of endeavor, he will find it difficult to bask in the luxury of a purely aesthetic viewpoint. Yet it has happened, on occasion, as in jazz, where a Bill Evans is admired for the sheer poetry he projects with his piano—and he imitates no one. Perhaps it can happen again in other areas of music. But in the interim the black, in his unceasing struggle for survival of his *self,* more than of his physical being, will lend his music to that struggle as he has from his earliest days on this continent. Already there are indications of the way this might alter the shape of soul to come.

Certainly, this was one of the motivating factors behind a significant theatrical event that took place in Chicago during the summer of 1967. The musical production recalled here did not open to a burst of critical reviews and Broadway did not know of its existence, though its importance far exceeded that of the frothy entertainments enjoying long runs before well-heeled audiences. It happened so far off Broadway that few people ever saw it, and the presentation did not even take place in a theater but in a church, deep in the heart of one of the most ravaged sections of the South Side ghetto. This was Oscar Brown Jr.'s production, *Opportunity, Please Knock,* which was sponsored by Chicago's notorious youth gang known as the Blackstone Rangers. Brown had written most of the music and, with the assistance of his collaborator, Jean Pace, staged the production using neighborhood talent, displaying it in a place where denizens of the ghetto might be exposed to it.

At the time, Brown had two other original musical shows running simultaneously in less forbidden sections of the city, but he donated his energy and formidable talent to this effort because it had a more important meaning. This meaning shone through loud and clear when teen-age girls and boys, garbed in brilliantly colored costumes designed especially for them, strutted up and down the aisles of the Woodlawn area's First Presbyterian Church, singing of the hidden glories of *Mother Africa,* imploring the whole world to please open the door of opportunity to them and chanting to blacks and whites in the audience that they were "Lookin' for a *soul* brother . . . all a-*round* me" who would stand by them. In this way, they tried to impart a sense of conviction to those who might be in a position to help and a sense of identity, of unity, of self-pride to those who'd never known such things. But the show also was designed to transmit a certain set of personal values to those in the cast and the maligned gang youths who had supported it. This production did not entirely succeed in doing all these things and its painfully protracted course was a stormy one, but it set an example others might well consider when they speak of "reaching" alienated ghetto youths.

The use of music to convey ideas and to motivate certainly is a fundamental principle in the work of a little-known but highly regarded jazz pianist-composer named Charles Bell. As one of the rare black students of composition at Pittsburgh's Carnegie Institute of Technology (now Carnegie-Mellon University) in 1958, he formed the now defunct Contemporary Jazz Quartet that took top honors in the Intercollegiate Jazz Festival competition in 1960 and waxed a first recording that was given *Downbeat* magazine's highest rating, five stars—all of which success caused Bell to wonder whether or not he was moving in the right direction. After graduating from Carnegie, he performed a commissioned jazz-symphonic work with the Pittsburgh Symphony Orchestra under William Steinberg. In those days, he was so steeped in classicism that his music was considered "third stream," or an amalgamation of the jazz and classical styles, as most notably set forth by Gunther Schuller, a composer and French horn player who expounded this approach in collaborations with the Modern Jazz Quartet and who now serves as president of the New England Conservatory of Music.

That was the early Charles Bell, whose music was often oblique and difficult to follow. Finding it almost impossible to earn a living as *this* kind of musician in a city such as Pittsburgh, which has spawned many outstanding artists but never has harbored experimentation, Bell took a job as a music teacher at an inner-city junior high school. He credits his students with having turned him on to the early soul tunes they liked so much. Then it was he realized that these same students who could not be stimulated by the traditional songs and formal melodies set forth in the regular course syllabus *could* be moved to great interest when the elements of theory were demonstrated in terms of the music they already knew. His first major effort along this line was the formation of a one-hundred-voice "rock 'n' roll" choir that performed at the city's annual high school music festival but presented, instead of the usual fare, their own renditions of hit tunes, such as the Supremes' *Come See about Me.* Very little rehearsal time had been required since the youngsters were able to fill in all the voicings and proper harmonies through their familiarity with the music. This writer, for one, was there and the sound was truly stunning.

Since 1964, Bell has lived in New York City, where he has performed, on rare occasions, as a jazz pianist-composer-leader, and each of these appearances is carefully followed and reported on by *Downbeat* and the *New York Times.* However, his main activities have been in the area of music education, where he has devised a method whereby the elements of grammar can be taught through pop-soul tunes he composes specifically to present the principle at hand. Like a handful of jazz musicians, among them trumpeter Donald Byrd, who is musician-in-residence at Rutgers University, Bell now teaches prospective teachers, training them in his methods at Hunter College. His approach has been demonstrated in a "rock" opera entitled *Big Time Selfish,* based on Dickens's *A Christmas Carol.* And he is at work on a major "rock-soul" opera called *The Golden Spook,* which will be sung by black and Puerto Rican youngsters to the instrumental accompaniment of their peers.

This is, perhaps, the shape of soul to come: the use of music as a functional art directed toward definite problems of contemporary life. All of these pursuits will not and have not been aimed exclusively at the needs of the young, for there are others who also hunger for a sense of pride and identity. And all of these things are taking place in separate but inseparable areas of music.

Yet, on another level, one comes to that which crosses the boundaries of various arts, where all things seem to come together. A singular achievement in this vein has been *Brer Soul,* a record album conceived and produced by Melvin Van Peebles, a "brother" from the States who has gained some renown as a film director in France, though he remains in closer contact with his black roots than many who never left the continent. In *Brer Soul,* he speaks of the verities of black life in the ghetto lingo, having written all the poems for this album as well as the music, which is arranged and conducted by Warren Stevens and Coleridge Perkinson. Though the music is infectious on the surface and the poems merely engaging, one can sense within them the urgency of black life and its fundamental nature, as captured in the joys of sex, the woes of jealousy, the anxiety of self-doubt and the plight of the persecuted. There is a universal ring in his pressing "Boom–taka." It is the call of life, the call of soul and the cry of mankind as man reaches out toward the life that is most meaningful to all.

DISCOGRAPHY

The following records are suggested for listening as a means of demonstrating many of the points made in this book. This list should not be considered complete to the exclusion of other recordings, for there are simply too many soul sounds for all to be included. All are long-playing albums (some tracks, of course, being better than others), and, with the unfortunate exception of the work of Dinah Washington, all are easily available. The liner notes should not be overlooked.

General Background

Folk Music of Ghana, Folkways Records FW 8859
Leadbelly . . . From Last Sessions, Verve Folkways FT-3019
Odetta Sings Ballads and Blues, Tradition Records TLP 1010
Erskine Hawkins: *After Hours,* RCA Victor LPM 2227
Duke Ellington with Mahalia Jackson: *Black, Brown and Beige,* Columbia CS 8015
The Freedom Singers Sing of Freedom Now!, (for *We'll Never Turn Back*) Mercury SR 60924
The Bessie Smith Story, 4 Columbia CL-85578
Dinah Washington: *After Hours with Miss "D"*, Mercury 36028

Gospel

Mahalia Jackson: *Newport 1958,* Columbia CS 8071
James Cleveland and the Cleveland Singers, Savoy MG-14131
Edwin Hawkins Singers: *Let Us Go into the House of the Lord,* BPS-10001

Rhythm and Blues

Atlantic's History of Rhythm and Blues: *Vol. 1, The Roots,* SD 8161; *Vol. 2, The Golden Years,* SD 8162; *Vol. 3, Rock and Roll,* SD 8163; *Vol. 4, The Big Beat,* SD 8164
Apollo Saturday Night, Acto 33-159
Chuck Berry: *Greatest Hits,* Chess 1485
Sam Cooke: *The Man Who Invented Soul,* RCA Victor LSP-3991

Ray Charles

Ray Charles Story, Vols. 1 and 2, Atlantic A-900 (8063/4)
Ray Charles In Person, Atlantic 8039
The Genius of Ray Charles, Atlantic 1312
Genius + Soul = Jazz, Impulse (S) 2
Modern Sounds in Country and Western, ABC (S) 410

Contemporary Blues

B.B. King Live at the Regal, ABC (S) 509
B.B. King: *Lucille,* Bluesway S-6016
B.B. King: *Live & Well,* Bluesway BLS 6031

Albert King: *Live Wire/Blues Power,* Stax STS 2003
Junior Wells: *It's My Life, Baby!,* Vanguard VSD 79231
Muddy Waters: *Brass and the Blues,* Chess LP 1507

Motown Sound

Diana Ross and the Supremes Join the Temptations, Motown MS679
The Supremes: *Where Did Our Love Go* (original hit album), Motown 621
Martha and the Vandellas: *Dance Party,* Gordy 915
The Miracles: *Greatest Hits from the Beginning,* Tamla 254
Stevie Wonder: *Greatest Hits,* Tamla 282
Four Tops: *Baby, I Need Your Loving,* Motown 622
Mary Wells: *Greatest Hits,* Motown 616
Marvin Gaye: *In the Groove,* Tamla 285

Otis Redding and Memphis Sound

History of Otis Redding, Volt (S) 418
Otis Redding: *The Dock of the Bay,* Volt (S) 419
Otis Redding and Carla Thomas: *King and Queen,* Stax 716
Stax Volt Revue Live in London, Vol. 1, Stax (S) 721
Soul Explosion, Stax STX-2-2007
Steve Cropper, Pop Staples, Albert King: *Jammed Together,* Stax STS 2020
Booker T. and the M.G.'s: *Hip-Hug-Her,* Stax (S) 717
Booker T. and the M.G.'s: *Up Tight,* Stax STS 2006

Soul-Folk

The Staple Singers: *Soul Folk in Action,* Stax STS 2004
Richie Havens: *Something Else Again,* Verve Forecast FT-3034

Nina Simone

Nina Simone in Concert (with *Mississippi Goddam!*), Philips 600-135
Nina Simone: *Wild Is the Wind* (with *Four Women*), Philips 600-207
Nina Simone: *High Priestess of Soul,* Philips 600-219
Nina Simone: *'Nuff Said!,* Victor LSP-4065

Aretha Franklin

I Never Loved a Man the Way I Love You, Atlantic SD 8139
Lady Soul, Atlantic S-8176
Aretha Now, Atlantic SD 8186
Soul '69, Atlantic S-8212

James Brown

Say It Loud, I'm Black and I'm Proud!, King 5/1047
Handful of Soul, Smash 67084

Selected Soul Artists

Dionne Warwick: *Anyone Who Had a Heart,* Scepter 517
Dionne Warwick: *Soulful,* Scepter 573
Lou Rawls Live!, Capitol ST 2459
Oscar Brown Jr.: *Between Heaven and Hell,* Columbia CS 8574
Oscar Brown Jr.: *Sin and Soul,* Columbia CCS-8377
The Sound of Wilson Pickett, Atlantic 8145
The Best of Joe Tex, Atlantic 8144
Della Reese: *I Gotta Be Me . . . This Trip Out,* ABC (S) 636
The Best of Little Anthony and the Imperials, Veep VPS 16512
The Impressions' Greatest Hits, ABC-515

White Soul Artists

José Feliciano: *Feliciano!,* Victor LSP-3957
Big Brother and the Holding Company with Janis Joplin: *Cheap Thrills,* KSC 9700
The Righteous Brothers: *Soul and Inspiration,* Verve V6-5001
Tom Jones in the Fever Zone, Parrot PAS 71019
Live Adventures of Al Kooper and Mike Bloomfield, 2 Columbia KGP-6
Elvis Presley in Memphis, RCA Victor LSP-4155

Soul In Jazz

Jimmy Smith's Greatest Hits, Blue Note BST 89901
Horace Silver: *Blowin' the Blues Away,* Blue Note 4017
Les McCann: *The Truth,* Pacific Jazz S-2
An Hour with the Ramsey Lewis Trio (for *Consider the Source*), Argo LP-645
Ramsey Lewis: *The "In" Crowd,* Cadet (S) 757
Young-Holt Unlimited: *Soulful Strut,* Brunswick 754144
Up with Donald Byrd, Verve 68609
Wes Montgomery: *Goin' out of My Head,* Verve 68642
Cannonball Adderley Quintet: *Mercy, Mercy, Mercy!,* Capitol ST 2663
Count Basie with Joe Williams, Verve 68488
Leonard Feather: *Encyclopedia of Jazz in the Sixties, the Blues* (for Oliver Nelson arrangement of *St. Louis Blues*), Verve V6-9677
Herbie Mann: *Memphis Underground,* Atlantic 1522
Melvin Van Peebles: *Brer Soul,* A&M SP 4161

Another Kind of Soul

John Coltrane: *A Love Supreme,* Impulse S-77
John Coltrane: *Ascension,* Impulse A-95
Pharoah Sanders: *Karma,* Impulse A-9181

INDEX